MW01169028

SOCIAL COMPUTING AND THE LAW

This innovative book sets itself at the crossroads of several rapidly developing areas of research in legal and global studies related to social computing, specifically in the context of how public emergency responders appropriate content on social media platforms for emergency and disaster management. The book – a collaboration among computer scientists, ethicists, legal scholars and practitioners – should be read by anyone concerned with the ongoing debate over the corporatization and commodification of user-generated content on social media and the extent to which this content can be legally and ethically harnessed for public safety in emergency and disaster management.

Khurshid Ahmad is Professor of Computer Science at Trinity College, Dublin. He specializes in artificial intelligence with research interests in information extraction from images and texts, fuzzy logic, sentiment analysis, neural networks and terminology and ontology. Ahmad holds a PhD in Theoretical Nuclear Physics from the University of Surrey. He is an elected Fellow of the British Computer Society and of Trinity College, as well as a Chartered Engineer. He has taught at the Universities of Karachi and Surrey and has been a Visiting Professor at Copenhagen Business School. Ahmad has published more than 250 research papers. His books include *Computers, Language Learning, and Language Teaching* (Cambridge, 1985), *Translator's Workbench: Tools and Terminology for Translation and Text Processing* (1995) and *Affective Computing and Sentiment Analysis: Emotion, Metaphor, and Terminology* (2011).

Social Computing and the Law

USES AND ABUSES IN EXCEPTIONAL CIRCUMSTANCES

Edited by
KHURSHID AHMAD
Trinity College, Dublin

CAMBRIDGE
UNIVERSITY PRESS

University Printing House, Cambridge CB2 8BS, United Kingdom

One Liberty Plaza, 20th Floor, New York, NY 10006, USA

477 Williamstown Road, Port Melbourne, VIC 3207, Australia

314–321, 3rd Floor, Plot 3, Splendor Forum, Jasola District Centre,
New Delhi – 110025, India

79 Anson Road, #06–04/06, Singapore 079906

Cambridge University Press is part of the University of Cambridge.

It furthers the University's mission by disseminating knowledge in the pursuit of
education, learning, and research at the highest international levels of excellence.

www.cambridge.org
Information on this title: www.cambridge.org/9781108428651
DOI: 10.1017/9781108575720

© Cambridge University Press 2018

First published 2018

Printed in the United States of America by Sheridan Books, Inc.

A catalogue record for this publication is available from the British Library.

Library of Congress Cataloging-in-Publication Data
NAMES: Ahmad, Khurshid, 1948–, editor.
TITLE: Social computing and the law : uses and abuses in exceptional circumstances /
edited by Khurshid Ahmad, Trinity College, Dublin.
DESCRIPTION: New York : Cambridge University Press, 2018. | Includes bibliographical
references and index.
IDENTIFIERS: LCCN 2018022356 | ISBN 9781108428651 (hardback)
SUBJECTS: LCSH: Computer networks – Law and legislation. | Computer networks – Social
aspects. | Microblogs – Social aspects. | Online social networks – Social aspects. | Interactive
computer systems – Social aspects. | BISAC: LAW / General.
CLASSIFICATION: LCC K564.C6 S554 2018 | DDC 343.09/99–dc23
LC record available at https://lccn.loc.gov/2018022356

ISBN 978-1-108-42865-1 Hardback

Contents

Figures

Contributors

Khurshid Ahmad School of Computer Science and Statistics, Trinity College, Dublin

Christian Berger University of Leipzig

Rob Corbet Arthur Cox LLC, Dublin

Paolo de Stefani University of Padova

Shane Finan School of Computer Science and Statistics, Trinity College, Dublin

Captain Brian Fitzgerald, Irish Naval Services

Paul Hayes Irish School of Ecumenics, Trinity College, Dublin

Linda Hogan Irish School of Ecumenics, Trinity College, Dublin

Damian Jackson Irish School of Ecumenics, Trinity College, Dublin

Stephen Kelly School of Computer Science and Statistics, Trinity College, Dublin

Colm Maguire Arthur Cox LLC, Dublin

Taiwo Oriola Ulster University

Xiubo Zhang School of Computer Science and Statistics, Trinity College, Dublin

Foreword

In 2012, as the Officer in Charge of Planning Policy and Enterprise in the Irish Naval Service, I became involved with a research project entitled Slándáil. This multi-national project was supported by the European Union's 7th Framework Programme for Research and Technological Development. From the outset it was obvious that there was a correlation between the 'human factor' and capability development that security services were advancing. I undertook the role of Chair of the Strategic Advisory Board for the project, and in this role represented emergency responders, monitoring the research and development of the team. Project Slándáil researched natural crises and analysed how social media can be better used to spread messages about the worst affected areas during these crises. The results of technological advances, end user responses and legal and ethical research from this project provided the motivation for this book.

As an end user of data such as social media, it was essential to understand how the project provided a better understanding of how an unwieldy, disruptive technology can be better harnessed to inform emergency responses to natural disasters. Towards the end of the project, I was appointed to command the flagship of the Irish Naval Service L.É. EITHNE to undertake a humanitarian mission to the central Mediterranean in response to the migrant crisis there. During this deployment, I witnessed first-hand the central role that modern communications systems play in life and death decisions on a grand scale, coordinating the rescue of several thousand migrants via an eclectic mix of international state and nongovernmental organisation assets. Central to the success of such a mission was the reliance on the communications modalities at my disposal. The gathering, analysis and dissemination of intelligence information were key to the humanitarian operations that ensued. In undertaking such analysis, data provenance, ethical issues and the use of language proved central to command decisions, and the experience from Project Slándáil proved invaluable.

Project Slándáil was amongst the first projects to see the dichotomy between the utility of social computing, especially in a disaster scenario and its potential abuse. This book discusses three key aspects of the law surrounding this area – internet law, copyright and data protection law, and human rights law. In doing so, it seeks to positively contribute to two divergent issues – the promotion of the use of social computing and the prevention of its abuse. The book also suggests a way forward through a legally based 'User Licence' which provides comfort to the entire spectrum of human beings involved – the citizens, the disaster prevention teams, the protection agencies and those who are interested in a balance between rights and duties.

In essence, this book represents a codification of ethics and law in social media for emergencies and outlines a system that is relevant to the needs of end users and society as a whole. Readers can look forward to charting a route through the rocky shoals of evolving human activity in emergency situations and the use of social media in a globalised world. Its content is invaluable.

If, as Napoleon Bonaparte reputedly once said, the secret of war lies in communications, then certainly the secret of peace, security and humanity does also.

Captain Brian FitzGerald
Irish Naval Service

Acknowledgements

The authors wish to acknowledge the support of the European Union's 7th Framework Programme for Research and Technological Development for funding Project Slándáil (Grant No. 607691, 2014–2017) and allowing us, the authors, to work together over a sustained period of time. We would like to thank all the partners in the project, especially emergency management partners who helped in specifying, designing and building Slándáil social media monitoring systems. These potential end users participated in workshop sessions on questions relating to ethics, emergency regulations and laws governing the internet, copyright protection and human rights. Our EU project officers, Dr Elena Manova and Dr Antonio Fernandez-Ranada Shaw of the EU Research Executive Agency, helped us throughout the project. Dr Tim Groenland (Trinity College) was involved in assisting with the editing, proofreading and layout of our book. Last but not least we thank Cambridge University Press for its help and support.

This project has received funding from the European Union's 7th Framework Programme for research, technological development and demonstration under grant agreement no. 607691. The material presented and views expressed here are the responsibility of the author(s) only. The EU Commission takes no responsibility for any use made of the information set out.

Abbreviations

BGH   Bundesgerichtshof (Federal High Court of Justice)
DMCR   Digital Millennium Copyright Act
ECJ   European Court of Justice
GCA   German Copyright Act
GCC   German Civil Code
GRUR   *Gewerblicher Rechtsschutz und Urheberrecht (Industrial Property and Copyright Law* [Journal]*)*
MMR   *Multi Media Recht (Multi Media Law* [Journal]*)*
TFEU   Treaty on the Functioning of the European Union, 2007
UrhG   Urheberrechtsgesetz (GCA)
ZUM   *Zeitschrift für Urheber- und Medienrecht (Journal for Copyright and Media Law)*

1

Introduction

Khurshid Ahmad
Trinity College, Dublin

Microblogging systems and social networking systems, sometimes referred to as types of social computing systems, generate enormous amounts of data that often contain specific information about persons, events and geographical locations. During exceptional circumstances, this data can, in principle, be invaluable – for example, in deploying scarce resources in times of emergency in order to save lives, rescuing and rehabilitating people and protecting property. Microblogs and social networking pages have become a mainstay of data dissemination in the public space and are used heavily by both citizens and authorities in times of crisis; they have been used, for example, by police forces for disseminating and seeking information about missing people, and by hospitals seeking blood. Twitter often carries the first messages of victims of atrocities (Paris 2015, Berlin 2016, London 2017 and Manchester 2017); Facebook is used to find missing relatives. Vast quantities of personal information floods microblogs and social networking pages. Although this data can help authorities to deploy resources where the need is greatest, it can also be used in wholesale surveillance. Social computing systems are now part and parcel of our interactions with others in good times and bad.

The ownership of the data in this space is disputed, and access to it remains a contentious issue. Social computing systems have all the hallmarks of a *disruptive* and *intrusive* technology, bringing unforeseen opportunities and challenges that cannot be faced by the existing ethical and legal order. The challenges related to the abuse of texts, images and spoken data available on social computing systems are all well-documented; the internet's ubiquity and transnational overreach can facilitate the appropriation of personal data and proprietary information across multiple social media platforms and national borders, anchored by multiple servers located in several countries, a scenario that inevitably raises jurisdictional issues in compliance and enforcement.

The scale of social computing means that its analysis – extracting relevant information from noisy data, checking facts, avoiding duplications, eradicating "fake news", recognising people and objects in grainy and shaky images – can only be adequately handled by yet another disruptive and intrusive technology, *artificial intelligence* (AI). AI techniques can be more effective than experts in revealing connections between people and between objects. The ethical and legal issues raised by the use of AI have just begun; imagining the combined use of the two intrusive and disruptive technologies is a challenge the authors of this volume have researched severally and collectively over the past number of years.

Project Slándáil (2014–2017) was an EU FP7-funded project (project #607691) that leveraged social media data for emergency management. The technologies developed on Project Slándáil were supported by the legal and ethical research discussed in this book. As a follow-up to this project, Trinity College, Dublin has developed a plan to commercialise text and image analytic systems, gratefully supported by Enterprise Ireland (contract #CF-2017–0778-P) and the European Regional Development Fund (2014–2020).

1.1 A NOTE ON TERMINOLOGY

We all use, in one form or the other, systems that facilitate social interactions. These interactions include the establishment and sustenance of friendships or animosities, the exchange of goods and services at an individual or organisational level, the creation or destruction of communities (howsoever defined), the conduct or blockage of political debate, and individual or governmental crossing of societal norms. The term *social computing systems* is evolving, and social computing systems essentially comprise two types: social media systems and social networking systems (Parameswaran & Whinston, 2007; Wang, Carley, Zeng & Mao, 2007). According to the Oxford English Dictionary:

> *Social media*. Noun. Websites and applications which enable users to create and share content or to participate in social networking. (In use since c. 2004.) [Exemplars of social media systems include Twitter, Flickr, Instagram, Snapchat, and YouTube]
>
> *Social network*. Noun. A system of social interactions and relationships; a group of people who are socially connected to one another; (now also) a social networking website; the users of such a website collectively; cf. social networking n. (In use since c. 1845.) [Exemplars of social networking systems include the ubiquitous Facebook; more specialised systems include professional networking systems such as LinkedIn, personal networking systems for dating, and those for finding long-lost friends]

Social computing is used for technologies that enable people to store for free their (highly unstructured) data in expensive, large databases (usually meant for structured data). Social computing systems process the unstructured data by using advanced computer systems involving thousands of computers working together with state-of-the-art technologies such as AI and machine learning, and distribute the processed data or information to the world in microseconds. These technologies tag unstructured data using details of the creator, the subject matter keywords, the machines used in generating the data, the geo-location of the creator and by annotating images and other seemingly innocuous metadata so that such data can be stored and retrieved systematically and efficiently (King, Li & Chan, 2009; Zeng, Wang & Carley, 2007). This involves the use of expensive and advanced information extraction systems but is, for users, all free.

Social computing systems "mine" the data of users, learning complex patterns within the data to mine more effectively. A symbiotic relationship exists between technology and data: larger datasets help systems to learn better, thus enabling better and even larger datasets to be mined.

Social computing systems connect disparate items of data in very complex ways:

- The **biographical data** of a person can be linked to their shopping habits, as displayed when they *crawl* shopping websites, or to inform them about private and public events.
- **Biometric data** is used by governments to plan and deliver health and social services, or to enforce immigration control.
- *Merged* or *fused* **biographical and biometric data** are used for rescuing and rehabilitating internally displaced people; disaster-struck people can be tracked by drones and by geo-locating their social computing messages in text and images.

Social computing systems connect disparate items of data together in ways sometimes referred to as *dataveillance*. There are two overlapping definitions here (Hu, 2015: 774):

(i) "In the intelligence context, it appears that 'collect-it-all' tools in a big data world can now potentially facilitate the construction, by the intelligence community, of other individuals' digital avatars. The digital avatar can be understood as a virtual representation of our digital selves and may serve as a potential proxy for an actual person".

(ii) "This construction may be enabled through processes such as the data fusion of biometric and biographic data, or the digital data fusion of the 24/7 surveillance of the body and the 360° surveillance of the biography".

The central question for us is why we, the citizen/users, make these systems so powerful? Two reasons come to mind. First, for small gains – free email, free software, free phone calls – and sometimes out of necessity – booking airline tickets, buying online, bidding in electronic auctions; we give away one of the most important assets we have, namely our biographical details. The second reason relates to the prolixity of legislation by many state agencies and the verbosity of service-provider forms, meaning that a vast quantity of biographical and biometric data is being continuously demanded of individuals. These vast silos continue to lose data, may contain data the silo should not have and can miss out on vital data.

Social computing systems are a classic example of disruptive technology and deft sales tactics. Disruptive technologies are paradigm-busting developments: a current technology (and some of its users) are discarded for a relatively untested new technology that creates its own, bigger user groupings. Disruptive technologies often emerge through a collaborative effort of like-minded, usually technocratic, persons and are marketed using nimble phrases such as "shareware" and "freemium". Most social computing enterprises have emerged during the past ten years or so.

Social computing systems have grown organically, and as such the ethics and legality of their use will continue to be debated by legislators and scholars. States and federations have struggled to adapt their legal systems to the developing technological systems; there appear to be few explicit rules, regulations, laws or directives for the development of these technologies, nor are there well-defined ethical frameworks for assigning rights and duties to the developers, end users and the individuals whose data is being acquired and disseminated.

EU Data Protection Regulations have just been released for consultation; Fair Use Legislation is lagging behind; national security organisations appear to have carte blanche for mounting surveillance on all known communications technologies while private security organisations are not far behind (Barnett, 2015; Bekkers, Edwards & de Kool, 2013; Galicki, 2015). Recent changes in EU law, such as the landmark developments in the EU's General Data Protection Regulation (2016/679) and the EU Law Enforcement Data Protection Directive (2016/680) together with the recently invalidated US-EU Safe Harbour framework and the EU-US and Swiss-US Privacy Shield Frameworks, approved in 2016 and 2017, respectively (Ni Loideain, 2016; Weiss & Archick, 2016), demonstrate the contested and evolving nature of the legal environment.

Social computing systems become even more powerful when coupled with *geographical information systems* and emerging *geospatial information systems*. In the OED, we find:

> **geographic information system**. Noun. An information system which allows the user to analyse, display, and manipulate spatial data, such as from surveying and remote sensing, typically in the production of maps.

The general-purpose maps produced by cartographers comprise many themes – political boundaries at national and local levels, population distribution, vegetation and soils, transportation networks and elevation. The term "geospatial" is defined by the OED as follows:

> **geospatial**. Adjective. Of or relating to geographical distribution or location; esp. designating data associated with a particular geographical location; relating to or involving such data.

The introduction of geospatial data related to these themes, which is kept updated to minute levels – such as location-based details of individual houses, the number of trees on major road-networks, and census data at a very fine grain of detail – will provide opportunities and challenges that perhaps will be equal to or greater than those made available by web-search systems and their coupling with social computing systems (Groot & McLaughlin, 2000; Lo & Yeung, 2007). Social media systems comprise links to documents on the web, and news sources use social media and networking messages on their website. *Geospatial* search engines allow for the linking of data about place-based assets with other such data, and one can use social media systems to discover how to access and provide such informational data. The scope of the ethico-legal debate appears to be wider than simply respecting the factual and provenance of textual and image-based documents.

The United States is in the vanguard for exploring and exploiting the use of spatial data and has developed a web-accessible National Spatial Data Infrastructure (NSDI) to ensure "that place-based data from multiple sources (Federal, state, local, and tribal governments, academia, and the private sector) are available and easily integrated to enhance the understanding of our physical and cultural world".[1] The NSDI has been developed since the 1980s and is now being used as a backbone for crawling programs that will search and aggregate geospatial data in an unprecedented manner. Like the commonly available text (and some image) search engines, the advent of *geospatial search engines* (Bone, Ager, Bunzel & Tierney, 2016) will provide commercial, policy and public protection opportunities much as the earlier text/image search engines did, and will bring perhaps greater ethico-legal problems.

European countries have their own GIS and geospatial databases in different states of availability and development. However, more recently, the EU has created a policy framework and concomitant directives for the creation of an infrastructure of spatial information across Europe (INSPIRE) covering thirty-four data themes, ranging from the conventional themes found in most maps and GIS systems to data on sites of special scientific interest, human health and safety, atmospheric conditions, socio-economic data and so on (Bartha & Kocsis, 2011; Vandenbroucke, Zambon, Crompvoets & Dufourmont, 2008). The INSPIRE Directive was released in 2007, and the completion date of this large geospatial database for all twenty-seven EU countries is 2021 (at the time of this writing). The EU states have been mandated to make all this information available, at cost, to people across the EU and beyond (provided national security considerations allow for this).

The coupled use of GIS and geospatial data was initially planned for policy development covering areas vulnerable to flooding, fire, strong winds, poverty alleviation and economic and social development. With the advent of efficient, low-cost remote sensing equipment that generates data in real-time, such coupled systems have been used in disaster management, the monitoring of epidemics and logistics management, to name but a few applications. GIS and geospatial data manipulation have been extensively used by the military and security agencies to monitor the movement of people, vehicles, arms and military machinery (Brewer & McNeese, 2003; Coleman & McLaughlin, 1998; Sui, 2008).

Social computing systems were initially used for crowdsourcing data for thematic maps, and human sensors were used to capture geospatial data (Heipke, 2010). Now, with the help of global positioning systems, we can track the activity of a person who is online and monitor mobile phones which have their "location finder" option on (Agarwal & Lau, 2010; Ryder, Longstaff, Reddy & Estrin, 2009). Tracking a person's communication equipment, mapping it onto geo-locational maps and observing its proximity to other people carrying mobile devices, facilitates monitoring of their movements and related activities. The computer systems of many law enforcement agencies are, as a result, filled with data resulting from legal or illegal surveillance of citizens going about their legitimate business (L. M. Austin, 2014; Greenwald, 2013; Kerr, 2002; Lyon, 2006; Pell & Soghoian, 2014).

1.2 SECURITY, PRIVACY AND DIGNITY DURING AN EMERGENCY

Systems are being developed that can process texts and images in conjunction with geospatial data in order to extract information that can be used during emergencies, using social media as a bi-directional communication aid between authorities and vulnerable citizens (Alexander, 2014; Simon, 1982). The authors of this book were involved in the development of such a system (Ahmad, 2017). In tandem with the project's technical work, we conducted an ethical analysis to ensure that the inviolable rights of citizens related to privacy and dignity, the concomitant proprietary rights of the individual to his or her social media texts and images, and the constitutionally mandated duty of the authorities to protect lives and property, were all given due consideration.

One important design consideration for us, therefore, was to ensure that the social-media informed emergency management system was licensed according to the current laws that allow safe use of the internet, protection of data available on social computing systems and, above all, that the rights of the citizens, whose life and safety are in peril during a disaster, were not violated whilst the emergency managers performed their mandated duties. We have developed a *licence* for the use of such systems wherein the user agrees to abide by the law of the land and international laws for an authorised use of the system.

A number of questions guided our investigations. Is there an ethical basis for an institution to examine an individual's interaction with others that is within the bounds of ethical norms and is permitted by the law? Can enterprises and agencies provide a legal basis for surveillance of citizens in cases where monitoring and harvesting of data has the potential to contribute to the public good? Both in the provision of opportunities and the posing of challenges, one question keeps recurring: who "owns" the data, those who generate it or those who store it and make it available on demand? *Social Computing and the Law* explores these questions, presenting a comparative transnational overview of the legal ramifications of harvesting social media data on the internet in the United Kingdom, the European Union and the United States.

Our team of lawyers worked with four emergency managers (two police forces, one in the UK and the other in Ireland), two civil protection organisations (in Italy and Germany), and two software companies (based in Germany and Italy), together with experts in human rights and ethics (in Ireland and Italy) and computer scientists (in Irish, German and UK universities) to chart the ethical and legal landscape surrounding the use of social computing data in exceptional circumstances. Our three lawyers – one a professor in internet law, another in copyright and data protection law, and the third in human rights laws and conventions – researched these areas for the use of social computing in exceptional circumstances; they were counselled by a professional law firm in Ireland and by academic experts in value pluralism.

We found that disaster management represents an invaluable case study for processing social computing data in exceptional circumstances, demonstrating the way in which information ordinarily considered private may be monitored and harvested for limited time periods in the interests of the public good. Social media allows an unprecedented look into the activities and environments of individuals and communities, presenting information that can be invaluable to emergency managers in each phase of disaster response. The potential for abuse of this data, however, is considerable, and it should and can be managed in the first instance by having a licence governing terms and conditions attached with the sale and use of a social media monitoring system that can be used in an emergency.

Social Computing and the Law presents key findings of our research on internet governance, data protection, copyright and human rights, together with a discussion of key motivating ethical issues concerning the problems of competing rights and the delegation of power to authorities. We look at ethical deliberations on how to reconcile the conflicting needs of two groups and consider the governance of the internet, as exemplified in relevant legislation and protocols, to ascertain the rights and duties of the vendors of these systems. We explore how copyright protection may be of help in protecting the rights of the citizens who generate data. We consider how international human rights laws and protocols provide an overarching umbrella for the protection of privacy and dignity as cardinal principles of governance. The incorporation of international human rights law within national legislative machinery can counterbalance the tendency of nation-states to curtail citizens' freedom.

The synthesis of these three legal analyses has led us to develop a template software licence drafted by professional lawyers (see Appendix A), with an accompanying legal checklist (see Appendix B), that provides a legal framework for the safe and transparent deployment of social computing systems, especially during exceptional circumstances. The book concludes by presenting these documents, showing how a practical and enforceable legal agreement can incorporate the ethical concerns and competing rights surrounding the use of social computing data in exceptional circumstances.

1.3 OUR CONTRIBUTION: DISASTERS, TECHNOLOGY, LAW AND ETHICS

Our book sets itself at the crossroads of several rapidly developing areas of research in legal and global studies relating to social computing. The advent of the internet has influenced all manner of legal and regulatory frameworks, including the protection of individual rights such as privacy, data protection and intellectual property; the explosion of social media has further expanded the challenges for such fundamental rights. *Social Computing and the Law* highlights complex legal challenges to these rights and considers how public emergency responders could legally appropriate content on social media platforms for emergency and disaster management. In the process, the book makes significant contributions to the ongoing debate on the corporatisation and commodification of user-generated contents on social media and the extent to which these can be legally and ethically harnessed for public emergency and disaster management.

Recent work on the societal impact of social media in exceptional circumstances has led to position papers on the ethical and legal aspect of using social media; see, for example, Hiller & Russell (2017). There is a growing discussion surrounding the ethical and legal challenges of using data gathered during a disaster as well as on the effect of EU Data Protection Directives, the 2016 version thereof (Rizza, Büscher & Watson, 2017). Our book contributes to this evolving literature by providing an extended exploration of the relevance of internet law, copyright and data protection law (with a focus on the changing legal landscape of the EU) and human rights laws to the propriety of using personal data in crisis management. Our checklist of legal obligations and ethical issues (and the accompanying discussion) will provide a valuable contribution in this regard.

Existing monographs on the use of social media in emergencies show a distinctive focus on emergencies affecting states in connection with armed conflicts, terrorist threats and similar political predicaments (see, for example, Gupta & Brooks, 2013; Nissen, 2015). Natural disaster scenarios have remained comparatively less studied, despite the pervasiveness and societal impact of such situations, and the significant role that technology played in them. The reflection on the appropriate use of big-data analysis and data mining in connection with natural disaster scenarios has just begun. In addition to the enormous positive potential for emergency response managers arising from such a shift in natural disaster management, legal and ethical risks may arise if disaster response operators fail to consider privacy and data protection as crucial human rights concerns.

The book benefits from the multifaceted work produced in the Project Slándáil, which combined theoretical and practical approaches; as an interdisciplinary work that draws on ethics, law, computer science and disaster management, it has very few competitors. Moreover, major works in the field of ethics of disaster management make few if any references to the ethical and legal challenges of social media harvesting – for example, in the area of disaster relief (Caron, Kelly & Telesetsky, 2014) or in disaster response (De Guttry, Gestri & Venturini, 2012). Works on ethics and social media explore key questions of *data/information* and *ethics* in a broad, general setting (Ess, 2013; Floridi, 2013; Taddeo & Floridi, 2017; Vallor, 2016) rather than deal with the special case of emergencies – something we have attempted to do (Jackson & Hayes, 2016).

The existing legal literature takes a rather generalised approach to the treatment of the preceding issues (De Franceschi & Lehmann, 2015; Lloyd, 2017; Stewart, 2017) and seldom has examined in detail the possible legal challenges posed to the altruistic uses of commodified user-generated contents on social media by public emergency responders. Works on data protection, copyright law and privacy law are many, but these either tend to focus on one aspect of the law or fail to attend to the situations of crisis or emergency management [Bently & Sherman, 2014; Citron, 2014; Mayer-Schönberger & Cukier, 2013; Reed, 2012; also D. K. Citron's *Hate Crimes in Cyberspace* (2014)].

The work carried out in Project Slándáil in building an emergency management system that receives actionable data (namely, data that is filtered, relevant and geo-located) from social computing systems involved extensive use of major branches of AI. Our system accepts data from social computing systems and from other digital streams comprising newspapers. The data is processed for information sharing with due regard to its copyright and due regard to the processed information for saving lives and property, but it is also capable of revealing identities of people and places. The processed information is analysed further to its context: information about the location (of a disaster) and the situation in which people and places may be. Finally, the processed information is aggregated for issuing warning, and for this knowledge for mitigating the impact of a disaster. In the final phases the system ensures that it is not distributing copyrighted material and that it is protecting the identities (see Figure 1; details are in Zhang, Kelly & Ahmad, 2016). These included natural language processing and computer vision systems, together with advanced geographical information systems. The use of these systems can generate information that can potentially violate the privacy and dignity of individuals, and concerns about the ethics of using AI systems has recently been aired in, for example, Emanuelle Burton et al.'s "Ethical Considerations in Artificial Intelligence Courses" (2017). Burton and colleagues make a concrete contribution to this literature by dealing with the real-world integration of AI technology into disaster management.

Engagement with legal practitioners adds a practical dimension to our work, which endeavours to translate ethical and legal principles into enforceable norms. The book, at the intersection between human rights law, internet law and disaster law, provides a holistic, thoughtful and timely contribution to a fast-growing debate.

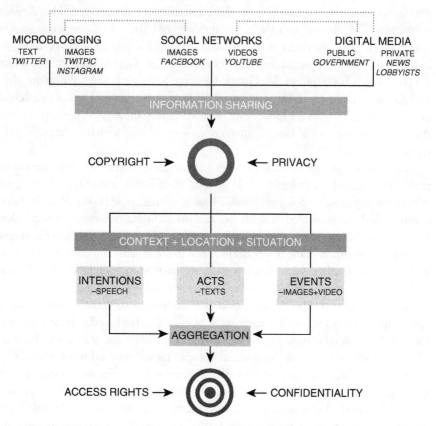

FIGURE 1 The complexity of using social media for emergency management, including sources and types of data. Acknowledgement of the legal landscape, including copyright and privacy, affect both the collection of data and the sharing of actionable information to emergency management teams. (Image courtesy of Project Slándáil – EU-FP7 Project #607691)

1.4 STRUCTURE OF THE BOOK

Chapter 2

We focus on social computing systems that deal with texts and images and will refer to geospatial information in passing. We begin with a discussion of the nature of the internet – the interconnected system of networked computing assets including processors, databases and graphical user interfaces – and discuss laws and conventions governing its use, particularly in the EU. The internet's ubiquity and transnational overreach could facilitate the appropriation of personal data and proprietary information across multiple social media platforms and national borders, anchored by multiple servers located in several countries. This inevitably raises jurisdictional issues regarding compliance and enforcement contexts. This scenario compels a comparative transnational overview of the legal ramifications of the operational deployment of a system that harvests social media data on the internet in the United Kingdom, the European Union and the United States.

Chapter 2 contains a consideration of the key ethical challenges posed by the use of data harvested from social computing systems: we suggest, drawing on ethical theory, that the notions of *value pluralism* and *state of exception* are an appropriate ethical framework. The chapter concludes with an overview of the book's structure and concerns.

Chapter 3

Drawing on comparative case law, legislative instruments and relevant literature from the European Union, the United Kingdom and the United States, Chapter 3 explores the parameters of relevant applicable laws that govern internet contents, specifically personal data and proprietary information on social media. It highlights the limitations to these laws and explores the extent to which such software could safely be deployed by public emergency responders within the prescribed legal limitations. Practical ways by which software programmers and public emergency responders or end users could lawfully derogate from prescribed laws and avoid infringements of third-party rights in personal data and proprietary information on social media are also proposed.

Chapter 4

Ordinarily, posted texts, images, videos and other digital content enjoy protection under copyright law if they are the author's own creation. We examine the application of these laws in extraordinary situations, such as those following natural disasters, in which the needs of disaster victims are paramount. We discuss *whether special exceptions and limitations can justify the use of digital content for emergency and disaster management* and whether an implied consent applies to the use of social media postings concerning the effects of a disaster. Analysis has shown that within the EU member states, despite numerous directives in the area of copyright, no uniform structure for exceptions and limitations exists to date (Cook, 2012). Our analysis therefore focusses on copyright law in Germany, as a worked example of the analysis needed to assess the copyright implications of deployment of a system that harvests social media data to enhance emergency response decision support in an EU jurisdiction.

Data and information are protected within the scope of protection of personal rights, strongly enforced through basic human rights at a European as well as national level.[2] The new EU General Data Protection Regulation (which came into force on 25 May 2018) aims to unify data protection law within the EU but contains a number of exemption clauses, so that the laws of national regimes and National Data Protection Authorities continue to have relevance. This analysis focuses on the new General Data Protection Regulation, assessing the potential privacy impact of the automated harvesting and processing of social media data to support emergency response decision-making. The regulation refers explicitly to disaster situations and is therefore particularly suitable to test and develop the balance between civil protection purposes and data protection rights.

Chapter 5

Given the importance of human rights across the spectrum of human activities, and the extensive references to these rights in the laws, treaties, directives and decrees, related to the harvesting, storing, analysing and disseminating data available on information systems in general, it is important to note how such data may be treated in a state of exception. We noted earlier that the declaration of a state of exception is constrained by obligations under international human rights laws and treaties.

There are three important considerations in this context. First, we must take into account human rights laws as articulated in UN-sponsored conventions and protocols and in the EU Charter on Fundamental Rights. Second, we must be cognisant of international humanitarian law that is based on neutrality and nondiscrimination. The third factor is the emergent international law on disasters that sets out the duties and rights of all stakeholders – states, intergovernmental and nongovernmental actors, and displaced individuals and groups. We use disaster prevention and mitigation to illustrate the opportunities and challenges related to the interaction among ethics, the law and social computing systems.

Chapter 6

Our final chapter draws on the legal analysis in the preceding chapters and outlines a model licence agreement for a social media monitor to use in disaster management. The template licence (Appendix A) is accompanied by a checklist (Appendix B) of legal issues covering (a) data protection comprising identification of applicable law, lawful processing of social computing data, data security, procedural requirements, data transfer, penalties including fines; (b) legal issues related to privacy; (c) copyright issues and (d) human rights legal framework.

The discussion of these issues is based on a series of documents produced by the EU-sponsored Slándáil Project, which are available on request. The operational use of this licence is shown in the operation of Slándáil's social media monitoring system which, in turn, empowers an existing emergency management system that draws data from an EU-facilitated geospatial data infrastructural database (INSPIRE) and can be interfaced to major social computing systems. The Slándáil system incorporates a *privacy intrusion detector* (named the Intrusion Index) which records the extent to which data related to named entities, people, places and things, has been collected, and which generates an encrypted record of the names collected for reporting to privacy protection officials.

NOTES

1. www.fgdc.gov/nsdi/nsdi-brochure.pdf
2. Data protection rights are not only included as a human right in the European Convention on Human Rights (Article 8) and the EU Fundamental Rights Charter (Articles 7 and 8) and Functioning Treaty (Article 16), but also in numerous constitutions (such as those of Germany, Ireland and Poland) as well as at the legislative level both in Directive 95/46/EC on the protection of individuals with regard to the processing of personal data and on the free movement of such data and in national laws.

2

Social Computing Systems and Ethical Considerations

Khurshid Ahmad, Shane Finan, Stephen Kelly and Xiubo Zhang
School of Computer Science and Statistics, Trinity College, Dublin

Paul Hayes, Linda Hogan and Damian Jackson
Irish School of Ecumenics, Trinity College, Dublin

2.1 INTRODUCTION

This book concerns the opportunities provided and challenges posed by "social computing systems", a term encompassing micro-blogging systems such as Twitter and Snapchat – termed "social media" generally – and social networking systems such as Facebook and YouTube. The data available on social computing systems is generated by its users and is stored and disseminated by social computing enterprises. The opportunities such systems have generated have led to a boom in electronic trading by citizens in virtual markets, as vendors of goods and services become able to bring their products to mass markets in previously unimaginable ways.

Print and broadcasting media have revived themselves through social computing systems, by using these systems to both generate public awareness about media content and to validate that content. Politicians "talk" directly to the public, sometimes in 140–280 characters, and the public can respond to their politicians in ways hitherto totally unknown; social computing systems are used to launch and manage political campaigns, by (for example) generating "micro" donations, and social computing platforms may host political debates (Cogburn & Espinoza-Vasquez, 2011; Loader & Mercea, 2011). Systematic governmental use of social computing is increasingly common (with websites and social media networks being used to carry notices and public information) and organisations have discovered that citizens can express their views almost instantaneously, with online petitions having the potential to influence governmental actions (McCaughey & Ayers, 2013; Morva, 2016).

Perhaps the best example of the use of social computing systems has been in the area of disaster management, where it has affected how citizens and states deal with the onset of disasters, mitigate their effects, and organise recovery from their impacts. Disasters are characterised by a paucity of accurate and well-sourced information, a commodity needed to deploy scarce resources efficiently and in a cost-effective and timely manner. The importance of citizen-band radios has been recognised by authorities such as FEMA in the United States; for example, during a crisis, authorities will often have limited information about the affected areas, and the work of amateur radio operators has been shown to play a key role in maintaining communication and minimising harm (Coile, 1997; Stallings & Quarantelli, 1985).

This two-way communication has become an accepted pattern of interaction in the digital age, helping to establish a two-way interaction between the public and authorities as well as interactions among members of the public (Liu et al., 2008). Twenty-first century earthquakes, hurricanes, tsunamis and floods have demonstrated that social computing systems facilitate this communication enormously; for example, studies have explored methods for harvesting community-oriented information related to disaster alerts (Shih, Han & Carroll, 2014) and for aggregating tweets to profile and geo-reference an impacted area during a flood (Johnson, Ruess & Coll, 2016).

Social computing systems have all of the hallmarks of a *disruptive technology*, bringing unforeseen opportunities and challenges that cannot be faced by the existing ethical and legal order. The challenges relating to the abuse of the data available on social computing systems are all well documented, from cyber-bullying in small groups (Campbell, 2005; Mishna, Saini & Solomon, 2009) to the wholesale invasion of privacy and dignity by agencies created to protect these values (Landau, 2014; Lyon, 2014). Is there an ethical basis for an institution to examine an individual's interaction with others that is within the bounds of ethical norms and permitted by the law? Can enterprises and agencies provide a legal basis for (blanket) surveillance of people going about their day-to-day business?

Both in the provision of opportunities and the posing of challenges, one issue keeps recurring: the "ownership" of data by those who generate it or those who store it and make it available on demand (Hill, 2012; Stelter, 2009; Zimmer, 2010). Those who generate information may seek remedies in existing legal instruments on the assumption that more specific protections will be available once the impact of disruptive social computing systems has been further assimilated. Individual governments can change the law, sometimes at short notice, so that legal protections existing one day may disappear the next.

We have focused on situations in which the need for the protection of life and property are paramount in unforeseen circumstances, such as a natural disaster, in order to develop an ethical framework that will allow for the collection of data on social computing systems for a limited period of time. Disaster management represents a case study for processing social computing data in exceptional circumstances, demonstrating the way in which information ordinarily considered private may be monitored and harvested for limited time periods in the interests of the public good. This has wider implications, since the potential utility of social computing data as a resource to be used in the interests of the public good is not restricted to disaster management.

In recent years, information that might be considered personal data has been leveraged to positive effect in different fields. Researchers, for example, have incorporated data on the digital "symptomatic footprint" of patients in order to identify potentially harmful combinations of widely used prescription drugs; used "digital disease detection" techniques to predict the spread of illness among large populations; explored how to anticipate food shortages using variables such as migrations and movements gleaned from mobile phone communications; examined methods to monitor and control energy use based on "smart grid data", enabling more efficient and environmentally sustainable delivery of electricity; and generated so-called clouds of patient experience that can be used to identify instances of poor clinical care earlier than conventional measures of healthcare quality (Brownstein, Freifeld & Madoff, 2009; Greaves et al., 2013; Tene & Polonetsky, 2012). Big data analytics can, in these cases, deliver tangible benefits to the public.

We look at ethical deliberations on how to reconcile the conflicting needs of two groups and consider the governance of the internet, as exemplified in relevant legislation and protocols, to ascertain the rights and duties of the vendors of these systems. We explore how copyright protection may be of help in protecting the rights of the data generators: our focus here is on German copyright law, which has been an important source of knowledge in this area. The protections provided to citizens of nation-states may disappear due to changes in national or state-level legislative activities. However, almost all of these nation-states have voluntarily accepted a range of human rights laws, protocols and treaties: we look at how international human rights law, international humanitarian law and the laws relating to migration affect the legal environment surrounding the ownership and use of data.

The synthesis of these three legal analyses has led us to develop a template software licence drafted by professional lawyers, with an accompanying legal checklist, that provides a legal framework for the safe and transparent deployment of social computing systems, especially during exceptional circumstances (cf. Appendix I and Appendix II). Our work was complemented by the work of our colleagues in computer science and civil protection who were involved in building an emergency management system empowered by a social computing systems monitor. The novelty here is the treatment of textual and image data on an equal footing, and the synthesis of data sources for generating actionable information whilst protecting the copyright of users and vendors and assuring confidentiality. The architecture of the system was developed between 2014 and 2017 in the context of the EU-funded project Slándáil, which deals with the impact of social media during emergencies; we outline this system and its legal framework.

2.2 KEY ETHICAL CHALLENGES POSED BY SOCIAL COMPUTING SYSTEMS

The increasing use of the abundant data harvested using social media, social networking and geospatial information systems has prompted key questions concerning factual provenance (Hartig, 2009; Moreau et al., 2008). Equally important is the question of whether or not the data were ethically sourced, with due consideration for the privacy and dignity of individuals. The basis of factual provenance and ethical sourcing hinges upon establishing ownership of data and then understanding the overarching responsibilities upon those who harvest, analyse and disseminate the processed data. In this section, we present a consideration of the ethical challenges posed by the use of data harvested from social computing systems; we suggest, drawing on ethical theory, that the notions of *value pluralism* and *state of exception* are key concepts in this regard.

2.2.1 *Value Pluralism*

Value pluralism is a strand of ethics that flows from the claim that there are a plurality of genuine moral values. It was developed by the philosopher Isaiah Berlin in the essay *Two Concepts of Liberty* (Berlin, 1958)[1] and recognises that all of the many ethical frameworks and culturally varied value systems have intrinsic merit and cannot be reduced to one overarching system that can be used to determine the best course of action in a given circumstance.

Value pluralism asserts that all of these systems of value, which reflect the cultural, ethnic and social diversity of the community, need to be protected and fostered; the valuing of pluralism itself needs to be explicit. It seeks to make ethical decisions based on protecting the freedoms and rights of others, particularly those who are vulnerable, such as ethnic minorities. It represents a kind of value system equivalent to the oft-cited expression of the principle of free speech: "I wholly disapprove of what you say – and will defend to the death your right to say it".[2] Berlin would say that we have an ethical obligation to defend others' right to live according to their ethical value systems and cultures, even if we wholly disapprove of them, because the alternative is hegemony and domination.

In addition to its implications for the protection of pluralism at a societal level, value pluralism can be applied at the personal level of an individual's decision-making. As individuals, we hold many (a plurality of) values dear. These genuine values contend with one another in influencing our decisions and actions and will sometimes come into conflict. This value conflict does not mean that the values have been misunderstood, but that they cannot be simultaneously satisfied. This is going further than stating that values conflict *in our experience*, but rather asserts that certain values conflict *in principle*, whether the conflict is experienced or not (Overeem & Verhoef, 2014). It is important to remember that these value conflicts are not between "good" and "bad" values, but between values (objectively) regarded as "good" by the persons concerned. They are all desirable, their relative importance depends on the circumstances and conflict arises when it is not possible to logically reason that one or the other is superior in a specific set of circumstances.

Not only may it be impossible to say that one value is more important than the other, it may be impossible to compare them at all as they are incommensurable. There is no valid moral standard to compare their moral worth, as they are qualitatively different and irreducible. A consequence of this is that, in certain circumstances, a decision must be made which cannot uphold both moral values, and (as the values are incommensurable) there is no rational moral basis on which to make a decision between them. Thus, the decision must be made nonrationally, or radically, and that decision will necessarily prefer one value over the other in a situation where they conflict.

Value pluralists assert that the dominant ethical theories skirt around the very real lived experience of moral dilemmas between cherished values; it recognises the unavoidable nature of such conflicts and engages with them. An argument regularly made in support of value pluralism is that moral dilemmas are very much a part of lived human experience; we find certain decisions difficult because no matter what we decide, some harm will result which goes against our principles or values. This is experienced as "the agony of choice". Berlin states that "[w]e are doomed to choose, and every choice may entail an irreparable loss" (Berlin, 2013: 14). The process of deliberating on such a choice is something that is experienced as painful.

John Kekes (1996: 10) claims that value pluralism "is not an uncommitted analysis of the relations of the types of values involved in good lives, but a theory motivated by a concern for human beings actually living good lives". It is this concern that provides the basis for deriving practical applications. What is desirable under value pluralism is a society structured to protect the ability of people to live out their cultural and ethical identities fruitfully.

In the context of an organisation, administration theorist Hendrik Wagenaar (1999) has advocated a practice-based approach in which practitioners "deal with" value conflicts using their experience and intuition, rather than "resolving" them. He argues that much literature in ethical theory caricatures value conflict as emotional and irrational and therefore advocates a rational, problem-solving response. Paradoxically as we have seen in this discussion, value conflict is generally exhaustively, rationally deliberated over (the agony of choice). When resolution is not forthcoming, the conflict is dealt with through a nonrational decision. This decision cannot be rational, as rational deliberation has not provided an answer. Thus, Wagenaar claims that in practice, value conflicts are not resolved, but instead are dealt with by administrators working intuitively, based on experience, in concrete and varying practical settings (Wagenaar, 1999). The implication here is that organisations ought to foster an environment that facilitates the virtues of wisdom and courage, and engenders learning from experience.

Power relations within the organisational structure also need consideration, as they are a potential factor in the context of decisions made by people in an organisation. Value pluralism enables people to understand that the "approach should begin ... with a recognition that the application of power can narrow the bounds of administrative and political discourse and, in doing so, can serve to restrict the range of values brought to bear in such discourse" (Spicer, 2001: 521). Dissent must be acceptable and contrary opinions considered.

Michael Spicer argues that value pluralism has implications for the cultivation of virtues, as does Paul Nieuwenberg, claiming that facing up to the agony of choice requires the cultivation of the virtues of honesty, truthfulness and courage (Nieuwenburg, 2004). Wagenaar maintains that value pluralism is applied all the time in "dealing with" value conflicts experienced in everyday life. He states that value pluralism has application in the recognition that experience has a role to play in ethical decisions, as reason alone is sometimes inadequate where incompatible and incommensurable values are affected in a particular context when a decision is required (Wagenaar, 1999).

The pluralist values that are particularly relevant to this area are the privacy of an individual (public data on social media) and the duty of care to save lives and property (held by emergency management teams during major disasters). This pluralist value system led us to consider what is *legally* allowed during an emergency and what is *ethically* justifiable. State of Exception theory helps to define the nuances of emergency management, whereas following a legal framework is paramount for emergency management teams at all times.

2.2.2 *State of Exception*

Cases of massive cyber-surveillance have been justified by governmental organisations, from local to the state level and onwards to multinational organisations, due to the existence of a "present danger". Details of the present danger is known usually to a few, and the danger should be dealt with almost immediately, otherwise the present order will tumble, with extraordinary consequence. All-embracing cyber-surveillance of individuals and disparate groups can be mounted by individuals, news organisations, the entertainment industry and those with criminal intent, within and across national boundaries.

This nexus of ethical issues of privacy and dignity, political questions of governance and assurance of protection of a whole population and the extant and emerging legal frameworks for protecting values, life and property, confronts groups large and small many times in their existence. In the twentieth century this nexus has been discussed under the rubric of *states of exception*. The "state of exception" denotes "a legal regime in which public institutions are vested with extraordinary powers to address existential threats to public order" (Criddle & Fox-Decent, 2012: 44). Some political scientists have argued that a "paradigm case for emergency powers has been an imminent threat to the very existence of the state, which necessitates empowering the executive to take extraordinary measures" (Ackerman, 2003: 1031).

From a human rights perspective, the state of exception bears important consequences on the mechanism of derogation. The leading international and regional human rights covenants regulate states' entry into, conduct and accountability before, during and after the state of emergency. The cornerstones of these covenants are their derogation clauses, which permit states to restrict some human rights in exceptional times – but only where this is strictly necessary to address serious threats to the life, independence or security of the nation and its members. The suspension of those human rights is subject to a carefully calibrated system of limitations, safeguards, notifications and review procedures. International human rights law affords states the power to impose heightened restrictions on certain human rights during emergencies (Ackerman, 2004).

A state of exception, which relates to the notions of a state of emergency, state of siege and public emergency, is used to "emphasise that, situations in which domestic authorities may take special measures to deal with a difficult crisis and possibly derogate from international human rights obligations, *is by nature inherently exceptional*, a fact that is considered by the concept 'states of exception'" (Svensson-McCarthy, 1998: xxiv). This is very important if a mass surveillance operation is launched to protect against natural or human-made disasters; states can change domestic laws almost at will when faced by a real or perceived *exception* norm. Note that almost all modern states have signed and more or less discharge their international treaty and legal obligations in order to protect human rights, including the protection of an individual's privacy at all times.

Thus, international laws and treaties, particularly those dealing with human rights, disaster relief and geospatial locations, act as a constraint on the national prerogative of using all the instruments in their command to protect their people, moral values and beliefs, existing order and sociocultural norms, during a period of crisis. An important caveat to the derogation mechanism exists in the form of a qualitative discrimination between "non-peremptory" and "peremptory" human rights. During national crises, governments may derogate from non-peremptory human rights norms such as the freedoms of expression, movement and peaceable assembly, but not from "non-derogable" human rights such as the right to life, prohibition of torture, freedom from slavery and the right to recognition before the law.

Recognising the dangers attached to a period of national emergency, international human rights laws limit the circumstances under which states may legally derogate from their international obligations. These dangers were addressed in 1985 by jurists, human rights experts, labour law experts and others, which led to the formulation of the Siracusa Principles for limiting and derogating provisions (United Nations Commission on Human Rights, 1984, paragraph A.10; Siracusa Principles 1985). The international and regional conventions on civil and political rights[3] provide criteria to evaluate the lawfulness of the suspension of human rights initiated by state members, including the following key factors:

Justification and strict necessity: All suspensions of human rights will be legally permissible only where "genuine public emergencies undermine the institutional prerequisites for the enjoyment of human rights by imperilling the life, independence, or security of the state".[4] A state's failure to provide a reasoned justification for particular emergency measures renders those measures unlawful, as the UN Human Rights Committee has recognised (Criddle & Fox-Decent, 2012).

Last resort: Suspending non-peremptory human rights obligations must represent the last resort.

Proportionality: States are required to use "only those measures that minimally restrict the freedoms ordinarily protected by the suspended treaty rights" (Criddle & Fox-Decent, 2016: 129).

Notification: Leading covenants on civil and political rights oblige states to notify the international community promptly when they suspend their human rights obligations during national crises, and when the suspension comes to an end.

Temporal scope: States must also provide a clear timeframe (a sunset clause) for the state of emergency; "only a truly extraordinary crisis that lasts for a relatively brief period of time can be a derogation-justifying emergency" (Gross & Aolain, 2001: 644).

Contestation: Decisions to suspend ordinary human rights must be open to public contestation to ensure that emergency powers are not held or abused so as to dominate the state's subjects.

It can, perhaps, be argued that the observance of these principles affords an appropriate respect for individual dignity, mitigating concerns that emergency powers will be employed in a manner inconsistent with the fiduciary authorisation of public power. The European Court of Human Rights has provided states a wide margin to decide both when a situation calls for derogation and the nature and scope of the measures required to tackle the emergency.

2.3 TECHNOLOGY-MEDIATED PROTECTION OF DATA AND PERSONS

From the preceding discussion one may draw a conclusion: When a person or a group of persons face danger during a disaster, then others acting as fellow citizens or as government/nongovernmental agencies are encouraged by their value systems to help those that are in peril. What is prohibited in *normal times* is allowed in *exceptional circumstances*. In civilised societies, there are laws that enable government agencies to look after the well-being of the citizens, and sometimes personnel in agencies have to risk their life and safety to help others. To save another from peril, it is important to have data about the person or persons at risk, – including age, location, infirmity, health, educational attainment, wealth, ethnicity and so on. Lack of this data often hampers evacuation (Elliott, 2014; Elliott & Pais, 2006) and rehabilitation (Chamlee-Wright & Storr, 2009). The collection of this personal and place data without the knowledge and consent of the citizens is sometimes regarded as a part of a mass surveillance aided and abetted by *Big Data* technology (Bigo et al., 2013; Brayne, 2017). It is important that there is no denudation of the trust between emergency managers and the citizens. Trust is the key to the successful resolution of conflicts related to place and person (Hardin, 2002), especially in a disaster situation.

The ethical landscape that affects the use of social media in disasters is not exhaustive – the chosen case studies of *value pluralism* and *state of exception* are two important areas where theory can be assessed. However, ethical theory is not enforceable, and in order to develop clear guidelines for emergency management practitioners, such as rescue services and police, it is necessary to assess the ethical theory within the frame of existing legal systems. In Project Slándáil we recognised that emergency management teams need clear guidelines through existing legal systems that show what is permissible by law in order to act on ethical principles. Thus, the expertise of legal practitioners in four EU countries (Ireland, the UK, Italy and Germany) was sought, and the following chapters represent the results of their analyses.

If we assume that the data collection for emergency management will be within legal bounds, we still have one outstanding problem: How can the data be protected against illegal retrieval? Anonymisation techniques, which are designed to protect the privacy of individuals whose data is held in large databases by deleting information such as names and Social Security numbers, was motivated by a desire for balances producing safe data (no names, addresses or other identifying characteristics) whilst maintaining useful data (e.g., data that can yield insight into disease prevalence, purchasing preferences).

Nevertheless, there are well-documented cases of large anonymised datasets being hacked and personal identities revealed by innocuous correlations (Sweeney, 2002) leading to the claimed "failure of anonymisation". The challenge from within legal circles centres on a lack of understanding about the limitations of anonymisation algorithms and solutions (Ohm, 2010, 2012). The pro-anonymisation researchers and developers have been boosted by the EU's Working Party (Advisory Board) on data protection and privacy (Opinion 5/2014) (El Emam & Álvarez, 2014). Despite the fact there are assurances about the strength of anonymisation technologies (Cavoukian & Castro, 2014), the debate on the efficacy of anonymisation shows that much more progress is needed, especially in the context of data from social computing systems, before we can trust data anonymisation algorithms to protect the data against attacks on privacy (Peng et al., 2014; Xu et al., 2014).

A technological solution for the safe use of systems that can potentially violate human rights of a person or persons will be very welcome, but it may take time to develop these solutions. In the meantime there is a need to introduce the notion of controlled use of systems that can access and process vast quantities of (personal) data in an emergency.

2.4 CONCLUSION

We conclude by noting that technological developments in all areas of human endeavour involve a reconsideration of established ethical norms and an assessment of their impact on societal values and power relations. Recent developments in information and communications technology (ICT) – namely, the advent of social media and social networks together with the maturing of technologies for the mining of large scale datasets, termed "Big Data Analytics" – have transformed the amount of information available to state authorities and offer the potential to improve the quality of actionable information derived from these data.

This transformation can be a boon to people in adversity, since vast quantities of data can be sieved in a matter of seconds to produce actionable information for the purposes of rescuing persons and property and ensuring the continuation of civil order. Equally, it challenges the notions that create civil order – rights to life, property and opportunity and the privacy of the individual – and there are fears that mass surveillance, aided and abetted by Big Data Analytics, may yet give life to the dystopian scenario symbolised by Orwell's "Big Brother".

We believe that the interaction and exchange of ideas between professional and academic lawyers, computer scientists and software professionals, human rights scholars and those responsible for implementing the law and protecting people and property, can aid in developing operational norms for the use of exciting new technological developments.

A social media monitoring system requires a legally robust foundation for the collection of personal data, and software developers and vendors must mitigate the risk of infringement of the human rights of the data subjects or owners, the copyright of the data owners without adequate justification, or the relevant personal data protection and privacy provisions of the EU or equivalent national or international law. The following chapters explore the legal frameworks that will enable the monitoring and harvesting of social computing data; the final chapter, a model licence agreement for a social media monitor for emergency management, represents an attempt to distil our findings into a practical and enforceable agreement.

We have synthesised ethical analysis and legal research not only to create technical solutions to the difficulties of monitoring and harvesting social computing data, but also to outline a viable legal path for a social media monitor. We have synthesised research into different legal frameworks – internet law (Chapter 3), copyright and data protection law (Chapter 4) and human rights law (Chapter 5) – in order to present a comprehensive picture of the legal environment in which social computing can be used safely.

NOTES

1. Berlin did not offer a succinct definition of values. He used the terms "values", "ideals" and "goals" more or less – but not quite – interchangeably. Values, for Berlin, are ideas about what it is good to be and do – about what sort of life, what sort of character, what sort of actions, what state of being it is desirable to aspire to (see Cherniss & Hardy, 2004, for a discussion about Berlin's work).
2. This quotation is often attributed to Voltaire, but it was actually written by a biographer, Evelyn Beatrice Hall, to illustrate Voltaire's ideas on freedom of speech (see Kinne, 1943: 534–535).
3. That is, the ICCPR, African Charter on Human Rights, American Convention on Human Rights (ACHR), Arab Charter on Human Rights (Arab Charter) and European Convention on Human Rights (ECHR).
4. For instance, the European Commission on Human Rights understands a "public emergency crisis" as a danger that is (1) present or imminent, (2) exceptional, (3) concerns the entire population and (4) constitutes a "threat to the organised life of the community".

3

Internet Laws

Taiwo Oriola
Ulster University

3.1 INTRODUCTION

Our strategy is to investigate both extant personal and proprietary data protection laws and regulations that will impact on a system that harvests data from social media. Adopting a conception of the Internet as a socio-technical system, we address different systems of governance including self-regulation, technical and government regulation (Section 3.2). Subsequent discursive sections address legal protections for personal data (Section 3.3) and for proprietary information (Section 3.4) on social media according to the jurisdictional scope of our work (Section 3.3.1). Our analysis is based on the interpretation of the existing law and key landmark cases in each area. Findings are then summarised in Section 3.5.

3.1.1 *Key Concepts Underlying the Research*

The Internet is a network of global computers, linked together by Internet Protocol Address, which anchors the World Wide Web application that provides an 'information space' for digital texts, pictures, audios and videos that are linked by hypertexts. Social media is an integral part of the World Wide Web applications, comprising platforms that host personal data and other proprietary information, and often serving as data storage and communication tools for subscribers who voluntarily surrender personal data and other proprietary information, in exchange for free use of social media platforms such as Twitter and social networking platforms like Facebook. 'The Internet' is often used generically in common parlance to describe a network of global computers, the World Wide Web and its constituent social media and numerous commercial and non-commercial digital platforms. Upon its operational deployment, harvesting and monitoring software would have to be a part of Internet ecosystems in order to access social media contents for disaster management.

In its broad generic sense, the Internet is transnational and transcendental of geography and physical barriers. Invariably, the transnational nature of the

Internet makes imperative the prospects for the application of multiple laws, norms and principles from across numerous countries. Additionally, the applicable laws are not in any way generic, but disparate, covering subjects as diverse as copyright, encryption, data protection, database protection and licensing rights. Thus, social computing providers, content generators and organisations and individuals who harvest data have to carefully navigate the parameters of these disparate laws from across multiple jurisdictions in order to determine the scope for lawful derogations and to avoid trampling third-party rights in personal data and proprietary information.

Internet governance systems are multifaceted, comprising self-regulation, market regulation, technical regulation and governmental regulation. Thus, data harvesters have to recognise the different categories of regulatory frameworks for the Internet, the exceptions to these regulations and the underlying safe harbours where they could lawfully derogate from prescribed norms, rules and laws that protect personal data and proprietary information on social media.

Social media comprise user-generated contents, volunteered by subscribers, in exchange for free use of social media platforms as storage and communication tools. Invariably, there are personal data and property rights in social media contents. Therefore, software programmers and users have to know the parameters of these laws, and be clear on the exceptions to prescribed laws that would allow for lawful derogations, in the operational deployment of harvesting and monitoring software for the appropriation of social media data.

3.1.2 *The Internet, the World Wide Web and Social Media: A Symbiotic and Generative Relationship*

Invariably, any social computing software would be deployed within the Internet ecosystem. Therefore, an understanding of the architectural dynamics of the Internet, the World Wide Web and the social media it anchors is crucial for the determination and analysis of the applicable laws and norms that underpin the governance of the Internet and its constituent social media.

The Internet is a global network of computers (Ziewitz & Brown, 2011). Each computer on the global network is assigned a unique address known as an 'Internet Protocol Address', which "can be used to identify the source of the connection to the Internet" (*Beyond Systems, Inc. v. Realtime Gaming Holding Company*, 2005). Thus, the Internet is an architectural and technical construct made up of networked computers that is distinct from, and is the gateway to, the World Wide Web, which is an 'information space' for the storage of texts, images, audio and videos that are linked by hypertext (McPherson, 2009).

Social media are the critical mass of the 'network society' and digital tools, which are anchored by the World Wide Web, and act as interactive digital applications that facilitate the creation, exchange and sharing of user-generated contents and other publicly available information (L. Austin, Fisher Liu & Jin, 2012; Fraustino & Ma, 2015).

Significantly, the relationship among the Internet, the World Wide Web and social media is largely symbiotic and generative, allowing for seamless production of user-generated contents and their derivatives, and sharing of value-added user-generated contents (Zittrain, 2006). This is exemplified by numerous parodies or pastiches on YouTube, and original 'tweets' and their 're-tweets' on Twitter.

The Internet evolved from the work of the Advanced Research Projects Agency Network (ARPANET), which was a research collaboration between US military defence contractors and US universities, on secured military communications systems via networked computers (Oriola, 2005). Therefore, the subsequent evolvement of the World Wide Web applications and social media platforms was largely serendipitous (McPherson, 2009). Nevertheless, the 'Internet', the 'World Wide Web' and 'social media' are routinely used interchangeably or synonymously in common parlance to denote the 'information space', where information or data is routinely shared, exchanged and traded (De Franceschi & Lehmann, 2015; Mayer-Schönberger & Cukier, 2013; Ramirez, Brill, Ohlhausen, Wright & McSweeny, 2014; Stieglitz & Dang-Xuan, 2013). This monograph implicitly adopts the common parlance description of the Internet, the World Wide Web and social media.

3.1.3 *User-Generated Content on Social Media*

A decade ago, coinciding with the advent of social networking and microblogging, experts in computer-mediated communications described three primary activities of the users of this new form of communication (Boyd & Ellison 2007: 211): first, for constructing a public or semi-public profile within a bounded system; second, for articulating a list of other users with whom they share a connection, and third for viewing and traversing their local network, or their list of connections, and more globally browsing the networks others have created. Social networking systems offer a set of 'tools' that, much like other artefacts, 'a society builds to create and maintain itself'. For example, users create their personal profiles, which are browsed and interacted with by others leading 'inexorably to the culture of sharing and voluntariness on social networks' (Stewart 2013: viii). The concepts of sharing and volunteering are 'difficult concepts for the law, which often seeks more rigid definitions and boundaries to regulate human affairs' (*Ibid.*). What starts as a noble act of sharing individual profiles and equally noble act of providing the infrastructure for the volunteers for free can cause major international ructions as in the case of targeting voters in elections and referenda in the US and UK in 2016 and 2017, respectively.

Perhaps a more functional and practical definition of social media and the nature of their platforms and contents was that proffered by a Maryland Court of Appeal in the case of *Independent Newspapers Inc. v. Brodie* (2009):

Social networking sites and blogs are sophisticated tools of communication where the user voluntarily provides information that the user wants to share with others. Web sites such as Facebook and Myspace, allow the user to tightly control the dissemination of that information. The user can choose what information to provide or can choose not to provide information. The act of posting information on a social networking site, without the poster limiting access to that information, makes whatever is posted available to the world at large.

Thus, characteristically, social media contents are essentially user-generated, and often voluntarily provided, with controlled or uncontrolled access by the general public. Typically, user-generated contents on social media comprise texts, pictures and audio-visual materials that are at once personal data and proprietary information, which are invariably subject to technical and legal protection measures under transnational and national legal frameworks, with concomitant legal implications for the deployment of software within Internet ecosystems.

Indeed, emerging case law and practices of social media operators would appear to tacitly acknowledge account holders' property rights in – and control over – their social media accounts, and, by extrapolation, the constituent information. For example, Facebook allows users, while they are alive, to designate a "legacy contact" or elect to have their accounts deleted following their death. The policy requires a designated family member or friend of the deceased Facebook account holder to complete an online form that would notify Facebook of the account holder's death. Facebook would then add a 'Remembering' tagline to the deceased user's name, and notify the 'legacy contact' accordingly. The legacy contact is expected to take over the control of the account and deal with the constituent information in accordance with the wishes of the deceased account holder. For example, the legacy contact could download information from the deceased user's account; write a memorial post for display on the deceased user's account; update profile photos or accept new friends.[1] Arguably, there is a parallel between Facebook's 'legacy contact' policy, and executors of the estates of deceased persons appointed under a will, which in parallel validates the proprietary notion of user-generated contents on social media.

The twin concepts of property rights in and control over social media contents by account holders recently received a judicial imprimatur in Canada in *The Amalgamated Transit Union, Local 113 v. Toronto Transit Commission (Use of Social Media Grievance)* (2016). The case involved the Twitter account owned by Toronto Transit Commission, which was used as a communication and feedback tool for its customers. Whilst most of the tweets were legitimate requests and feedback, the court found that a minority of the tweets were vulgar, offensive, racist, homophobic, abusive, sexist or threatening. The plaintiff sued the defendant on behalf of the defendant's employees, allegedly for its failure to take reasonable steps to protect its employees from abusive tweets (messages posted on Twitter). The main issue for determination centred on the extent to which the defendant was required to manage its social media accounts in a way that would protect its employees from harassment. The court agreed with the plaintiff that the defendant did not take all reasonable and practical steps to protect its employees from abusive tweets in the circumstances, but rejected the plaintiff's request that the defendant shut down its Twitter account. Rather, the court suggested that both parties establish mutually agreed strategies for dealing with inappropriate and abusive tweets posted on the defendant's Twitter account by its customers. The case certainly demonstrates that social media account holders have a degree of control and ownership of the constituent information.

However, social media platform operators such as Facebook, Twitter, Instagram, etc. equally have some degree of control over, and proprietary interests in, user-generated contents on social media. These control and proprietary interests are typically secured via contractual terms of use. With regards to control over social media contents, for example, social media platform operators reserve the right to shut down an account that breaches a term of use. For example, in early February 2016, Twitter deleted more than 125,000 accounts that were linked to the Islamic State and other terror organisations (Yadron, 2016).

Similarly, the proprietary interests of social media operators are contractually secured in the routine commodification and exploitation of social media account holders' personal data and other proprietary information via targeted advertisements that continually provide steady revenue streams for social media operators (Andrejevic, 2011; De Franceschi & Lehmann, 2015). Thus, the *quid pro quo* for the commodification of user-generated contents by social media proprietors is the free use of social media platforms as information storage and as a communication tool by social media account holders. This contractual arrangement is aptly articulated by Sebastian Sevignani thus: "People are not only using social networking sites, but they are also producing something that is appropriated by the social networking site's owners and sold to others in order to realize profit. Therefore, we can speak of users as *prosumers*, a portmanteau of producer and consumer" (Sevignani, 2013: 325).

Inevitably, whether at the research or commercial phase, software for monitoring and harvesting social computing data has to engage with the commodified user-generated contents on social media, which are subject to the control of account holders and social media operators. Both account holders and social media proprietors rely heavily on technical and legal protection measures under transnational and national legal frameworks for the protection of their proprietary interests. Thus, the appropriation of commodified user-generated contents on social media management could have legal ramifications for users under the current regulatory framework, the nature of which is examined and analysed in the next section.

3.2 INTERNET GOVERNANCE SYSTEMS: SELF-REGULATION, TECHNICAL REGULATION AND GOVERNMENTAL REGULATION

Regulation of the Internet is a contentious topic. The very idea frequently invokes polemical views that are the hallmarks of Internet governance discourses. There are those who are opposed to any form of regulation for fear that it could impinge upon free speech. This indeed was one of the central arguments canvassed by plaintiffs in *Reno v. ACLU* (US, 1997). The US Supreme Court unanimously upheld the argument, and held *inter alia* that section 223 of the Communications Decency Act, which prohibited minors from accessing indecent material on the Internet, was unconstitutional. In particular, the US Supreme Court observed that the use of the word 'indecency' in the act was overboard and vague, and a content-based restriction, "which raises special First Amendment concerns because of its obvious chilling effect on free speech".

Indeed, the virtues of free speech, and the imperatives for its protection in the online environment, are a recurring theme in Internet governance discourses, and are generally perceived as a major constraint to delimiting the parameters of online hate speech (Burns, 2015; Citron, 2014). Even so, there are compelling circumstances for regulatory interventions in the Internet environment, which include combating cybercrimes and enforcement of intellectual property rights (Reed, 2012).

Similarly, there are others who favour self-regulation and continually pine for a cyberspace 'Wild West' that is bereft of governmental regulatory intervention (Netanel, 2000). However, given that the online world is no less than the mirror-image of the regulated brick-and-mortar world of commerce, taxation, sundry crimes, friendship, etc., the utopian vision of a lawless and self-regulatory cyberspace would arguably remain an unrealisable fantasy (Oriola, 2005).

Yet, there are those who favour technical regulation (Lessig, 2006), whilst some argue for governmental regulation to infuse order into the "vast wasteland" of "hate, violence and porn" (Henderson, 2013: 7). The reality, however, is that Internet governance systems are a mixture of self-regulation, market regulation, technical control measures (technical regulation) and governmental regulation (Lessig, 1999; Longworth, 1999).

Therefore, following the operational deployment of harvesting and monitoring software on the Internet, programmers have to grapple with all forms of Internet governance systems: self-regulation, market regulation, technical regulation and governmental regulation. In the following paragraphs, the categories of regulatory measures are explored in relative detail as a background to Section 3.3, which explores the regulatory framework for Internet contents governance in greater depths.

3.2.1 *Self-Regulation/Market Regulation*

Self-regulation typically involves operational norms and customs of social media communities, such as negative ratings or ostracism for misbehaviour (see, for instance, Solove (2007: 76–102), who cites examples of the reactions for and against 'shaming and the digital scarlet letter'), or blocking of access by social media operators such as Facebook and Twitter, for prohibited or unacceptable behaviour by users (Luca, 2016; Trudel, 2000). For example, online market operators such as Amazon and eBay rely heavily on their users for feedback and rating systems to build reputation, rein in dishonesty and impose a sense of order and trust between sellers and buyers (Reed, 2012).

Similarly, social media operators typically have terms of use for subscribers and third-party software developers who use their platforms. This is exemplified by the Twitter Developer Agreement, which targets harvesting and monitoring software that would "interact with Twitter's ecosystem of applications, services, website, web pages and content". Notably, noncompliance with the terms of the developer agreement are deemed as "policy violations," or "violations of the Developer Agreement" that could potentially lead Twitter to block the erring third-party software developer from trawling their website.[2] For example, as previously noted in Section 3.1.3, in early February 2016, Twitter deleted more than 125,000 accounts, including applications that were linked to the Islamic State and other terror organisations (Yadron, 2016).

In addition to unilateral revocation of an erring social media account, a social media operator could seek judicial intervention in blocking third-party software or applications for noncompliance with agreed terms of use, as exemplified by *Craigslist, Inc. v. 3 Taps, Inc.* (2013). Craigslist is a popular website that hosts classified advertisements from across the United States. The defendants, 3 Taps. Inc., partnered with other companies to provide an alternative user interface software for browsing the Craigslist website for housing advertisements datasets. However, Craigslist disapproved of the practice and subsequently blocked the companies' IP addresses, and served them with a cease-and-desist letter, leading to a significant reduction in traffic to the defendants' website. Nevertheless, 3 Taps, Inc. continued to harvest housing advertisement datasets from the Craigslist website, and Craigslist had to sue 3 Taps, Inc., claiming that the latter's actions were tantamount to a violation of the Computer Fraud and Abuse Act, a breach of Craigslist's terms of use policy and copyright infringement. The court found for the plaintiff (Craigslist), and held *inter alia* that the cease-and-desist letter, coupled with the blocking of the defendants' IP addresses, constituted sufficient notice under the Computer Fraud and Abuse Act, and a clear indication that Craigslist had revoked its authorisation to the defendants to access its website. Consequently, deploying software to monitor and harvest social computing data might require navigating terms-of-use and access policies imposed by social media operators.

Significantly, a self-regulatory custom or practice could be induced by market imperatives, allowing for an overlap between self-regulation and market regulation, as exemplified by the aforementioned online feedback and rating systems that help build reputations and trust between disembodied online buyers and sellers. Yet another example is social media operators' putative business model, which makes digital storage and communication tools freely available to the public in exchange for the trading of users' personal data and proprietary information for advertising revenues. Users are typically bound by enforceable terms of service agreement that allow social media operators to freely profile and target them with advertisements for goods and services that might be of interest to users (Andrejevic, 2011; De Franceschi & Lehmann, 2015).

However, a self-regulatory norm or custom infused by market paradigms could ultimately carry commercial and proprietary connotations, with clear legal implications for the deployment of harvesting and monitoring software on the Internet. This scenario is again exemplified by *Agence France Presse v. Morel* (2013) in which a US federal jury found that Agence France-Presse and Getty Images had wilfully violated the US Copyright Act when, without prior consent, they used photos of the earthquake in Haiti taken by Daniel Morel in his native Haiti, in the aftermath of the 2010 earthquake that killed more than 250,000 people. The defendants had culled the photos from Morel's Twitter account without authorisation, and the federal jury ordered the defendants to pay $1.2 million in damages to the plaintiff (Morel).

In Section 3.3 we will highlight practical ways by which software vendors and users could avoid similar legal pitfalls; we analyse the legal boundaries within which software for harvesting and monitoring social computing data could lawfully be deployed without encroaching on third-party rights in personal data and proprietary information.

3.2.2 *Technical Regulation*

Technical regulation involve using codes, which are an integral part of Internet architecture, to mediate or regulate access to social media contents, or filter or block abusive postings or copyright-infringing file-sharing software. For example, in September 2016, Instagram, a social media platform, introduced a comment moderating application designed to filter or block abusive trolls. According to Instagram, the contents filtering tool was designed "to empower each individual … and promote a culture where everyone feels safe to be themselves without criticism or harassment" (Mlot, 2016). Similarly, Google Chrome and Firefox browsers were reconfigured to block access to The Pirate Bay website, a notorious file-sharing software application typically used to share copyright-protected audio-visual digital files (Millman, 2016).

Other examples of technical regulatory practices include the routine use of encryption software for mobile devices and servers, respectively, by manufacturers of mobile devices and operators of cloud-based computing services to protect and erect barriers or bar access to web-based information. For example, in *Government's Ex Parte Application for Order Compelling Apple Inc. to Assist Agents in Search (Apple Inc. v. FBI)* (2016), Apple rejected the FBI's request for the creation of a special software that would enable the FBI to unlock and access the contents of an iPhone 5C device, owned by one of the couple involved in the San Bernardino terrorist attack that killed fourteen people and injured twenty-two on

5 December 2015. On the eve of the hearing scheduled for 22 March 2016, before the US District Court for the Central District of California, the hearing was postponed at the instigation of the FBI, and the case was subsequently withdrawn by the FBI on grounds that an overseas third-party security researcher had helped the FBI to access the information contained in the iPhone.

Similarly, in *Microsoft Corporation Inc. v. United States of America* (2016), Microsoft challenged a warrant issued by a New York District Court judge under section 2703 of the Stored Communications Act, compelling Microsoft to produce all e-mails and information about a certain account hosted by Microsoft Servers in Dublin, Ireland. On 14 July 2016, the US Court of Appeals for the Second Circuit upheld Microsoft's argument and held that the Store Communications Act should not have an effect outside of the United States, although the warrant would have been valid if the e-mails had been stored on a Microsoft Server based in the United States.

Whilst some scholars have argued that protecting digital contents or privacy by code or encryption software is superior to the protection afforded by regulation (Edwards, 2009: 861–872), it is often necessary to have back-up laws that would prohibit or punish computer hacking or anti-circumvention measures. In the European Union, for example, there is a legal obligation on the providers of publicly available electronic communications networks and services to provide security and encryption of personal data and proprietary information (Article 29 Data Protection Working Party, 2012; Article 29 Data Protection Working Party: Preliminary EDPS Opinion on the review of the ePrivacy Directive 2002; Directive 2002/58/EC ePrivacy Directive, 2002).

With regards to encryption protection for copyright works, Articles 6 and 7 of Directive 2001/29/EC on Copyright and the Information Society, provide safeguards against the circumvention of encrypted copyright in musical and audio-visual works. Similarly, Articles 2, 3, 4, 5 and 6 of the Council of Europe Convention on Cybercrime generally criminalise computer hacking by respectively prohibiting 'illegal access', 'illegal interception', 'data interference', 'system interference' and 'misuse of devices'.

Even so, there are exceptions to anti-circumvention legislations protecting personal data and proprietary information, as evidenced by *Case C-335/12 Nintendo and Others v. PC Box Srl and Others* (2014), in which the Court of Justice of the European Union (CJEU) ruled that circumventing a protection system of a games console may, in certain circumstances, be lawful under Directive 2001/29/EC on Copyright and the Information Society. In particular, the court noted that digital right management legal protection under Directive 2001/29/EC covered only technological measures intended to prevent or eliminate unauthorised acts of reproduction, communication, public offer or distribution, for which authorisation from the copyright holder was required. The court further observed that digital rights management must respect the principle of proportionality without prohibiting devices or activities which have a commercially significant purpose or use, other than to circumvent the technical protection for lawful purposes.

Thus, whilst harvesting and monitoring software could potentially be blocked from accessing crucial data on social media by encryption software, it cannot be prohibited outright simply because it is capable of infringing third-party rights in data and proprietary information, in light of its commercially significant and dual non-infringing and public interest uses (*CBS Songs Ltd. v. Amstrad Consumer Electronics PLC*, 1988; *Sony Corp. of America v. Universal City Studios, Inc.*, 1984).

Moreover, there could be circumstances where it may be lawful for software programmers to circumvent encryption and access crucial data and information on social media. In Section 3.3, we will highlight the parameters of lawful derogation under which software vendors and users could lawfully circumvent encryption software barriers to social media data and information that are crucial for disaster management.

3.2.3 *Governmental Regulation*

There is no generic set of laws that regulate the Internet as such. Rather, applicable Internet laws are as varied, disparate and transnational as there are countries connected to the Internet, due to the variations in national laws, attendant legal issues, as well as the transnational overreach and ubiquity of the Internet (Rowland, Kohl & Charlesworth, 2016). For example, the use of harvesting and monitoring software on the Internet could trigger disparate legal issues that range from copyright, data protection, encryption laws to licensing rights that protect web-based user-generated contents across multiple countries. This chapter analyses these legal issues in relative detail in Section 3.3, and the extent to which those harvesting and monitoring social computing data could lawfully derogate from the prescribed laws, in the operational deployment of software on the Internet.

We will review relevant and analogous literature on Internet regulation and governance systems in the context of the operational deployment of social computing systems. Whilst acknowledging that applicable Internet laws are as diverse as the countries connected to the Internet worldwide, we focus on literature and laws from selected jurisdictions: the Republic of Ireland, Italy, Germany, the UK, the EU and the US. The narrowness of the scope of jurisdictions selected for analysis is informed by relevance of literature and the sheer impracticality of analysing the laws of all the countries connected to the Internet globally.

3.3 OWNERSHIP OF PERSONAL DATA HARVESTED FROM SOCIAL COMPUTING SYSTEMS

There are two recurring themes here that the operational deployment of social computing systems have to legally grapple with: these, in broad terms, are personal data and proprietary information, which are the critical mass of the information on social media. However, the transnational and transcendental nature of the Internet (Rowland et al., 2016) compels a transnational approach to the analysis of the legal implications of Internet laws for the operational deployment of monitoring and harvesting software by programmers and end users (Reed, 2012). Therefore, this chapter will focus on relevant literature and selected international laws, UK laws, EU laws and US laws.

3.3.1 *Limited Jurisdictional Scope*

Even though the Internet is transnational and transcendental with global coverage, and it is most likely that harvesting and monitoring software could engage social media contents outside of the Western hemisphere, nevertheless, this section confines the scope of relevant laws for analysis to those from applicable international treaties or norms, the United Kingdom, the European Union and the United States for two main reasons. First, the sheer volume of disparate national laws and norms involved make such an exercise impractical. Second, most of the social media operators whose platforms harvest and monitor software would invariably engage with are headquartered in the United States, with operational servers and subsidiaries located respectively in the United States and Europe (*Microsoft Corp. v. United States*, 2016). Therefore, for practical purposes, the scope of applicable laws would necessarily be limited to that of applicable international treaties and the laws of the United Kingdom, the European Union and the United States.

In structural terms, the section is divided into two broad categories comprising 'personal data' and 'proprietary information'. Each of the two broad categories is subdivided into four jurisdictions: (a) transnational laws, (b) UK laws, (c) EU laws and (d) US laws. Moreover, for each jurisdictional category, where applicable, we note the nature of the norm or law in question – that is, whether it is self-regulation, market regulation, technical regulation, governmental regulation or a combination of the aforesaid categories.

Moreover, due to the wide scope of jurisdictions under consideration, this section of the chapter focusses exclusively on 'black letter law' – that is, relevant legislations and selected case law that interpreted the legislations, and the extent to which the said laws could be applicable to harvesting and monitoring software. This section also highlights the parameters of lawful derogations from the laws protecting personal data and property rights in data and information, and how harvesting and monitoring software programmers and users could lawfully appropriate personal data and proprietary information on social media.

Chapter 4 deals comprehensively with EU and German copyright laws for the operational deployment of social computing systems, and with the implications of EU human rights laws, in the context of personal data protection. We focus here on how relevant and applicable Internet laws, broadly defined, could impact the operational deployment of harvesting and monitoring software, and it highlights the boundaries of lawful derogations from the laws protecting personal data and proprietary information on social media.

3.3.2 *Social Computing Systems and Internet Law*

The laws protecting personal information in the broadest sense would invariably protect personal data and data privacy. In legal literature, 'personal data', 'data privacy' and 'personal information' are often used synonymously and interchangeably because the concepts are overlapping, with similar legal connotations (Rowland, Kohl & Charlesworth 2016: 333–337). Article 4(1) of the General Data Protection Regulation, defines personal data as "any information relating to an identified or identifiable natural person (data subject)". Samuel Warren and Louis Brandeis defined privacy as the "right to enjoy life: the right to be left alone" (Warren & Brandeis, 1890). Thus, there are correlations among personal data, personal information and data privacy.

Within the context of social computing systems, the pertinent questions are: What is personal data or data privacy, and the laws protecting private or personal information? Would it be reasonable for users to expect privacy protection for self-disclosed personal data or information on social media? We address these questions as a background to the analysis of the implications of data protection and privacy laws in selected jurisdictions, for the harvesting of social computing data.

3.3.3 *International Laws*

International privacy standards invariably frame personal data protection or data privacy as a human right. In this section we highlight the framing of personal data or data privacy as a human right under selected international laws and treaties, their enforceability and implications for operational deployment of social media platforms and networking systems.

Article 12 of the Universal Declaration of Human Rights (1948) provides: "No one shall be subjected to arbitrary interference with his privacy, family, home or correspondence, nor to attacks upon his honour and reputation. Everyone has the right to the protection of the law against such interference or attacks". Although the Universal Declaration of Human Rights is not a treaty document, and is therefore unenforceable, it was adopted by a number of international treaties, including the International Covenant on Civil and Political Rights (ICCPR).

Article 17 of the ICCPR expressly states that everyone has the right to the protection of the law against unlawful or arbitrary interference with their privacy. It has been suggested that the term 'unlawful' implied that no interference could take place "except in cases envisaged by the law", and that "interference authorized by States can only take place on the basis of law, which itself must comply with the provisions of the International Covenant on Civil and Political Rights". Similarly, it has been suggested that the term 'arbitrary interference' could only extend to interference provided for under national law, and that the concept of 'reasonableness' should indicate that "any interference with privacy must be proportional to the end sought and be necessary in the circumstances of any given case" (Report of the United Nations High Commissioner for Human Rights: The Right to Privacy in the Digital Age, 2014).

Article 2 of the ICCPR requires each signatory state to respect and ensure to all persons within its territory and subject to its jurisdiction, the rights recognised in the covenant without distinction of any kind, such as race, colour, sex, language, religion, political or other opinion, national or social origin, property, birth or other status. Article 2 paragraph 3(b) of the covenant further enjoins signatory states "to ensure that any person claiming such a remedy shall have his right determined by competent judicial, administrative or legislative authorities, or by any other competent authority provided for by the legal system of the State, and to develop the possibilities of judicial remedy".

The foregoing provisions clearly demonstrate that the ICCPR overly relies on signatory states for enforcement nationally. This could be problematic, where a signatory state or its agency is responsible for privacy rights violations. Thus, although international human rights laws such as the ICCPR contain ample provisions for the enforcement and implementation of the right to privacy, prevailing evidence shows "a lack of adequate national legislation and or enforcement, weak procedural safeguards, and ineffective oversight, all of which have contributed to a lack of accountability for arbitrary interference in the right to privacy".[3]

Therefore, in order to ameliorate a possible lack of enforcement at the state level, the ICCPR established two Optional Protocols to the Covenant. The first Optional Protocol, which is relevant to this discourse, establishes an individual complaints mechanism, which allows individuals to complain to the United Nations Human Rights Committee about the violations of the provisions of the covenant. The UN Human Rights Committee must then bring the complaint to the attention of the relevant state, which must respond within six months. Even so, anonymous complaints are barred, and complainants must have exhausted all domestic remedies prior to lodging complaints before the UN Human Rights Committee (UN, 1976).

Even with the First Optional Protocol that allows individual complainants to bypass the might of the state, not all states are parties to the Optional Protocol, which currently has 115 parties and 35 signatories (UN Treaty Collection, Status of the First Optional Protocol to ICCPR), making the enforcement of individual rights under the ICCPR a major challenge under international human rights law.

Yet another major challenge to the enforcement of the ICCPR is the failure of some sates to ratify the treaty. According to the Charter of the United Nations, in order for international treaties such as the ICCPR to be binding on a signatory state, it must be registered with the United Nations, signed, ratified, with an enforcement date (UN, 1945).

Moreover, in order to be enforced nationally, some states require that international treaties such as the ICCPR be adopted by national parliament as a domestic law. For example, the United States has refused to be bound by the provisions of the covenant, which have not been incorporated into domestic laws by the US Congress (Cruz & Krausmann, 2013).

Moreover, even if a data privacy–related treaty was duly registered with the United Nations, and duly signed and ratified by signatory states, it is not necessarily binding on the ratifying parties vis-à-vis individuals and corporate bodies, and it can only be enforced by consent of signatory states before the International Court of Justice; an aggrieved individual or corporation could not sue before the United Nations Court System (i.e., the International Court of Justice) due to the court's limited jurisdictional oversight over disputes between states, rather than between individuals or corporate entities (Giegerich, 2012; UN, 1945). Even if an aggrieved individual took advantage of the provisions of the First Optional Protocol and filed a complaint before the UN Human Rights Committee under Article 1, Optional Protocol 1, ICCPR 1976, the decision of the UN Human Rights Committee is not necessarily binding on the state concerned.

Therefore, in the context of harvesting of data from social computing systems that could impinge individual personal data or privacy rights, an aggrieved individual party, whose personal data or information on social media was engaged by software without prior consent, is unlikely to succeed in a cause of action predicated on the provisions of international treaties guaranteeing protection for personal data or data privacy rights. However, aggrieved individual parties could sue under national laws with comparative provisions before national courts with the requisite jurisdiction. Even then, however, the aggrieved individual parties would not be suing under international treaties on privacy as such, but under national privacy laws as implemented by a national parliament. Therefore, there is no scope for an enforceable cause of action for aggrieved individuals under international treaties on personal data or data privacy protection.

3.3.4 *European Union Laws*

Within the European Union, the legal foundation for the protection of personal data, data privacy or personal information is arguably Article 16(1) of the Treaty of the European Union 2010 (TFEU), which provides that "[e]veryone has the right to the protection of personal data concerning them". Article 16(2) of TFEU then provides for the methods and procedures by which the European parliament and the council would establish rules that would protect the processing of personal data of individuals "by Union institutions, bodies, offices and agencies, and by the Member States when carrying out activities which fall within the scope of Union law, and the rules relating to the free movement of such data". It has been argued that Article 16(1)(2) of TFEU was the primary legislation on which the auxiliary legislation – that is, General Data Protection Regulation 2016 – was ultimately predicated (De Hert, 2015). Even so, there are other complementary EU laws which protect personal data by proxy (i.e., via the privacy route) and would notably include Article 8(1) of the European Convention on Human Rights, which provides that "[e]veryone has the right to respect for his private and family life, his home and his correspondence". The implications of the provisions of Article 8(1)(2) of the European Convention of Human Rights for harvesting and monitoring software are analysed extensively in Chapter 5.

The current law on personal data protection in the European Union is Directive 95/46/EC on the Protection of Individuals with Regards to the Processing of Personal Data and on the Movement of Such Data. However, the directive was replaced in May 2018 by the General Data Protection Regulation 2016/6W79 (GDPR). Therefore, this section analyses key provisions of the GDPR, and the extent to which software programmers and users could lawfully derogate from the prescribed rules on personal data processing and data retention.

3.3.4.1 Personal Data under the General Data Protection Regulation

To the extent that it regulates personal data on social media, the General Data Protection Regulation 2016 falls into the category of governmental regulation as described in Section 3.2.3.

Article 4(1) of the GDPR 2016, defines 'personal data' as "any information relating to an identified or identifiable natural person ('data subject')". An identifiable natural person "is one who can be identified, directly or indirectly, in particular by reference to an identifier such as a name, an identification number, location data, an online identifier or to one or more factors specific to the physical, physiological, genetic, mental, economic, cultural or social identity of that natural person".

Social media users routinely volunteer and post 'personal data' by which they could be identified directly or indirectly. These range from real names, pseudonyms, photos, texts, videos, location data, to online identifiers such as email address. Indeed, some social media platforms such as Facebook operate a "real-name-system" policy, which requires users to subscribe with real names and addresses, with a view to weeding out scammers and ghost subscribers in order to ensure the safety of the Facebook community and to maximise its market or stock value and advertisement revenues (Holpuch, 2015; Lee, 2014).

Inevitably, the social computing data harvesting systems would process 'personal data' in its various forms and engage Article 4(1) of the GDPR. The pertinent question therefore is: how could harvesters avoid identifying their data subject directly or indirectly, whilst processing their 'personal data'? The answer to that question is for software programmers to 'code privacy' into the application (Edwards,

2009) and thereby enable personal data anonymisation, a technological solution that fits into the technical regulation narrative previously discussed in Section 3.2.1.

According to the 2006 Report of Privacy Technology Focus Group, data anonymisation is defined as:

> Technology that converts clear text data into a nonhuman readable and irreversible form, including but not limited to preimage resistant hashes (e.g., one-way hashes) and encryption techniques in which the decryption key has been discarded. Data is considered anonymized even when conjoined with pointer or pedigree values that direct the user to the originating system, record, and value (e.g., supporting selective revelation) and when anonymized records can be associated, matched, and/or conjoined with other anonymized records. (US Department of Justice, 2006)

Additionally, social computing platform owners or data harvesters could program the software to enable personal data pseudonymisation, which is defined by Article 4(5) of the GDPR as

> the processing of personal data in such a manner that the personal data can no longer be attributed to a specific data subject without the use of additional information, provided that such additional information is kept separately and is subject to technical and organisational measures to ensure that the personal data are not attributed to an identified or identifiable natural person.

Indeed, Article 40(2)(d) of the GDPR encourages personal data controllers and processors to adopt 'pseudonymisation of personal data' as a code of conduct or good practice. Moreover, Article 11(1) of the GDPR highlights the beneficial effect of adopting personal data anonymisation or pseudonymisation techniques as follows: "the controller shall not be obliged to maintain, acquire or process additional information in order to identify the data subject for the sole purpose of complying with this regulation".

Therefore, to the extent that it is technically feasible, software programmers and users should enable personal data anonymisation and pseudonymisation techniques in the processing of social media data and information. This is good practice and a veritable bulwark against unwitting disclosure of personal data that could directly or indirectly identify data subjects.

3.3.4.2 Key Principles for Personal Data Protection under the General Data Protection Regulation

Article 5 of the GDPR stipulates six key principles for the protection of personal data: (a) personal data should be processed lawfully, fairly and in a transparent manner; (b) personal data must be collected for specified, explicit and legitimate purposes, and must not be processed in a manner that is incompatible with those purposes, whilst simultaneously legitimising "further processing for archiving purposes in the public interest, scientific or historical research purposes or statistical purposes"; (c) personal data must be adequate, relevant and limited to what is necessary in relation to the purposes for which they are processed (data minimisation); (d) personal data must be accurate, and where necessary, kept up to date, whilst reasonable steps must be taken to erase or rectify inaccurate data without delay; (e) personal data must be kept in a form which permits identification of data subjects for no longer than is necessary for the purposes for which the personal data are processed; however, personal data may be stored for longer periods provided the data would only be processed for archiving purposes in the public interest, scientific or historical research purposes or statistical purposes inaccurate personal data free movement of personal data within the European Union (Article 1(1)(2)(3) of GDPR 2016).

Notably, Article 5 of the GDPR appears to be a delicate balancing act by acknowledging the imperatives for archiving personal data for public interest, scientific, historical, research or statistical purposes. In the context of harvesting data from social computing systems, the key question here is the extent to which those trusted with our safety and security could take advantage of this data retention or archiving exception under Article 5 of the GDPR.

This question becomes pertinent, for example, in our consideration of an emergency or disaster scenario: it might be necessary, cost-effective and beneficial for a monitoring system for security responders to store personal data for a relatively longer period of time. There could be no doubt that personal data retention or archiving for emergency and disaster management would be in the public interest, but would this, therefore, be within the ambit of Article 5 of the GDPR?

For an answer, we have to look to the judgment of the CJEU in Cases C-293/12 and C-594/12 Digital Rights Ireland and Seitlinger and Others (2014). In the two consolidated cases, an Irish High Court and an Austrian Constitutional Court challenged the validity of Data Retention Directive 2006/24/EC, the primary objective of which was to ensure that data were available for serious crime detection, investigation and prosecution. The directive had prescribed a data retention period of a minimum of six months to a maximum of twenty-four months. Nevertheless, the CJEU held that Data Retention Directive 2006/24/EC was invalid because "by requiring the retention of those data and by allowing the competent national authorities to access those data, the directive interferes in a particularly serious manner with fundamental rights to respect for private life and to the protection of personal data". Significantly, the court noted that by adopting the Data Retention Directive, the EU legislature had exceeded the limits imposed by compliance with the principle of proportionality in light of Articles 7, 8 and 52(1) of the EU Charter of Fundamental Rights. Article 5(4) of the Treaty on European Union (TEU) provides that, under the principle of proportionality, the content and form of EU action must not exceed what is necessary to achieve the objectives of the treaties. This means that the EU legislator must not enact laws if this is not necessary, appropriate or proportionate in a strict sense.

Thus by extrapolation, users of a social computing monitoring and harvesting system cannot retain personal data indefinitely, notwithstanding the 'public interest' personal data archiving exception under Article 5 of the GDPR. Therefore, any retention period would have to be justifiably necessary and proportionate in the circumstances. It is, however, possible that such a system might be able to retain personal data for a relatively longer period of time, if the data were anonymised or pseudonymised, as safeguards against the risk of abuse and unlawful access and use.

3.3.4.3 Lawful Processing of Personal Data under the General Data Protection Regulation

Article 4(2) of the GDPR defines 'processing' as

> any operation or set of operations which is performed on personal data or on sets of personal data, whether or not by automated means, such as collection, recording, organisation, structuring, storage, adaptation or alteration, retrieval, consultation, use, disclosure by transmission, dissemination or otherwise making available, alignment or combination, restriction, erasure or destruction.

Inevitably, the social computing monitoring system would process personal data on social media within the statutory meaning of Article 4(2) of GDPR 2016.

However, processing of personal data is not prohibited as such, provided it is lawful. Therefore, within the context of the operational deployment of systems to harvest data from social computing systems, processing would be lawful under Article 6(1) of GDPR 2016 in the following circumstances: (a) if the data subjects gave consent to the processing of their personal data; (b) if processing was necessary for compliance with the legal obligation to which the controller is subject; (c) if processing was necessary for the performance of a task carried out in the public interest, or in the exercise of the official authority vested in the controller; and (d) if processing was necessary to protect the vital interests of the data subjects or of other natural persons. It is therefore legally conceivable that personal data could be appropriated from personal data under the aforementioned scenarios in Article 6(1) of GDPR 2016.

3.3.4.4 Restrictions on the Right of Data Subject under GDPR 2016.

There are specified general legal restrictions on the right of data subjects to object to the processing of their data under Article 23(1) of GDPR 2016. However, such restrictions must respect "the essence of fundamental rights and freedoms and is necessary and proportionate measure in a democratic society to safeguard: (a) national security; (b) defence; (c) public security".

Arguably, as seen in our case study (Chapter 6), a monitoring system for emergency and disaster management would fall within the purview of national security, defence or public security exceptions. However, such restrictions could not ride roughshod over fundamental freedoms, and must be necessary and proportionate in a democratic society. Therefore, software for monitoring and harvesting social computing data should be used responsibly within clear and accountable guidelines.

3.3.5 *Laws of the United Kingdom.*

In the United Kingdom, there is no written constitution that guarantees the right to privacy of individuals, and there is no general common law right to privacy. However, since the enactment of the Human Rights Act 1997, which was based on the European Convention on Human Rights, UK courts have used the provision of Article 8 of the Convention Rights on the right to family life, to secure privacy rights for individuals. In *Campbell v. MGN Ltd* (2002), the claimant was photographed coming out of a Narcotics Anonymous meeting on the King's Road, London. The *Mirror* newspaper published these photographs with the faces of other attendees at the meeting pixelated to protect their identities. The accompanying article claimed that Naomi was a drug addict. Naomi sued for damages for breach of confidentiality and compensation under section 13 of the Data Protection Act 1998. The High Court ruled in favour of Naomi, but the ruling was set aside by the Court of Appeal. However, the House of Lords overruled the Court of Appeal by a three-to-two majority, and held *inter alia* that the additional information was confidential as its publication would have caused substantial offence to a person of ordinary sensibilities in the claimant's position. The court held further that the claimant's Article 8 rights outweighed the defendant's Article 10 rights, so that publication of the additional information was an infringement of the claimant's Article 8 rights, for which she was entitled to damages.

3.3.5.1 Personal Data or Data Privacy Protection in the UK Post-'Brexit'

For the June 2016 referendum, the majority of UK voters chose to leave the European Union, The implication of the referendum for the UK data protection law is that when it becomes effective in May 2018, the General Data Protection Regulation 2016, would not automatically apply to the UK, unless the UK remains within the European single market; in that case the UK would have to comply with GDPR 2016. This view was echoed by the UK Information Commissioner, Christopher Graham, after the referendum:

> Over the coming weeks we will be discussing with Government the implications of the referendum result and its impact on data protection reform in the UK. With so many businesses and services operating across borders, international consistency around data protection laws and rights, is crucial both to businesses and organisations and to consumers and citizens. The ICO's role has always involved working

closely with regulators in other countries, and that will continue to be the case. Having clear laws with safeguards in place is more important than ever given the growing digital economy, and we will be speaking to government to present our view that reform of the UK law remains necessary (Graham, 2016).

The current data protection law in the UK is the Data Protection Act 1998, which was based on the European Data Protection Directive (95/46/EC).[4]

3.3.5.2 Personal Data under the UK Data Protection Act 1998

Other than the provision of Article 8 of the European Convention on Human Rights, the primary legislation for the protection of personal data in the UK is the Data Protection Act 1998.

Section 1(1)(e) of the Data Protection Act 1998 defines 'personal data' as

data which relate to a living individual who can be identified – (a) from those data, or (b) from those data and other information which is in the possession of, or is likely to come into the possession of, the data controller, and includes any expression of opinion about the individual and any indication of the intentions of the data controller or any other person in respect of the individual.

Section 1(1) of the Data Protection Act 1998 defines 'data processing' as

obtaining, recording or holding the information or data or carrying out any operation or set of operations on the information or data, including – (a) organisation, adaptation or alteration of the information or data, (b) retrieval, consultation or use of the information or data, (c) disclosure of the information or data by transmission, dissemination or otherwise making available, or (d) alignment, combination, blocking, erasure or destruction of the information or data.

3.3.5.3 Processing of Personal Data under the UK Data Protection Act 1998

Schedule 1 of the Data Protection Act 1998 contains eight principles that regulate how personal data should be handled. These principles apply to both online and offline data, and they require that (1) personal data shall be processed fairly and lawfully; (2) personal data shall be obtained only for one or more specified and lawful purposes, and shall not be further processed in any manner incompatible with that purpose or those purposes; (3) personal data shall be adequate, relevant and not excessive in relation to the purpose or purposes for which they are processed; (4) personal data shall be accurate and, where necessary, kept up to date; (5) personal data processed for any purpose or purposes shall not be kept for longer than is necessary for that purpose or those purposes; (6) personal data shall be processed in accordance with the rights of data subjects under the act; (7) appropriate technical and organisational measures shall be taken against unauthorised or unlawful processing of personal data and against accidental loss or destruction of, or damage to, personal data; (8) personal data shall not be transferred to a country or territory outside the European Economic Area unless that country or territory ensures an adequate level of protection for the rights and freedoms of data subjects in relation to the processing of personal data.

3.3.5.4 Rights of Data Subject and Others under the UK Data Protection Act 1998

In part II of the Data Protection Act 1998, the data subject and others have rights that range from the right to access personal data; the right to prevent processing likely to cause damage or distress; the right to prevent processing for purposes of direct marketing; rights in relation to automated decision-taking; the right to compensation for failure to comply with certain requirements; to the right to rectification, blocking, erasure and destruction.

3.3.5.5 Restrictions on the Right of Data Subject under the UK Data Protection Act 1998

Certain exceptions are made to the strict protection of personal data. The most relevant to the monitoring and harvesting software include section 28 of Data Protection Act 1998, which provides for 'national security' exception from the provisions of data protection principles "for the purpose of safeguarding national security". Although what constitutes 'safeguarding national security' is not defined in the Data Protection Act, it could conceivably include national emergency scenarios such as natural disasters or an outbreak of infectious disease. Arguably, the national security safeguard exception is analogous to the national security exemption in Article 23(1) of GDPR 2016 previously discussed in Section 3.3.4.4. It appears that monitoring of, and harvesting of data from, social computing systems should be subject to the exemption, whilst taking precautions in using monitoring or harvesting software responsibly, and if technically feasible, with anonymisation techniques to safeguard the dignity of data subject.

3.3.6 *Laws of the United States*

The United States does not have a single federal data protection legislation or privacy laws, unlike in the United Kingdom and the European Union. Rather, there are disparate and overlapping federal and state laws that protect data and privacy rights. Similarly, there is no single dedicated authority with general oversight over data protection in the US. Rather, there are disparate data and privacy-related laws that include the Fair Credit Reporting Act, the Children Online Privacy Protection Act, and the Driver's Privacy Protection Act. Most importantly, "there is no law of general application regarding privacy and information security in the US, and thus there are no derogations, exclusions, or limitations of general application as there are in other jurisdictions" (Hartzog, 2012; Sotto & Simpson, 2015). The pertinent question therefore is: What does the lack of a coherent and uniform data and privacy law in the US mean for the operational deployment of monitoring and harvesting software for the appropriation of personal data on social media that are mostly headquartered in the United States?

3.3.6.1 No Reasonable Expectation of Privacy in Publicly Available Social Media Postings in the US

There is a general consensus in the emerging case law in the United States that there could be no reasonable expectation of privacy in publicly available postings on social media. In *People of the State of New York v. Malcolm Harris* (2012), the defendant, Malcom Harris, was charged with disorderly conduct for allegedly marching on the Brooklyn Bridge roadway during the Occupy Wall Street protest. In January 2012, the New York District Attorney's office subpoenaed Twitter for Malcom Harris' account information and tweets in the course of its criminal investigation of Malcom Harris. However, Twitter declined to release Malcom Harris' tweets. The court then ordered Twitter to disclose Harris' account information, but Twitter filed an application to quash the court's order. The key issue for determination before the court was whether the order for disclosure of Harris' account information violated his privacy under the Fourth Amendment. The court held that the order for disclosure did not violate the Fourth Amendment because there was no physical intrusion into Harris' personal property; nor was there a violation of Harris' reasonable expectation of privacy because Harris voluntarily "broadcast [tweets] to the entire world into a server 3000 miles away".

Similarly, in *Largent v. Reed*, Case No. 2009–1823 (2011), the two plaintiffs sued for personal injury and claimed "serious and permanent physical and mental injuries, pain, and suffering". At the deposition of one of the plaintiffs, defence counsel learned that the plaintiff Jennifer Largent had a Facebook account and used her account regularly. Therefore, defence counsel requested information about the account, but Ms Largent refused to provide the information, and the defence counsel filed an application to compel Ms Largent to disclose information in her Facebook account. However, Ms Largent raised the following four objections to disclosing her Facebook information: (1) the information was irrelevant to the case and not subject to discovery; (2) the information was privileged; (3) the information was protected by the Stored Communications Act; and (4) the request for the information was unreasonably embarrassing or annoying.

The court however dismissed the arguments and held *inter alia* that the defendant was requesting information that was properly subject to discovery under Pennsylvania law. Furthermore, the court noted that Pennsylvania law does not provide for a "confidential social networking" privilege and stated that "there is no reasonable expectation of privacy in material placed on Facebook".

Furthermore, in *Nucci v. Target Corporation*, 162 So. 146 (2015), Maria Nucci petitioned for *certiorari* relief to quash a 12 December 2013 order compelling discovery of photographs from her Facebook account in a personal injury case. The photographs sought were reasonably calculated to lead to the discovery of admissible evidence about the alleged injury suffered by Nucci. A Florida appellate court ruled that there was no reasonable expectation of privacy in information posted on social media:

> We agree with those cases concluding that generally, the photographs posted on a social networking site are neither privileged nor protected by any right of privacy, regardless of any privacy settings that the user may have established. Such posted photographs are unlike medical records or communications with one's attorney, where disclosure is confined to narrow, confidential relationships. Facebook itself does not guarantee privacy. By creating a Facebook account, a user acknowledges that her personal information would be shared by others. Indeed, that is the very nature and purpose of these social networking sites else they would cease to exist. Because information that an individual shares through social networking web-sites like Facebook may be copied and disseminated by another, the expectation that such information is private, in the traditional sense of the word, is not a reasonable one.

Therefore, the monitoring of social computing systems for appropriation of personal data in the United States would not lead to violations of personal data or privacy, provided said social media contents are publicly available and accessible to the whole world. However, if the said information is not publicly accessible to the world, then there would be a reasonable expectation of privacy (*Government's Ex Parte Application for Order Compelling Apple Inc. To Assist Agents in Search* (*Apple Inc. v. FBI*), 2016; *Microsoft Corp. v. United States*, 2016).

3.3.7 *Conclusions*

Legal protection for personal data and privacy for social media contents vary from country to country. Whilst there is no reasonable expectation of privacy in the United States for publicly available postings on social media (*Largent v. Reed*, 2011; *Nucci v. Target Corporation*, 2015; *People of the State of New York v. Malcolm Harris*, 2012), the situation is different under EU and UK laws due to relatively stronger personal data and privacy laws. Therefore, users of software for harvesting and monitoring social computing data must be aware of these differences and avail themselves of the exemptions under EU and UK data and privacy laws. However, the key difference in the United States, as exemplified by emerging case law, is that the information on social media must be made publicly available in order for the account holder to forfeit any reasonable expectation of privacy in the information. Conversely, if the social media account settings were set to 'private', for example, and the information was not publicly available or accessible to the entire world, then the owner would retain his or her privacy rights in the information.

3.4 PROTECTION FOR MONITORING AND HARVESTING INFORMATION ON SOCIAL MEDIA

We briefly explore the proprietary nature of user-generated social media contents, and how account holders and social media operators could simultaneously have proprietary interests in the same information, due to social media operators' business model of commodifying user-generated contents, by targeting them with advertisements (De Franceschi & Lehmann, 2015; Sevignani, 2013). In the following paragraphs, we will explore the categories and scope of legal protection for proprietary rights in user-generated contents on social media, and the extent to which they are enforceable under applicable transnational laws, the laws of the European Union, United Kingdom and the United States.

The legal categories of applicable property rights would include copyright and associated licensing rights, and database rights. Because copyright is a part of the applicable Internet laws, the following paragraphs will briefly explore copyright and database rights strictly from the perspective of Internet governance systems under four different jurisdictions: transnational laws, EU laws, UK laws and US laws. The subject of copyright is discussed in detail in Chapter 4, where we use the laws of the Federal Republic of Germany as an example.

3.4.1 *WTO TRIPS Agreement 1994*

The WTO TRIPS Agreement of 1994 is perhaps the most significant international intellectual property treaty to date, due to its enforceability by the WTO TRIPS Council amongst signatory countries and its incorporation of key provisions of the Berne Convention for the Protection of Literary and Artistic Works 1886 (Bently & Sherman, 2014; WTO, 1995).

Notably, copyright, like all intellectual property rights, is inherently territorial and is ultimately conferred by national laws. Thus, although there are numerous international treaties on copyright, there is nothing like international copyright as such, but national copyright. Therefore, it is up to national governments to enforce the terms of international copyright treaties in their national laws (Ginsburg, 1999). Even so, the copyright provisions of TRIPS agreement are binding on national governments, who are obliged to observe a minimum level of protection in their national laws (WTO, 1995).

The following sections will focus analysis on key copyright provisions of the TRIPS Agreement, and their relevance for monitoring and harvesting software and its operational deployment on social media.

3.4.1.1 Monitoring/Harvesting Data from Social Computing Data and Copyright under WTO TRIPS Agreement 1994

Article 10(1) of TRIPS Agreement 1994 provides that "computer program, whether in source or object code, shall be protected as literary works". Consequently, software for harvesting and monitoring social computing data is protected as a literary work, and software programmers shall be deemed as authors in the absence of any contrary agreement. In addition, Article 11 of TRIPS Agreement 1994 confers rental right on authors of such software, who shall have the right to authorise or to prohibit the commercial rental to the public of originals or copies of the software.

Article 12 of TRIPS Agreement 1994 provides for a term of copyright protection that shall not be less than fifty years. In effect, programmers of software for monitoring and harvesting data would have a minimum of fifty years of exclusive authorship or monopoly right to rent or licence or sell such software. However, Article 13 of TRIPS 1994 acknowledges that member states could impose limitations or exceptions on the exclusive copyright conferred by Articles 10, 11 and 12 of TRIPS Agreement 1994 "to certain special cases which "do not conflict with a normal exploitation of the work, and do not unreasonably prejudice the legitimate interests of the rights holder".

It is clear from the foregoing that monitoring/harvesting software is protected as a property right in its own right. However, within the context of the social media in which such software would ultimately be deployed, there are other works that are potentially subject to copyright protection under TRIPS Agreement 1994.

3.4.1.2 Copyright Protection for Social Media Contents under WTO TRIPS Agreement 1994

Invariably, the software for harvesting and monitoring data would have to engage social media contents that range from photos, drawings and texts to audio-visual works that could potentially qualify as literary, dramatic, artistic, musical or broadcasting rights under Articles 1–21 of the Berne Convention 1886 as amended in 1971, which provisions have now been incorporated into the TRIPS Agreement via Article 9(1). For example, Article 2(1) of the Berne Convention as incorporated into TRIPS 1994 by Article 9(1), defines 'literary and artistic works' as including "every production in the literary, scientific and artistic domain, whatever may be the mode or form of its expression, such as books, pamphlets and other writings, lectures, addresses, etc." This definition will clearly cover the sort of materials that such software would invariably engage on social media. Consequently, unless a prior consent is obtained, there is a potential for copyright infringement, if the software is used to appropriate information and materials that are subject to copyright protection.

3.4.1.3 Limitations on Copyright Monopoly Right under WTO TRIPS Agreement 1994

Article 10(1) of the Berne Convention, as incorporated into WTO TRIPS 1994, provides for free uses of copyright work for the purposes of quotations and teaching. Furthermore, Article 10bis (1) provides for free uses of certain articles, works of broadcast, or works seen or heard in relation to current events. The aforementioned body of works could potentially include regular materials on YouTube, Facebook and Twitter. Thus, a combined reading of Articles 10(1) and 10bis (1) could provide lawful derogations and lawful uses of social media contents that fall within the ambit of the Articles, and thereby prevent copyright infringement by monitoring and harvesting data from social computing systems.

3.4.1.4 Legal Protection for Database Right under WTO TRIPS 1994

Article 10(2) of TRIPS 1994 offers protection for database rights, otherwise known as

> compilations of data or other material, whether in machine readable or other form, which by reason of the selection or arrangement of their contents constitute intellectual creations shall be protected as such. Such protection shall not extend to the material itself, shall be without prejudice to any copyright subsisting in the data or material itself.

The preceding provision clearly requires some degree of originality in the 'selection and arrangement' of contents as a condition for legal protection. In the context of operational deployment of software for monitoring and harvesting social computing data for the appropriation of proprietary information, it is possible that a number of social media platforms could qualify for protection, provided that the 'selection and arrangement' of their contents constituted 'intellectual creation', thus meeting the copyright originality threshold. In that case, users might need prior consent of the proprietors of the social media in question, before appropriating proprietary information on their digital platforms.

However, it is conceivable that users of a monitoring and harvesting system could benefit from the limitations and exceptions on exclusive copyright monopoly right under Article 13 of TRIPS 1994, provided the exceptions sought fall under "special cases, which do not conflict with a normal exploitation of the work and do not unreasonably prejudice the legitimate interest of the right holder". Users of the software considered in Chapter 6, for example – a social media monitor for emergency management – should arguably be able to satisfy the preceding criteria on the following grounds: First, it is conceivable that using social media contents for emergency management would constitute 'special cases' due to the underlying public security and safety issues. Second, using social media contents for non-commercial emergency management and response measures would not conflict with normal commercial exploitation of the contents or be prejudicial to the legitimate commercial interests of the proprietors of the social media in question.

3.4.2 *European Union Copyright Law*

We now focus, in summary, on the aspects of EU copyright laws that deal with the Internet ecosystems, especially in the context of copyright protection for software, hyperlinking, encryption issues and database rights.

3.4.2.1 The Scope of Copyright Protection for Harvesting and Monitoring Social Computing Data under EU Laws

The primary legislation for copyright protection of computer programs in the European Union is Directive 2009/24/EC on the legal protection of computer programs (OJ L 111/16, 5.5.2009), which harmonises the national laws on copyright protection for computer programs across the European Union. Recital 7 of Directive 2009/24/EC defines 'computer program' as including programs in any form, including those which are incorporated into hardware. This term also includes preparatory design work that leads to the development of a computer program.

Article 1(2) of Directive 2009/24/EC deals with the scope of what can be protected by copyright in software: "Protection . . . shall apply to the expression in any form of a computer program, including those which underlie any element of a computer program, including those which underlie its interfaces, are not protected by copyright under this Directive". It is clear from this that algorithms are not protected by copyright, and that without a doubt, harvesting and monitoring software would qualify as a computer program under Article 1(2) of Software Directive 2009/24/EC.

In *SAS Institute Inc. v. World Programming Limited* (C-406/10), the key question before the court was the extent to which the developer of a computer program may lawfully replicate the functions of an existing computer program, and the materials that he may lawfully use for that purpose. SAS had produced a computer software language and system for statistical analysis, together with supporting manuals. The defendants had produced software which was intended to mimic SAS software in part. SAS alleged copyright infringement.

The CJEU held that the functionality of a computer program, nor the programming language nor the format of data files constituted a form of expression, and so were not protected by copyright under Article 1(2) of Software Directive 2009/24/EC. The court observed further that under Article 5(3) of Software Directive 2009/24/EC, a licensee of a computer program could study its operations in order to understand its underlying principles without the authorisation of the copyright owner, provided that the exclusive right of the copyright owner was not breached. The court further noted that licensing agreements could not be used to protect un-protectable elements of a computer program, such as ideas, principles and algorithm.

Finally, the court held that under Article 2(a) of Information Society Directive 2001/29/EC, the reproduction of certain elements described in the user manual of a computer program in a different computer program or user manual would constitute an infringement of the former manual, and that it was up to the national court to determine whether the reproduction did infringe copyright.

3.4.2.2 The *SAS Institute* Case and Third Party Commercial/Open Source Software

The *SAS Institute* case has clear implications for developers of a monitoring and harvesting system vis-à-vis third party software, whether proprietary or open source. The Internet ecosystems into which such a system would invariably be deployed are a jungle of codes and applications, making the achievement of interoperability with other software applications a key challenge for harvesting and monitoring software developers. Therefore, of necessity, developers would have to study the functionality or the programming language of third party code or software (including web-based applications or platforms such as Twitter and Facebook) with a view to achieving software interoperability, security and resilience, without necessarily infringing copyright or licensing rights. This is made possible by the *SAS Institute* judgment of the Court of Justice of the European Union.

Furthermore, under Software Directive 2009/24/EC, third party software penetrating testing for interoperability, security and resilience could be lawful without prior authorisation of vendor. For example, Article 6(1)(a) (b) (c) of Software Directive 2009/24/EC provides: "authorisation of the right holder shall not be required where reproduction of the code and translation of its form … are indispensable to obtain the information necessary to achieve the interoperability of an independently created computer program with other programs". However, the aforesaid activities could only be performed if the researcher has a licence or permission of the right holder to use a copy of the program, the information necessary to achieve interoperability has not previously been readily available to the researcher, and the researcher's activities are confined to the parts of the original program which are necessary to achieve interoperability. Most importantly, the researcher cannot use the information obtained in the process for goals other than to achieve interoperability of the independently created software, nor use the information to develop, produce or market a computer program that is substantially similar in its expression to the one used for his or her research.

However, contractual or licensing complications could arise from the incorporation of open source code into a potentially commercial or quasi-commercial applications such as software for harvesting and monitoring social computing data. Therefore, software developers must be aware of the underlying terms and types of their licensing agreement for expressly using or incorporating third party codes, because such an activity would not be covered by the authority of the *SAS Institute* case in which the CJEU acknowledged the possibility that SAS programming language or data files could be copyright protectable under Information Society Directive 2001/29/EC on their own rights as 'works' (provided copyright originality requirements are satisfied), rather than as codes or computer programs.

Since developers of a harvesting system are more likely to have access to open source software codes than proprietary codes, they must be aware of the types and terms of underlying licence. For example, whilst MIT and BSD licences place almost no restrictions to the use of codes other than acknowledgement and inclusion of licence, the terms of a GPL licence for open source codes are not as generous (GNU, 1991).

3.4.2.3 Encryption, Circumvention, Anti-circumvention Copyright Rules and Harvesting and Monitoring Software

Encryption generally involves encoding messages and information as a barrier to access for unauthorised parties, whilst circumvention is a process of bypassing technological barriers to required data or information. EU copyright laws have anti-circumvention provisions designed to discourage bypassing of technological barriers to data and information (Information Society Directive 2001/29/EC). This is a classic example of technical and governmental regulatory framework discussed earlier in Sections 3.2.2 and 3.2.3.

Within the Internet environment, software for harvesting and monitoring social computing data would invariably come across encrypted web-based data and information. The pertinent question here is the extent to which the software could, if necessary (and if technically capable), circumvent such barriers under Information Society Directive 2001/29/EC.

Article 6(1) of Information Society Directive 2001/29/EC requires that "Member States shall provide adequate legal protection against the circumvention of any effective technological measures, which the person concerned carries out in the knowledge, or with reasonable grounds to know, that he or she is pursuing that objective".

However, Article 6(4) of Information Society Directive 2001/29/EC also enjoins member states to take necessary measures to ensure that copyright holders do not use anti-circumvention provisions in Article 6(1) of Information Society Directive 2001/29/EC to deprive beneficiaries of copyright exceptions contained in Article 5(2)(a), (2)(c), (2)(d), (2)(e), (3)(a), (3)(b) or (3)(e), which comprise reproduction rights for lawful users. Arguably, this is a public policy provision designed to prevent copyright holders from using encryption and technological barriers to block access to data and information that lawful users would otherwise be legally entitled to have.

It is therefore arguable that if copyright holders deliberately and wrongfully blocked access to data or information on social media platforms such as Facebook or Twitter by erecting technological barriers, any circumvention activities taken by a lawful user in the circumstances could be justifiable under Article 6(4) of Information Society Directive 2001/29/EC. Thus, by extrapolation, users of the software could, subject to technical capability, circumvent any technological barriers to web-based data or information that they are lawfully entitled to under Article 6(4) of Information Society Directive 2001/29/EC.

3.4.2.4 Text and Data Mining Right in the Proposed Digital Single Market Directive 2016

Article 3 of the proposed Digital Single Market Directive 2016 enjoins member states to

> provide an exception to the rights provided for in Article 2 of Directive 2001/29/EC, Articles 5(a) and 7(1) of Directive 96/9/EC and Article 11(1) of the Digital Single Market Directive for reproductions and extractions made by research organisations in order to carry out text and data mining of works or other subject-matter to which they have lawful access for the purposes of scientific research.

Article 1(1) of the proposed Digital Single Market Directive 2016, defines a 'research organisation' as

> a university, a research institute or any other organisation the primary goal of which is to conduct scientific research or to conduct scientific research and provides educational services (a) on a non-for-profit basis or by reinvesting all the profits in its scientific research; or (b) pursuant to a public interest mission recognized by a Member State; in such a way that the access to the results generated by the scientific research cannot be enjoyed on a preferential basis by an undertaking exercising a decisive influence upon such organisation.

Article 1(2) of the proposed Digital Single Market Directive 2016 defines 'text and data mining' as "any automated analytical technique aiming to analyse text and data in digital form in order to generate information such as patterns, trends and correlations".

In the context of the operational deployment of software for harvesting and monitoring social computing data for appropriation of personal data and proprietary information on social media, the proposed text and data mining research exception is very significant, especially at the research or experimental or developmental phase for the software. The programmers working on such software would of necessity be engaged in trial runs and experimentation with proprietary information and datasets, and this exception would provide legal cover from potential copyright or database right infringement. There could be no doubt that such a software project satisfies the requirements of Article 3, Article 1(1) and Article 1(2) of the proposed Single Market Directive.

3.4.2.5 Database Rights and Harvesting Systems under EU Laws

Databases are compilations of data, digital or otherwise. Invariably, software for harvesting and monitoring social computing data would trawl digital databases on social media such as Facebook and Twitter for information. However, just like Article 10(2) of TRIPS Agreement 1994 discussed in Section 3.4.1.4, Database Directive 96/9/EC offers copyright and *sui generis* protection for databases (Oriola, 2004). The pertinent question, therefore, is: What is the extent to which such software could legally make use of protected datasets or information in legally protected database?

Article 1(2) of Directive 96/9/EC defines a database as "a collection of independent works, data or other materials arranged in a systematic or methodical way and individually accessible by electronic or other means". Article 4 of Directive 96/9/EC defines the author of a database as "the natural person or group of natural persons who created the database". This is exactly how social media platforms such as Facebook and Twitter are set up: they are no more than a repository of independent works and materials posted by users, set up by natural persons, at least initially, prior to market capitalisation.

With regards to the use of datasets or information in a database by harvesting/ monitoring software, the extent of access would depend on whether the dataset is protected by copyright or as a *sui generis* right under Database Directive 96/9/EC. In order to qualify for copyright protection, Article 3 of Database Directive 96/9/EC provides that a database must "by reason of the selection or arrangement of their contents, constitute the author's own intellectual creation". For a database protected by copyright, the author would have an exclusive right to carry out or authorise temporary or permanent reproduction, translation, distribution and any communication, display or performance to the public (Article 5 Database Directive 96/9/EC).

If a database fails to satisfy copyright originality requirement in Article 3 of Database Directive 96/9/EC, it could still be protected as a *sui generis* right under Article 7(1) of Database Directive 96/9/EC, provided the maker of the database could show "that there has been qualitatively and/or quantitatively a substantial investment in either the obtaining, verification or presentation of the contents to prevent extraction and/or re-utilization of the whole or of a substantial part, evaluated qualitatively and/or quantitatively, of the contents of that database" (*Ryanair Ltd v. PR Aviation BV*, C-30/14).

There are, however, exceptions to *sui generis* database rights. For example, Article 9 allows lawful users to extract data for private purposes, for illustration for teaching or for scientific research, provided proper attribution is made and the use is non-commercial. Also, extraction or re-utilization is permissible "for the purposes of public security or an administrative or judicial procedure".

Therefore, under Article 9 of Database Directive 96/9/EC, users of software for harvesting and monitoring social computing data could, on grounds of 'public security', use datasets that are subject to *sui generis* rights for emergency and disaster management without prior authorisation from its maker.

3.4.3 *UK Copyright Law*

United Kingdom copyright laws are currently on a par with that of the European Union with regards to the issues discussed in Section 3.4.2. For example, the *SAS Institute* case discussed in Section 3.4.2.2 originated from the UK and was referred to the CJEU by UK courts. Therefore, it would not be necessary to repeat these issues under this section dealing with UK copyright laws. Moreover, due to time and space constraints, it would be fruitless to speculate at this point on what the state of UK copyright law will be following proposed final exit from the European Union.

3.4.4 *US Copyright Law*

The following paragraphs will discuss selected issues under US copyright laws that could potentially impact the operational deployment of software for harvesting and monitoring social computing data in the Internet environment. The issues will be similar to those raised under EU copyright laws in the preceding paragraphs, but are particularly relevant for operational deployment of software for harvesting and monitoring social computing data on social media platforms such as Facebook and Twitter, which are owned by US businesses and whose servers are located in the United States.

As previously noted in Section 3.4.1, copyright, like all intellectual property rights, is inherently territorial and is invariably conferred by national laws. The United States has recently abolished the compulsory requirement for the registration of copyright works as precondition for protection under US copyright laws. Nevertheless, registration is still required for all authors and proprietors, prior to filing lawsuit for copyright infringement in the United States.[5] Therefore, it would be advisable for harvesting system programmers or vendors to do voluntary registration with the US Copyright Office.

3.4.4.1 Encryption, Anti-circumvention and Software for Harvesting and Monitoring Social Computing Data under US Copyright Law

It is pertinent to discuss encryption and anti-circumvention measures under US copyright laws because harvesting systems would invariably engage social computing content on digital platforms anchored on US-based servers that are subject to US laws (*Microsoft Corporation Inc. v. United States of America*, 2016).

In the United States, the Digital Millennium Copyright Act prohibits circumventing access-control measures [17 U.S.C. § 1201(a)(1)]. Thus, it is illegal to circumvent technological measures used to prevent unauthorised access to copyrighted works, including copyrighted books, movies, videos, video games and computer programs.

Most importantly, there is no fair-use exception to the anti-circumvention law in the United States. Thus, unlike the European Union, the United States does not have equivalent provisions of Article 5(2)(a), (2)(c), (2)(d), (2)(e), (3)(a), (3)(b) or (3)(e) and Article 6(4) of Information Society Directive 2001/29/EC, which allow for derogation on grounds that users are lawfully entitled to certain reproduction rights in the encrypted works.

However, 17 U.S.C. § 1201(2) instructs the Librarian of Congress to make determinations in a rulemaking proceeding every three years, upon the recommendation of the Register of Copyrights, evaluating and, as appropriate, adopting limited exemptions from the general prohibition against circumvention of access controls.

As previously noted in Section 3.4.2.3, most US-based social media platforms such as Facebook and Twitter (with which the harvesting software would invariably interact) do not, as a matter of business policy, use anti-circumvention access-control measures. Rather, they are open platforms that actively encourage users to post data and information, which are routinely used to profile data subject for the purposes of advertising (De Franceschi & Lehman, 2015). Therefore, it is highly unlikely that users of software for harvesting and monitoring social computing data would face anti-circumvention control-measures on US-based social media.

3.4.4.2 Monitoring and Harvesting Social Computing Data and Database Rights in the United States

In the United States, databases are protected by copyright on condition that they satisfy the originality requirement (*Feist Publications, Inc., v. Rural Telephone Service Co*, 1991). The US Supreme Court rejected the argument that copyright should subsist in telephone white pages comprising names, phone numbers and addresses, noting that the information were facts, and that under section 103 of US Copyright Act 1976, facts were not copyrightable. It is therefore unlikely that users of the harvested data could have database rights problem with the US-based social media with which they would invariably engage. However, separate copyright could subsist in individual works, comprising photos, drawings, texts, etc. Therefore, users should pay particular attention to social media terms-of-use policy to avoid possible copyright infringement.

3.4.5 *Conclusions*

We have looked at the literature, case law and legislative instruments on Internet contents governance in the context of personal data and proprietary information. Sections 3.3 and 3.4 have delved into the protection of personal data and data privacy, and the protection of proprietary information, respectively. Section 3.3 explored relevant transnational laws, EU laws, UK laws and US laws on personal data and privacy, and how the said laws could impact the operational deployment of a monitoring/harvesting system on social media. This chapter highlights the key differences between the European Union and the United States and notes that whereas US data and privacy laws are fractured, and there is generally no expectation of privacy on publicly available personal information on social media, the EU has perhaps the strongest data and privacy protection regime in the form of the newly minted General Data Protection Regulation 2016.

In Section 3.4, we highlighted applicable Internet laws on selected issues that range from copyright, encryption and anti-circumvention measures to database rights under international law, EU law, UK law and US law. We highlighted potential legal challenges for developers and users of software for harvesting and monitoring social computing data on issues including using third party code and programming language, navigating copyright and database rights, and dealing with personal data and privacy issues under selected EU, US, UK and international laws.

3.5 SUMMARY FINDINGS

This chapter explored the full ramifications of varied Internet laws on the operational deployment of the software for harvesting and monitoring social computing data on the Internet for software programmers and vendors. The applicable norms and laws that govern Internet contents are technical, customary, national, regional and transnational in nature, and they cover a range of issues that include encryption and anti-circumvention measures, copyright, licensing right, data protection and database protection. This chapter explored the parameters and limitations of these laws, and the extent to which software programmers and vendors could safely and lawfully derogate from prescribed laws without infringing third party rights in personal data and proprietary information on social media.

NOTES

1. See Facebook's website: https://www.facebook.com/help/408044339354739?helpref=faq_content (last accessed 25 March 2018) for details.
2. Twitter Developer Agreement, available at https://dev.twitter.com/overview/terms/agreement-and-policy (last accessed on 27 March 2018).
3. Report of the Office of the United Nations High Commissioner for Human Rights (2014: 15–16).
4. Brexit negotiations are ongoing at time of publication. This section documents the currently existing-laws at time of publication.
5. US Copyright Office, https://www.copyright.gov/ (last accessed 26 March 2018).

4

Copyright Law and Data Protection Law

Christian Berger
University of Leipzig

4.1 INTRODUCTION

Having looked at internet laws, particularly as they relate to harvesting, analysing and disseminating data, we now turn to the question of social computing. This chapter examines the extent to which the monitoring and use of digital content on social media is compatible with applicable copyright law.

Ordinarily, posted texts, images, videos and other digital contents enjoy protection under copyright law if they are the author's own creation. This is often the case for very short texts and simple photographs. The chapter examines how these laws apply in exceptional situations, such as natural disasters. We consider disaster management as an area in which data ordinarily considered to be private might be considered as a resource to benefit the public good, and in which social computing data may be viably monitored and harvested. It should be borne in mind that social computing data streams contain key information about the nature and extent of a disaster: this information can help to save lives and property, and this is the mandate given to emergency managers.[1]

Our motivation here is ethical, since data rights in general have come to be thought of as an important human right: the ethical and factual provenance of social media data is our concern. Within this context, the question arises as to who holds the intellectual property rights to the works. It appears that according to the creator principle, social media *users* generally hold the rights. However, on the basis of their general contractual terms and conditions, social media *operators* also claim transferred ownership of the rights.

The rights to reproduce and to communicate to the public are of special relevance as possible rights which could be affected by a system that harvests social media data. It must be emphasised, however, that in copyright law, the establishment of an infringement does not mean that the respective action violates copyright laws. Indeed, it is necessary to assess, in a further step, whether the infringement is justified. This leads to a discussion of *whether special exceptions and limitations can justify the use of digital content for emergency and disaster management.* Within the EU member states, despite numerous directives in the area of copyright, no uniform structure for exceptions and limitations exists to date. This analysis is therefore limited to copyright law in Germany because a worked example of the analysis needs to assess the copyright implications of deployment of a system that harvests social media data to enhance emergency response decision support in an EU jurisdiction.

4.1.1 Issues in Data Protection Law

Copyright law is designed to protect the rights of an author to original works of authorship from the moment of the work's creation – personal intellectual creations. Data protection law safeguards the right of an individual to his or her personal data, in particular in the Charter of Fundamental Rights of the EU (Article 8). The definition of "original work" is independent of the medium (analogue or digital); similarly the definition of "personal data" is independent of whether it is held digitally or in analogue fashion. The constitutional basis of both laws has been under scrutiny, and the laws have been challenged in courts around the world. This challenge has become more intense as data storage and data distribution technologies enable unprecedented levels of violation of the rights of the author (Menell, 2016) and intrusion into the privacy of the individual (Barnett, 2015).

Data protection law involves the protection of personal information. To this end, and specifically for the EU General Data Protection Regulation (GDPR) (2016)[2] "personal data"

> means any information relating to an identified or identifiable natural person ('**data subject**'); an identifiable natural person is one who can be identified, directly or indirectly, in particular by reference to an identifier such as a name, an identification number, location data, an online identifier or to one or more factors specific to the physical, physiological, genetic, mental, economic, cultural or social identity of that natural person.[3] [emphasis added]

Note that the General Data Protection Regulation (2016) was adopted in April 2016 and became enforceable as of 25 May 2018.

It is also important to know when personal information can be "processed". In the context of the GDPR (2016), General Data Protection Regulation (2016), "processing" means

> any operation or set of operations which is performed on personal data or on sets of personal data, whether or not by automated means, such as collection, recording, organisation, structuring, storage, adaptation or alteration, retrieval, consultation, use, disclosure by transmission, dissemination or otherwise making available, alignment or combination, restriction, erasure or destruction[.][4]

According to the preceding, the mere "selection" of information could already be relevant.

Furthermore, GDPR has looked at the definition and scope of the term "restriction of processing" as "the marking of stored personal data with the aim of limiting their processing in the future" (GDPR 2016, Article 4(3)). It may be of interest to the reader that the GDPR (2016) takes a strict view of "profiling", based on automated processing of any information relating to an identified or identifiable natural person with a view to predict the behaviour of the data subject (GDPR 2016, Article 4(4) and Articles 21 and 22).

If data is anonymised, however, data protection no longer applies. The legal prerequisites for anonymisation, however, are not evident from the General Data Protection Regulation. In particular, the question arises as to whether de-anonymisation can be carried out.

An additional issue is posed by "pseudonymisation", which, we paraphrase, is the processing of personal information in such a way that the information can no longer be associated with a specific person affected without required additional information, as long as this additional information is stored separately and is subject to technical and organisational measures which ensure that it cannot be allocated to a specific or specifiable person.[5]

4.1.2 *Data Protection and Copyright*

The precise data protection challenges that arise in the use of software for harvesting and monitoring social computing data are user-dependent. For example, a user who only processes anonymous data using such software is not exposed to a data protection risk. However, a user who uses the software to obtain and retain large amounts of pictorial or other personal data will need to conduct a data protection impact assessment before deployment.

More complex is the issue of access to copyright and associated trademarks by software for harvesting and monitoring social computing data. With regard to the limitations of copyright in the interest of disaster protection, no more than a very weak protection can be determined. Exemptions for the use of works under copyright do not seem to give sufficient latitude for software that harvests and monitors social computing data. It seems likely therefore that users will be required to obtain copyright licences from copyright owners such as social networks. The terms of these licences will be determined by reference to the proposed scope of use, the relevant territories and other factors.

It may be that, when it comes to deployment, the promoters of software for harvesting and monitoring social computing data could explore with some of the main social networks whether or not they would be prepared to offer open source–type licences for users committed to using such software for humanitarian, non-commercial purposes. If so, this could enable users to streamline their deployments of software for harvesting and monitoring social computing data without getting impeded by negotiating individual licence agreements.

Based on the risk analysis in the area of copyright discussed earlier, it is necessary to reinforce weak legal foundations through contractual agreements with the parties involved. One of the tasks in the context of software for harvesting and monitoring social computing data, therefore, is to precisely identify the relevant parties, the copyrights and other intellectual property rights in order to be able to enforce them.

To this end, we begin by examining the situation as regards social computing data in the area of EU copyright law (Section 4.2). We go on to consider the ontology of copyright law, examining what can be protected and how ownership can be determined (Section 4.3). We then discuss copyright and exceptional circumstances, examining how copyrights such as reproduction and distribution rights are affected by the use of social computing data in exceptional circumstances such as disaster management (Section 4.4). We then examine exceptions and limitations, examining the issues of implied consent and considering the circumstances in which exceptions may be granted (Section 4.5).

4.2 EU COPYRIGHT DIRECTIVES AND GERMAN COPYRIGHT LAW

There are, with due qualifications, provisions in copyright law that may allow the use of digital content on social media for emergency and disaster management. However, these provisions are limited in scope in some cases and do not capture all conceivable scenarios. Nevertheless, one can often assume an *implied consent* on the part of social media users to allow the use of their content. Data ownership questions are typically addressed under copyright law. In German, this law is referred to as *Urheberrecht* and in Italian it is named *diritto d'autore*. The English term literally refers to the protection against illegal copying, whereas the German and Italian terms refer specifically to the rights of an author. We note the nuances here to highlight the fact that the differences show how laws may differ in letter, whilst keeping the European spirit. There is no unified approach to copyright law at the European level. While copyright law is governed by various EU directives, these are not directly applicable to individuals, corporations and state agencies because they are not binding on the member states. The differences need further appraisal, so an assessment of German law will be undertaken in this section.

Similarly, questions related to the protection of data against unauthorised use have been addressed under *Data Protection Acts* or *Bundesdatenschtzgesetz*, or *Codice in materia di protezione dei dati personali*, or *dlí um chosaint*. The nuances, commonalities, interpretations and opinion about these currently differ at a national level. However, the EU General Data Protection Regulation (2016) provides more consistent legal foundations across the EU in relation to data protection law.

We have examined copyright and data protection legislation initially within the framework of German law, in close consultation with lawyers from Ireland, Italy and the UK, to get an EU-wide perspective. In this chapter, we consider disaster management as a field that demonstrates the competing legal demands upon the monitoring and harvesting of data from social computing systems. We refer to judgements made in the rapidly evolving field of laws governing computers and social media. We note possible risks that may be faced by a public or private authority intending to use a commercial product that is an operational version of a system for harvesting and monitoring social computing data.

This chapter is written as a legal opinion about issues of copyright law in the framework of social computing data harvesting; our opinion is based on European and German case law and on findings reported in the academic literature. However, since the legal questions we consider concern a completely new area of copyright law, the quantity of case law and relevant academic research papers is relatively low. Thus, we also address related areas of copyright law.

4.2.1 *Overview of Copyright Law in Software Development*

The systematic and time-unlimited use, by any enterprise, of social media content for disaster management involves the collection, reproduction, distribution, transfer and communication of copyright-protected works (social media texts, images and videos) to the public. Thus, the question arises as to whether copyright law caters to the needs of enterprises which use social media content.

As a first step, we present an overview of the data protection law which is relevant to the monitoring and harvesting of social computing data:

1. The social media data harvested by a software system can comprise written texts, still images and videos, and audio tracks; each of these harvested items may be protected by copyright laws.
2. The processing of the legally sourced copyrighted data may require transmission of the data to other computer systems including database systems for storage or specialist processing systems.
3. The user converts legally sourced data into knowledge, possibly including the public. Ensuring the legality of the use of the contents of the generated information is ultimately the responsibility of the user.

Based on these three parameters, we now examine more closely the copyright implications of software for harvesting and monitoring social computing data.

To begin, a distinction must be made between the research phase and the deployment phase of software for harvesting and monitoring social computing data. The *research phase* relates to the activities which are of relevance under copyright law during the (academic) research. In particular, this relates to the creation and testing of computer programs and databases. The *deployment phase* encompasses application-oriented questions of software for harvesting and monitoring social computing data from the end-user's viewpoint. The focus here is on the saving, reproduction and distribution (including communication to the public) of materials protected by copyright law.

The analysis under copyright law is carried out from the various perspectives of the respective stakeholders involved. Stakeholders include the designers of software for harvesting and monitoring social computing data, users, emergency responders, formal media and media outlets, governmental organisations and members of the general public.

Neither the research phase nor the deployment phase may be allowed to lead to an infringement of applicable copyright law. The analysis of copyright law questions primarily serves to ensure that the project is feasible from a legal viewpoint. The stakeholders involved should be provided with a reliable basis, which allows them to recognise the legally permissible applications of software for harvesting and monitoring social computing data and to act accordingly.

Three perspectives come to the fore here:

– Activities within the scope of software for harvesting and monitoring social computing data relate to content which is not yet protected under copyright law; for instance, pure information and data are not protected as such;
– Activities within the scope of such software relate to copyrights, but are allowed and legally admissible through statutory exceptions and limitations;
– Activities within the scope of such software are covered by the consent of the copyright holder and through licensing agreements and are therefore allowed and legally permissible.

The cornerstones for a licensing agreement concluded by the users of software for harvesting and monitoring social computing data should be determined simultaneously on this basis (see Chapter 6).

Because the topic of copyright and social computing has not been researched intensively to date, it is important to recognise that the legal questions addressed in this chapter concern a completely new area of copyright law; therefore the quantity of directly pertinent case law and the amount of relevant academic research papers is relatively small. Hence, what is considered here are additional case law and research that address relevant issues, albeit not specifically concerned with social media data itself, but from which we can learn by analogy.

4.2.2 Applicable Law

4.2.2.1 National Law, EU Law, International Agreements

The legal frameworks of copyright law in Europe and particularly within the European Union are complex. In the first place, copyright is (still) national law.

It is determined through the respective laws and provisions of other acts of law of member states and their courts. The national acts of law and court decisions generally take effect in the respective national territory only (principle of territoriality) (Dreier & Schulze, 2004; Ginsburg, 1994; Renda, Simonelli, Mazziotti, Bolognini & Luchetta, 2015).

In parallel, the European level of copyright law plays an increasingly important role (Berger, 2014; Loos, 2016; Renda et al., 2015). However, there are as yet no uniform copyright regulations which determine copyright issues as directly binding law. The enabling rule of Article 118 of the Treaty on the Functioning of the European Union (TFEU)[6] has not been applied to date (Van Velze, 2015). Also, the copyright aspects of the legal regulations and directives in conjunction with the digital domestic market are not aimed at providing a uniform copyright regulation.

At the European level, however, many directives in relation to copyright have been enacted. These directives, in particular Directive 2001/29/EC of the European Parliament and of the Council of 22 May 2001 on the harmonisation of certain aspects of copyright and related rights in the information society[7] deal thoroughly with the rights of the author and possible exceptions and limitations (Loos, 2016; Van Velze, 2015). It must be noted here that an author's rights of use have already been extensively harmonised on the basis of these directives. It seems to be somewhat different with regard to the exceptions and limitations. Here, the level of harmonisation is lower. Although Article 5 of Directive 2001/29/EC regulates "exceptions and limitations", in accordance with Article 5(2) and Article 5(3) of Directive 2001/29/EC, member states are entitled to decide at their own discretion whether they wish to recognise in their national law the limitations mentioned in these provisions (Manning, 2016). Questions of an author's personality rights and licensing agreement rights have not been harmonised.

Ultimately, with the international agreements for the protection of authors and their works, there is a third legal level which is directed primarily at the signatory states. The Berne Convention, the WIPO Copyright Treaty (WCT) and the TRIPS Agreement (which deals especially with copyright law in Articles 9–14) are particularly noteworthy in this respect (G. W. Austin, 2005; Manning, 2016). However, since all signatory states have implemented the requirements and obligations of the respective conventions into national law, it is not necessary to look at the conventions in detail here.

4.2.2.2 When Is the Respective National Copyright Law Applicable?

On the basis of the territoriality principle relating to copyright, the national laws for the protection of authors and their works only apply within the territory of the respective state. The question as to which national law applies to the infringement of copyright laws in a case involving international relations complies with Article 8(1) of Regulation (EC) No 864/2007 of the European Parliament and of the Council of 11 July 2007 on the law applicable to noncontractual obligations (Rome II):[8]

Infringement of intellectual property rights
1. The law applicable to a non-contractual obligation arising from an infringement
of an intellectual property right shall be the law of the country for which protection
is claimed.

Based on Article 8(1) of Regulation (EC) No 864/2007, the law in the respective country for which the copyright is being claimed applies (*lex loci protectionis*) (Kramer, 2008; van Engelen, 2008). In practical terms, this means that the questions of origin, first ownership, content and scope of the copyright as well as transferability of copyrights are based on the state for whose territory copyright protection is being sought (Dreier & Schulze, 2015).

The question of the applicable law in the infringement of copyrights must be distinguished from the substantial law which applies to contractual obligations, which is determined to a large extent by "Regulation (EC) No 593/2008 of the European Parliament and of the Council of 17 June 2008 on the law applicable to contractual obligations (Rome I)".[9] Contractual obligations are not in the scope of this work. Hence, the Rome I Regulation is not relevant in this chapter, but it will come into the focus in our final Licence Agreement (Appendix A), which deals with contractual obligations arising from license agreements.

4.2.2.3 Why (Only) German Copyright Law?

On the basis of Article 8(1) of Regulation (EC) No 864/2007 (Rome II, Kramer, 2008), within the scope of harvesting and monitoring of social computing data, the applicable law is the national copyright law of the state *on whose territory copyright-protected works are reproduced, transferred and communicated to the public*. In concrete terms, this means that the question of legality complies with French law in the case of a natural disaster in France and complies with Polish copyright laws in the case of the use of such a system in Poland, provided that the relevant acts of copyright usage are being carried out in the respective countries.

It is not possible to examine all national copyright laws of all (currently twenty-eight) member states within the scope of this project. Therefore, for the question of the compatibility of data monitoring of, and harvesting from, social computing systems, with national copyright laws, German copyright law is being taken as a worked example. Although the results cannot be directly transferred to other member states in their entirety, they provide valuable indications for possible risks in the use of social media content within the scope of disaster management as well as a potential model for analysis of copyright law within other member state jurisdictions.

4.2.3 *Overview of the Relevant Issues*

The use of data, information and content of social media for the purpose of disaster management raises numerous questions related to copyright law. The following questions are at the heart of the analysis of the harvesting and monitoring of social computing data from the viewpoint of copyright law:

- **Can social media content** (posts, tweets, texts, pictures, videos, etc.) **claim copyright protection at all?** In this regard, it must be taken into account that data, information, facts, ideas, etc. are not "works" (in the sense of copyright law) and therefore do not enjoy copyright protection in the first place. Data on the basis of databases enjoy protection as an exception. See Section 4.3.1 for details.
- **Texts, images, videos, music are only protected if they are the author's "own intellectual creation".** In this context, it is necessary to assess whether the required level of "individuality" (creativity) has been attained. This can be doubtful. In relation to social media content, the works are often very short, trivial or banal, and show a rather low level of creativity. In this respect, however, the decisions of the European Court of Justice (ECJ) in the *Painer* and *Infopaq* cases are significant. In the *Painer* case, the ECJ decided that even simple portrait photos can enjoy copyright protection,[10] while the *Infopaq* case recognises the possibility that as few as eleven words of a text can meet the prerequisites of being the author's own intellectual creation.[11] In this context, the most recent decision of High Court Cologne from 8 April 2016 (6 U 120/15) is significant. In this case, six words ("When the house has wet feet") were denied protected. See Section 4.3.1 for details.
- **Insofar as social media content enjoys copyright protection, this raises the question as to who holds the copyright.** In accordance with the "principle of creativity" the author of the work is the first holder of the copyrights. The "work made for hire principle", which applies in England[12] and the Netherlands, whereby ownership of works created within the scope of contractual and employment relationships may be assigned to the employer or the employee, is of no importance under German copyright law. However, in relation to the question as to who owns the copyright, **the contractual agreements concluded between the user and the operator must also be taken into consideration.** Ownership of the content is often transferred to the operator. In relation to licensing agreements, it is necessary to assess to what extent rights of use are granted, and whether corresponding compensation must be paid. See Section 4.3.3 for details.
- **Which of the usage rights are being infringed by the systematic and continuous use of social media for extreme cases, for example disaster management?** It must of course be emphasised here that establishing an infringement in copyright laws does *not* mean that the matter refers to an illegal act which violates copyrights. Rather, it must be assessed with regard to whether the infringement is

justified, either through a declaration of consent, legal exceptions and limitations or licensing agreements. See Section 4.4.1 for details.

– If the matter refers to reproducing, distributing or communicating the content to the public, **one must assess whether these actions can be justified through limitations on copyright and exceptions.** This conforms to national copyright law. In Germany, Sections 44a et seq. of the German Copyright Act (GCA) are relevant. In accordance with Section 5 of the GCA, for official works (i.e., works created by governmental bodies) copyright protection can be completely omitted. Therefore, it must be assessed to what extent data and materials which originate from public authorities rather than from private users enjoy copyright protection from the outset. See Section 4.5 for details.

– **Finally it must be assessed whether users of harvested social computing data grant a declaration of consent for the use of their posts.** However, an implied consent often comes into consideration. See Section 4.5.3 for details.

4.3 THE ONTOLOGY OF COPYRIGHT

4.3.1 *What Can Be Protected by Copyright in Social Computing Systems?*

The key concept in copyright law is that of the "work" (Schack, 2015), as protection under copyright law is only granted to "works." (Guibault, 2010; Lipton, 2001). In this sense, Article 2 of Directive 2001/29/EC contains the following statement regarding the reproduction right:

> "Member States shall provide for the exclusive right to authorise or prohibit direct or indirect, temporary or permanent reproduction by any means and in any form, in whole or in part: a) for authors, of their works [. . .]"[13]

Along these lines, Section 2 of the GCA sets out the following:
Protected *works*

(1) Protected works in the literary, scientific and artistic domain include, in particular:
  1. Literary works, such as written works, speeches and computer programs;
  2. Musical works;
  3. Pantomimic works, including works of dance;
  4. Artistic works, including works of architecture and of applied art and drafts of such works;
  5. Photographic works, including works produced by processes similar to photography;
  6. Cinematographic works, including works produced by processes similar to cinematography;

7. Illustrations of a scientific or technical nature, such as drawings, plans, maps, sketches, tables and three-dimensional representations.

(2) Only the author's own intellectual creations constitute works within the meaning of this Act.

The first conclusion we can draw from Section 2 of GCA is that – since they are not mentioned in the list and not an author's own "creation" – mere ideas or motifs, as well as scientific discoveries, teachings and theories enjoy as little protection as facts, information and data (Schack, 2015). Ideas and information must remain in the public domain and may not be monopolised in order to avoid limiting cultural and scientific exchange and the free flow of information through intellectual property rights (Wagner, 2003).

This raises the question as to what additional prerequisites denote that the material is a "work". At the European level, Directive 2009/24/EC on the legal protection of computer programs (Article 1), Directive 96/9/EC on the legal protection of databases (Article 3) and Directive 2006/116/EC on the term of protection of copyright (for the photographic type of work [Article 6]) are the only directives that provide details on the prerequisites for the protection of specific copyright-protected works (Rosati, 2013). All three directives refer to the *individuality of the work and the author's own intellectual creation* (Griffiths, 2011). Thus, for Germany, for the three types of work mentioned, the prerequisites for protection regarding the author's "own intellectual creation" were reduced, which became palpable in the early 1990s particularly in the area of copyright protection for computer programs. In addition, Directive 2001/29/EC contains no more specific stipulation as to what prerequisites a "work" must fulfil (Rosati, 2013).

4.3.2 Jurisprudence of the ECJ and German Courts

This statutory starting point has been modified by case law. However, the ECJ has repeatedly dealt with the question as to what prerequisites must be met for a work to merit protection. Both decisions are very relevant in that – since they pertain to very short sequences of text and simple photographs – they refer to work formats which often occur in social media.

4.3.2.1 The *Infopaq* Case

In the *Infopaq* decision of 16 July 2009, the ECJ dealt with the prerequisites of a general European concept of the work for the first time (Berger, 2012; Leistner, 2014). What had to be decided on was the question of whether the use of eleven words from a newspaper article constituted reproducing part of a work in accordance with Article 2 of Directive 2001/29/EC. A party of the Danish main proceedings is on the side of the plaintiff Infopaq, which deals with the analysis of print media. For its analysis, Infopaq scans newspaper articles and searches them for search terms specified by its customers (Griffiths, 2011; Margoni, 2014). In order to facilitate the process of finding a search term in its context, the term is combined with the five preceding and five subsequent words, then saved and printed. A printed out search text (for search word "TDC") looks like this:

> TDC: "the imminent sale of telecommunications group TDC whose takeover is considered likely"

Infopaq brought a claim against the trade association of the Danish daily newspaper on the basis that the procedure used in the media analysis was not permissible without the right-holder's permission.

On the Danish court's request, the ECJ had to assess the question as to whether the saving and printing of eleven words constituted "reproduction" (Griffiths, 2011; Guadamuz, 2016). The ECJ responded in the affirmative: "An action consisting of saving and printing an 11-word excerpt of a protected work can fall under the heading of a partial reproduction as defined by Art. 2 of Directive 2001/29/EC, if the parts which have been reproduced – which must be assessed by the national court – constitute the author's own intellectual creation" (mn. 51). In the justification, the ECJ refers to the wording of Article 2 of Directive 2001/29/EC, whereby acts of reproducing relate to "works", citing these as originals since they are their authors' "own intellectual creations" (mn. 37) (Waelde et al., 2013: 50). The ECJ says that parts of works are protected if they contain elements which constitute the author's own intellectual creative expression (mn. 39). Words "as such" do not constitute components subject to protection (mn. 46), but an excerpt from a written work does, provided it is an expression of the author's intellectual creativity. According to the ECJ this can also be the case in an excerpt containing eleven words (mn. 48).

However, in the *Infopaq* decision, the ECJ did not conclusively decide whether the 11 words which are the subject of the dispute fulfil the prerequisites of an author's own intellectual creation. The ECJ specifically emphasised that this decision was the duty of the national courts (Crackau, 2014). This would appear logical. After all, it relates to fact-finding and subsuming. Therefore, it may not be concluded on the basis of the *Infopaq* decision that 11 words fulfil the criteria of a copyright-protected work in all cases.

4.3.2.2 The *Painer* Case

The second decision which is key for the harvesting and monitoring of social computing data is the *Painer* case, which was decided by the ECJ on 1 December 2011. The case was in relation to claims brought by the photographer Painer against several European publications which printed portrait photographs of a kidnapping victim in their media agencies. The photographs at issue had been produced by the plaintiff, who photographs children in playgrounds as an independent photographer and who took several photographs of the kidnapping victim in this context and had "in the process designed the background, determined the position and facial expression, operated the camera and developed the photographs" (mn. 27). These photographs, which the plaintiff had made available to the police for the purposes of the search, were printed by the newspaper publishers (who were the defendants of the case) following the end of the dramatic kidnapping. Vienna commercial court asked the ECJ whether the portrait photographs enjoy copyright protection because they demonstrate only limited creative scope (Guadamuz, 2016; Handig, 2012; Margoni, 2014).

The ECJ remarked that a work was its author's "own intellectual creation" if the author's personality was expressed, because the author could express his or her creative abilities and therefore freely make creative decisions (recital 88 et seq.). The ECJ takes the distinguishing characteristic of the person captured in the work from recital 16 of the term of protection directive. The "personal touch" which is required in accordance with this recital is also possible in portrait photography as the creative scope is not necessarily reduced or must be reduced fully to zero (mn. 92 f.) (Guadamuz, 2016; Handig, 2012; Margoni, 2014).

4.3.2.3 US: *AFG v. Morel*

Although US copyright law is not the focus of this chapter, which deals with European and German copyright law (cf. 4.2.2), it completes the picture that under the Digital Millennium Copyright Act (DMCA) the United States District Court Southern District of New York in *AFG v. Morel* held that photographs taken in the aftermath of the 2010 Haiti earthquake enjoy copyright protection.[14] The case is of particular interest in the context of disaster management and social media: The author, a photographer based in Haiti, had uploaded the photos to Twitter, and another Twitter user had copied them, which allowed the Defendant – a press agency – to distribute them to customers around the world. Under these circumstances, the distribution of the photographs of the earthquake collected from Twitter violated the copyright on the photographs, and the owner of copyright could claim damages for violation of copyright.

4.3.2.4 Synthesis

We can conclude from the *Infopaq* and *Painer* cases that although the ECJ will not grant copyright protection for individual words, a mere few words within a sentence or relatively standard photographs can nevertheless enjoy protection under copyright law, but this is on condition that the material is the author's "own intellectual creation", which is met if a certain creative scope is available.

However, in a case on 8 April 2016 (6 U 120/15), the High Court of Cologne denied a copyright application for an advertising slogan consisting of six words. This case is also interesting in the context of harvesting and monitoring social computing data as it relates to social media. The respondent promoted a book on Twitter using the slogan "When the house has wet feet" ("Wenn das Haus nasse Füße hat"). The complaint, which was brought by a publishing house that also used this slogan, was dismissed. The court concluded that the slogan was not a "creation" subject to protection, that it contained no particularly original content, and that in fact it only described the content of the book.

If these criteria are transferred to social media content, then *texts, images, videos, drawings, etc. in this sphere should often be deemed subject to protection*. A certain creative scope is required, although it depends on the specific facts of the case (Reinemann & Remmertz, 2012), and in many cases, this will not be deemed existent (Wandtke, Bullinger, Block & Grunert, 2014). Nevertheless, it must be taken into account that a text will not be granted or denied copyright protection on the basis of its word count alone. Rather, copyright protection is conferred when the material is the author's "own intellectual creation" and a certain creative scope was present.

In individual cases, it may be difficult to determine whether copyright exists. However, it is reasonable to expect that the use of social media content on a mass scale often comprises the use of protected works and therefore requires a special justification.

4.3.3 Who Owns the Copyright?

4.3.3.1 First Ownership

Insofar as social media content enjoys copyright protection because it represents the author's own intellectual creation, one must ask who *owns* the copyright. Directive 2001/29/EC does not contain any regulation on first ownership of rights. Therefore, national law is definitive. In accordance with Section 7 of the GCA, "the author is the creator of the work". In German copyright law, there are no exceptions to this creator principle (Förster, 2014). Based on this stipulation, it follows that the natural person who created the work is the sole owner of all copyrights. Legal bodies (such as companies) cannot be copyright holders (Förster, 2014; Herzberg, 2006). The creator principle also applies to the employment relationship: the copyright holder and therefore first right-holder is always the employee. However, in accordance with Section 43 of the GCA, the employee is obligated to license rights of use to the employer (Förster, 2014; Fuchs, 2006).

The results in the area of rights to computer programs are very similar. Article 2 of Directive 2009/24/EC of the European Parliament and of the Council of 23 April 2009 on the legal protection of computer programs[15] sets out the following regarding the authorship of computer programs:

1. The author of a computer program shall be the natural person or group of natural persons who has created the program or, where the legislation of the Member State permits, the legal person designated as the right holder by that legislation.
   Where collective works are recognised by the legislation of a Member State, the person considered by the legislation of the Member State to have created the work shall be deemed to be its author.
2. In respect of a computer program created by a group of natural persons jointly, the exclusive rights shall be owned jointly.
3. Where a computer program is created by an employee in the execution of his duties or following the instructions given by his employer, the employer exclusively shall be entitled to exercise all economic rights in the program so created, unless otherwise provided by contract.

Since German law stipulates that legal entities cannot be copyright holders, the copyright to computer programs is always (jointly) held by the programmers (Förster, 2014; Herzberg, 2006). In the case of a computer program created within the scope of an employment relationship, the rights of use are held by the employer. This also applies to employment relationships in universities and research institutes.

Furthermore, the special feature of German copyright law, whereby the copyright as such is not contractually transferrable, must also be taken into consideration (Ensthaler, 2009). This principle is stipulated in Section 29(1) of the GCA. *This leads to significant legal difficulties, if "ownership" of the copyright or the work (e.g., on social media) is to be transferred through contracts* (Haupt & Marschke, 2005).

Under German law, only "rights of use" may be granted [Section 29(2) of the GCA]. These rights of use are also referred to as "licenses".

4.3.4 Contractual License Agreements

When considering to whom copyrights belong, the contractual agreements concluded between the user and the operator of social networks must be taken into consideration. In these agreements, *ownership of the contents is often assigned to the operator.*

The following analysis of ownership of social media content looks at the examples of Twitter and Facebook, based on their general contractual terms and conditions.

- Who owns the property rights of the content on Facebook/Twitter?
- What usage rights have Facebook/Twitter obtained?

a) **Facebook**, in its Statement of Rights and Responsibilities states as follows:

Paragraph 2: Sharing Your Content and Information[16]:
   You own all of the content and information you post on Facebook, and you can control how it is shared through your privacy and application settings. In addition:

1. For content that is covered by intellectual property rights, like photos and videos (IP content), you specifically give us the following permission, subject to your privacy and application settings: you grant us a non-exclusive, transferable, sub-licensable, royalty-free, worldwide license to use any IP content that you post on or in connection with Facebook (IP License). This IP License ends when you delete your IP content or your account unless your content has been shared with others, and they have not deleted it.

In accordance with this contractual clause, Facebook demands an unlimited, nonexclusive transferrable right of use to posted user content (both copyright and personality right – but copyright only when the user also holds a right of use). The following passage is slightly unclear: "You own all of the content and information you post on Facebook". Here, Facebook recognises the users' rights to their content. Thus, the user has ownership, but only to a limited extent, as the content and therefore also the rights of use are retained by Facebook if the content has been distributed by other users ("unless your content has been shared with others").

With regard to the effects of Facebook's general contractual terms, the *Kammergericht Berlin* (Higher Regional Court Berlin) determined the *invalidity of the terms* due to an infringement of the transparency clause of Section 307(1) of the German Civil Code (GCC):

Section 307 Test of reasonableness of contents
(1) Provisions in standard business terms are ineffective if, contrary to the requirement of good faith, they unreasonably disadvantage the other party to the contract with the user. An unreasonable disadvantage may also arise from the provision not being clear and comprehensible.

The court held that the license clause included in Facebook's Standard Terms does not meet the requirements of "being clear and comprehensible".[17] Furthermore, the grant of a non-remunerated usage right to Facebook is not in line with the principle of fair remuneration of authors.[18] Thus, the court deemed the license agreement between the operator of Facebook and the user of Facebook to be invalid and nonbinding. Consequently, under German law, the copyright of the user-generated content rests with the user.

b) Twitter (Terms of Service)
Paragraph 5 of the Twitter Terms of Service contains the following text:

You retain your rights to any Content you submit, post or display on or through the Services. By submitting, posting or displaying Content on or through the Services, you grant us a worldwide, non-exclusive, royalty-free license (with the right to sublicense) to use, copy, reproduce, process, adapt, modify, publish, transmit, display and distribute such Content in any and all media or distribution methods (now known or later developed).[19]

In accordance with this contractual clause, Twitter – like Facebook – acquires an unlimited, nonexclusive, royalty-free right of use.

Twitter is authorised to transfer the rights and content to other parties:

> You agree that this license includes the right for Twitter to provide, promote, and improve the Services and to make Content submitted to or through the Services available to other companies, organizations or individuals who partner with Twitter for the syndication, broadcast, distribution or publication of such Content on other media and services, subject to our terms and conditions for such Content use.

On this basis, it would be possible for software developers and users deploying a system which harvests social media data to, for example, acquire Twitter's rights to the posts.

However, the following terms of use are unclear:

> Twitter has an evolving set of rules for how ecosystem partners can interact with your Content on the Twitter Services. These rules exist to enable an open ecosystem with your rights in mind. But what's yours is yours – you own your Content (and your photos are part of that Content).

Clearly, Twitter wishes to allow the "ecosystem partners" access to the content, without limiting the users' ownership.

4.4 COPYRIGHT AND EXCEPTIONAL CIRCUMSTANCES: DISASTER MANAGEMENT

On the basis of the general contractual terms and conditions, Facebook and Twitter can be granted simple rights of use. However, based on the reasoning of the *Kammergericht* ruling, an operator's usage right is subject to the requirements of a simple and clear wording in the General Terms and the issue of reasonable remuneration of the author.

Users would thus have two possible means of acquiring rights of use in relation to the content: Firstly, by *concluding an agreement with the social media operators* in order to gain access to and use the data; however, one can rely on this approach only if the operator has obtained valid usage rights, which might be doubtful under the case law, in particular in the light of the *Kammergericht* ruling.[20] Secondly, responders could *contact the users directly* to obtain usage rights. The latter should be discarded for practical reasons. In light of this unclear legal starting point, the issue of a user's "implied consent" to their posts being used for the purpose of disaster management is the focus of interest (see Section 4.5.3).

4.4.1 *What Copyrights Are Affected by the Use of Social Media Content for Disaster Management?*

The use of copyright-protected content for the purpose of disaster management must not illegally infringe on the copyrights of social media users. However, it is worth emphasising that asserting an infringement under copyright law *does not necessarily mean that an illegal action* violating copyright has taken place. Rather, it is necessary to assess in a further step whether the infringement is justified, either through consent, legal exceptions and limitations or licensing agreements. The particular copyrights which could come into consideration regarding the harvesting of social media for emergency response decision support are analysed in the paragraphs that follow. These potentially relevant copyrights include the copyright holder's exclusive right to reproduce, distribute and publicly communicate the content.

4.4.2 *Reproduction Right*

The saving of copyright-protected works – for example, on servers – constitutes reproducing. The copyright holder is granted this right exclusively under Section 16 of the German copyright law (Hoeren, 2013).

Section 16 of the GCA reads as follows:

Right of reproduction:
(1) The right of reproduction is the right to produce copies of the work, whether on a temporary or on a lasting basis and regardless of by which means of procedure or in which quantity they are made.

(2) The transfer of the work to devices for the purposes of repeated communication of video and sound sequences (video and audio recordings), regardless of whether this is the recording of a communication of the work on a video or audio recording medium or the transfer of the work from one video or audio recording medium to another, also constitutes reproduction.

Section 16 of the GCA is based on Article 2 of Directive 2001/29/EC:

Reproduction right. Member States shall provide for the exclusive right to authorise or prohibit direct or indirect, temporary or permanent reproduction by any means and in any form, in whole or in part:
(a) for authors, of their works[.]

In concrete terms, this means that the act of making copies of social media content – provided that it is copyright protected – represents an infringement on the reproduction right, which requires justification.

The question as to whether displaying a copyright-protected work on a screen constitutes "reproduction" is currently unresolved (Berger, 2012; Bernhöft, 2009; Vitoria, Laddie & Prescott, 2011). The German Federal Supreme Court came to the conclusion that the display of a work on a screen does not infringe the author's reproduction right, since the reproduction right requires a "tangible" copy of the work.[21]. In contrast, the ECJ – in the case *Football Association Premier League Ltd v. Karen Murphy*[22] – held that

> Article 2(a) of the Copyright Directive must be interpreted as meaning that the reproduction right extends to transient fragments of the works within the memory of a satellite decoder and on a television screen, provided that those fragments contain elements which are the expression of the authors' own intellectual creation, and the unit composed of the fragments reproduced simultaneously must be examined in order to determine whether it contains such elements.[23]

Up to now, German courts have not had the opportunity to review their perception on this issue. However, in the light of the ruling of the ECJ, it can be expected that German courts will follow this opinion.

4.4.3 Distribution Right

The copyright holder reserves the exclusive right of distribution. The basis under European law is set out in Article 4(1) of Directive 2001/29/EC:

> 1. Member States shall provide for authors, in respect of the original of their works or of copies thereof, the exclusive right to authorise or prohibit any form of distribution to the public by sale or otherwise.

Section 17(1) of the GCA accordingly stipulates the following:

> Right of distribution
> (1) The right of distribution is the right to offer the original or copies of the work to the public or to bring it to the market.

In relation to the use of social media for disaster management, the right of distribution plays a small role. As a prerequisite, the copyright-protected work must be produced on the basis of a tangible copy of the work, which is not the case in social media which are based on digital networks (Hoeren, 2013).

4.4.4 Right to Communicate Works to the Public and Right to Make Works Available to the Public

In accordance with Article 3 of Directive 2001/29/EC, the copyright holder holds the exclusive right to communicate the work to the public – in particular the right to make the work available to the public:

> Right of communication to the public of works and right of making available to the public other subject-matter

1. Member States shall provide copyright holders with the exclusive right to authorise or prohibit any communication to the public of their works, by wire or wireless
means, including the making available to the public of their works in such a way
that members of the public may access them from a place and at a time individually
chosen by them.

Accordingly, Section 19a of the GCA stipulates as follows:

Right of making works available to the public
The right of making works available to the public shall constitute the right to make
the work available to the public, either by wire or wireless means, in such a manner
that members of the public may access it from a place and at a time individually
chosen by them.

The right of making works available to the public could play an important role in the
use of harvested social media. It grants the copyright holder – which are the authors
of the posts as first owners of copyright (cf. Section 4.3.3) – exclusive authorisation to
make the work available to the public on the internet or on other networks (Hoeren,
2013). This is the case if the work has been made available to an unspecified number
of potential recipients of a service.[24] Since copyright law grants *exclusive* rights to the
author, nobody but the author (and a licensee under a valid license agreement) can
make the post available to the public. If, for example, a member of the public who
has not been authorised by the author copies a Tweet onto a public digital bulletin,
that person infringes the author's copyright.

However, this preliminary finding is subject to exceptions and limitations, which
are discussed in the following section (Section 4.5).

4.5 EXCEPTIONS AND LIMITATIONS

As has already been emphasised, an infringement under copyright law does not
constitute a legal offence. In many cases, the use of a third party work is admissible
on the basis of limitations in copyright law.

4.5.1 *The European Legal Framework of Exceptions and Limitations*

The European legal framework of exceptions and limitations to copyright law is
Article 5 of Directive 2001/29/EC. This contains a list of exceptions to the respective
rights of the copyright owners. At first glance, a significant harmonisation of the
limitations appears to have been achieved here. However, it must be noted that, only
the limitation in Article 5(1) of Directive 2001/29/EC (temporary acts of reproduction) is obligatory for the member states. All other twenty limitations are *optional*
(Guibault, 2010; Kur, Planck & Dreier, 2013). This is provided for by the following
wording in the opening sentences in Article 5(2) and (3): "Member States *may*
provide for exceptions or limitations".

Thus, the European Commission sets out the following:

The fragmentation of copyright rules in the EU is particularly visible in the area of exceptions. The exceptions set out in EU law are, in most cases, optional for Member States to implement. Often exceptions are not defined in detail. As a consequence, an exception in the law of one Member State may not exist in a neighbouring one, or be subject to different conditions or vary in scope. In some cases the implementation of a given exception in Member States' law is narrower than what EU law permits.[25]

It follows that the member states may choose at their own discretion whether or not to implement a limitation (Guibault, 2010; von Lewinski & Walter, 2010).

Therefore, the harmonisation achieved by directive 2001/29/EC in relation to exceptions and limitations is minimal (Kur, Planck & Dreier, 2013). As a result, each individual member state must assess carefully whether the use of social media content in disaster management is covered by limitations and exceptions. The statements in the following section relate to copyright law in Germany only.

4.5.2 *Limitations and Exceptions Under German Copyright Law*

4.5.2.1 Introductory Remarks

The use of social media content for disaster management can touch on the reproduction right and the copyright holder's right to make works available to the public. The extent to which individual limitations may become relevant to the harvesting and monitoring of social media data is assessed herein.

As we have seen, Article 5(3)(e) of Directive 2001/29/EC empowers the member states to implement specific rules which allow the use of copyright-protected materials for the purposes of public security. This conclusion is also supported by recital 34 of Directive 2001/29/EC, according to which

Member States should be given the option of providing for certain exceptions or limitations for cases such as educational and scientific purposes, for the benefit of public institutions such as libraries and archives, for purposes of news reporting, for quotations, for use by people with disabilities, for *public security uses* and for uses in administrative and judicial proceedings. [emphasis added]

Without any doubt, disaster management maintains and improves public security. However, as we will see, German lawmakers have taken advantage of Article 5(3)(e) of Directive 2001/29/EC only to a very small extent.

In this regard it is also worth mentioning that German copyright law does not provide for a "fair use" or a "fair dealing" exception in the sense of a general permission to infringe copyright for specific purposes under certain conditions. *Fair use or fair dealing is not permitted as such.* What is required under German law is a precise statutory justification to use copyright-protected materials under specific conditions.

4.5.2.2 Section 5 of the GCA: Official Works

In accordance with Section 5 of the GCA, official works are not subject to copyright protection:

(1) Acts, ordinances, official decrees and official notices, as well as decisions and official head notes of decisions do not enjoy copyright protection.

(2) The same applies to other official texts published in the official interest for general information purposes, subject to the proviso that the provisions concerning the prohibition of alteration and the indication of sources in Article 62 (1) to (3) and Article 63 (1) and (2) shall apply mutatis mutandis.

Therefore, *if ownership of a work is ascribed to an administrating body with sovereign powers, copyright protection does not apply.* In this context, publicly accessible weather data of the German Weather Service may be considered official works in accordance with Section 5 of the GCA.[26] On the other hand, if governmental bodies such as the police are using copyright-protected materials created by users of social media, Section 5 of the GCA does not apply because the content remains protected.

4.5.2.3 Section 44a of the GCA: Temporary Acts of Reproduction

Under Section 44a of the GCA, temporary saving can be justified:

Article 44a Temporary acts of reproduction
Those temporary acts of reproduction shall be permissible which are transient or incidental and constitute an integral and essential part of a technical process and whose sole purpose is to enable

1. a transmission in a network between third parties by an intermediary, or
2. a lawful use of a work or other protected subject-matter to be made and which have no independent economic significance.

This limitation ensures that not all technical reproduction procedures which are required in the online transfer of works in digital networks, temporary storage and work storage fall under the right to reproduce (Dreier & Schulze, 2015; Hetmank, 2016). However, the prerequisite that the reproduction has no economic value and that the copy is automatically deleted again applies.[27]

4.5.2.4 Section 52a of the GCA: Making Works Available to the Public for Instruction and Research

The limitation in Section 52a of the GCA is particularly significant for the research phase of harvesting and monitoring social computing data:

(1) It shall be permissible for: ...

(2) published limited parts of a work, small scale works, as well as individual articles from newspapers or periodicals exclusively for a specifically limited circle of persons for their personal scientific research to be made available to the public, to the extent that this is necessary for the respective purpose and is justified for the pursuit of non-commercial aims.

Section 52a of the GCA echoes Article 5 Paragraph 3 no. 1 directive 2001/29/EC:

3. Member States may provide for exceptions or limitations to the rights provided for in Articles 2 and 3 in the following cases:

(a) use for the sole purpose of illustration for teaching or scientific research, as long as the source, including the author's name, is indicated, unless this turns out to be impossible and to the extent justified by the non-commercial purpose to be achieved[.]

Both, German and European limitation regulations provide for an exemption of copyright protection regarding scientific research. Thus, they are important primarily with regard to the research phase of software for harvesting and monitoring social computing data, but less relevant for the deployment phase.

However, even in the research phase, Section 52a of the GCA cannot absorb all risks. In particular, it is important to be aware of the fact that a research project is privileged only if it does not pursue a commercial purpose. Hence, the commercial use of research results gained would exclude the limitation provided in Section 52a of the GCA.

In addition, it should be mentioned that under Section 52a(4) of the GCA, financial compensation must be paid to the right holders for the use of their material (Bagh, 2007):

(4) An equitable remuneration shall be paid for making works available to the public in accordance with paragraph (1). Claims may only be asserted through a collecting society.

Therefore, to a significant extent, the relevance of Section 52a of the GCA depends on whether the use of data and information from social networks, insofar as they are copyright protected, constitutes making them publicly available. This depends heavily on the issue of whether the group of researchers is a limited circle of persons. Since (and to the extent that) the use of posts on Twitter and Facebook (and other social media) is accessed only within the group of researchers and made available only to them, the requirement is fulfilled.

Nevertheless, if a commercial use of the results of harvesting and monitoring data from social computing systems is intended, Section 52a of the GCA is not applicable. This raises the question of the requirements for a "commercial use". In this regard, commercial use means generating profits by selling software systems resulting from this research. Hence, if researchers intend to market results of the project to a company which includes small-to-medium-sized enterprises (SMEs), the research is done for commercial reasons and Section 52a of the GCA is not applicable. On the other hand, if the results are left to some commercial enterprises without remuneration, the requirements of a commercial research are not fulfilled and the researchers can rely on Section 52a of the GCA.

The issue of remuneration for the researchers, however, is not relevant here. The fact that a researcher is being paid for his or her work does not lead to the conclusion that the research is of commercial character.

4.5.2.5 Section 45 of the GCA: Administration of Justice and Public Security

In the deployment phase of software for monitoring and harvesting social computing data, Section 45 of the GCA can also only offer a narrow basis for the use of copyright-protected works:

(1) It shall be permissible to make individual copies of works for use in proceedings before a court, an arbitration tribunal or authority or to have such copies made.

(2) Courts and authorities may, for the purposes of the administration of justice and public security, make copies of portraits or to have these reproduced.

(3) The distribution, exhibition in public and communication to the public of the works shall be permissible under the same conditions as apply to reproduction.

Section 45(1) of the GCA allows authorities access to copyright-protected works. The authorities include not only public authorities, but also private individuals, provided they have been commissioned by an authority to fulfil official or governmental duties (Lutz, 2009). Therefore, any individual may produce a copy of copyright-protected material to communal authorities and, for example, private fire departments.

Under Section 45(2) of the GCA, "authorities" can reproduce photographs of people and make them publicly available (Poeppel, 2005). Therefore, police and other governmental authorities may use portraits for disaster management (i.e. if a person is missing and publicly searched for), but private institutions, unless they have been contracted for the purpose of public security, may not. To clarify the difference, it is important to keep in mind that under German law "authorities"

("Behörden") are always governmental bodies as opposed to private individuals and other private bodies such as private companies.

4.5.2.6 Justification Based on General Civil Law Rules

The use of works for disaster management can be justified under the specific copyright limitations. Nevertheless some gaps still remain. This begs the question of whether justifications based on general civil law rules may become relevant.

Section 904 of the GCC sets forth the requirements for justification of acts in the case of an emergency:

> The owner of any item is not entitled to prohibit the use by another person of that item if such use is necessary to ward off a present danger, and if the damage associated with such a danger is disproportionately great in relation to the damage suffered by the item's owner as a result of its use. The owner may require compensation for any damage incurred such use.

On this basis, the infringement may also be admissible in works of copyright law. However, Section 904 of the GCC emphasises the "thing" ("Sache"). In accordance with Section 90 of the GCC, only corporeal objects are "things" as defined by law, not intangibles.

However, it is necessary to assess whether the general legal reasoning on which Section 904 of the GCC is based can also be transferred to the copyright law. No legal precedent exists for this. One strong argument concerning the analogous application of Section 904 of the GCC to copyright works in disaster scenarios can be concluded from the underlying basic concept of Section 904 of the GCC. In the case of a collision of goods such as life or physical integrity on the one hand and property on the other, the owner of property has to tolerate the infringement of ownership.

One can offer this basic thought on the conflict of life and copyright in the case of a disaster: the owner of copyright has to tolerate the infringement of his or her ownership on the protected work if the infringement is exercised with the intension to save life and to protect the physical integrity of people in need. The fact that the wording of Section 904 of the GCC is limited to tangible property ("thing") does not exclude the analogous application: When the German Civil Code was adopted in the nineteenth century, the conflict of copyright in social media with the need to save lives was a completely inconceivable scenario. This statutory gap can be closed by an analogous application of Section 904 GCC. Hence it can be argued that *it is justified to use copyright-protected materials to safeguard life and physical integrity*.

However, the analogous application of Section 904 of the GCC is limited to the use of copyright in response management to a real and concrete risk scenario only. This follows from the wording of Section 904 of the GCC which requires a "present danger". Hence, Section 904 of the GCC does not justify the use of copyright materials in some sort of perpetual "background monitoring" of social media.

4.5.3 Implied Consent

Our analysis has shown that although a statutory limitation may allow the use of copyright-protected works for disaster management, emergency managers using harvested social media data can by no means in all circumstances rely on legal exception provisions. This raises the question of whether the users themselves can legitimise the use of their works, by way of consent, for the purpose of disaster management. As express written consent is rare, *implied consent* comes into consideration here.

In the *Google thumbnails* decision, the German Federal High Court of Justice deemed implied consent to be possible for the use of images in search engines. The Federal High Court of Justice stated the following:

> The clear conclusion is that the plaintiff's act of making the content of its website available to search engines without availing of technical means in order to remove images of its works from the search and display by image search engines in the form of preview images could objectively be understood by the defendant as operator of a search engine as authorization to use images of the plaintiff's works within the customary scope of image searches. An authorised party which provides free and unlimited access to texts or images on the internet must expect the acts of use which are usual under the circumstances.[28]

A corresponding authorization by implied consent can absolutely be assumed in social media posts also. Based on the presumed intention of anyone who posts information on disasters, photographs of specific catastrophe situations or calls for help in social networks of course *agrees that this content will be shared with other users* (Reinemann & Remmertz, 2012) (which is the purpose of social media networks) and in particular used for managing the disaster in every possible and necessary manner. This includes reproducing the material and making it publicly available.

On the other hand, the presumed intention of somebody who posts disaster-related content on social media is limited to the purpose of disaster management. Consequently, an implied consent does not justify the commercial use of postings. Furthermore, there is no authorization by implied consent to a preventive or precautionary monitoring of social networks. Finally, since implied authorisation relates to a concrete disaster situation, the consent is limited only to the time of the disaster management and requires that the copyright-protected works are no longer used after the disaster has ended.

4.5.4 *Implications*

The harvesting and monitoring of social computing data needs a stable legal frame-work. It is self-evident that the infringement of personal rights has to be avoided from the outset. There is no intention to develop a tool for the violation of the law and of personal rights. The responsibility to abide by privacy and copyright law rests with the researchers and users. In order to properly meet this responsibility, the legal analysis provided in this chapter clarifies the legal framework and addresses some potential legal risks.

The main questions and findings from the preceding discussion, and the implica-tions of these findings for a system for harvesting and monitoring social computing data can be summarised as follows:

Q: *Can the content of social media be protected by copyright law?*

A: Yes. Although not every short text containing a few words or a simple photograph ("snapshot") is copyright protected, the user of software for harvesting and monitor-ing social computing data has to take into account that the use of social media content can infringe copyright-protected materials.

Q: *Is the use of social media in emergency response justifiable by any limitations in German copyright law or German civil law?*

A: The justification of the use of copyright-protected material under German law can be argued in particular on Section 904 of the GCC, according to which the owner of property is not entitled to prohibit the use by another person of the property if the use is necessary to ward off a present danger (e.g., for life and physical integrity).

Q: *Is the use of copyright-protected material justified in response management only, or can the use in event detection (which may entail background monitoring) also be justified?*

A: Section 904 of the GCC requires a "present danger" (to life, physical integrity and property); hence permanent background monitoring, which does not respond to and is not triggered by a concrete disaster scenario, cannot be justified by Section 904 of the GCC.

Q: *Can implied consent by copyright holders be deemed to have been given?*

A: Basically yes. In the core of social media lies the idea of "sharing" content, which implies a consent to make use of information placed on social media. Furthermore, if postings refer to a specific disaster scenario, an implied consent to usage can be assumed even more.

Q: *Will users have to negotiate contractual agreements with the rights holders?*

A: If users want a totally secure and stable basis for the use of social media content in disaster scenarios, a contractual agreement is the most preferable way.

Q: *With whom must a user conclude a contract?*

A: The contract has to be concluded with the holders of copyright.

Q: *Who are the copyright holders?*

A: First ownership of copyright belongs to the "authors" of the copyright-protected works (i.e., the members of the public who use social media). However, if ownership (or usage rights) is being transferred contractually to the operators of social media, the operators are the owners of copyright and thus the appropriate contractual partners for end-users. The question of whether there is a valid contractual assignment of ownership to the operators is an open question. It depends (inter alia) on the specific design of the general contractual terms and conditions.

4.6 SUMMARY

This chapter deals with the use and exploitation of digital content distributed on social media under European copyright law and in particular German copyright law. Its purpose is to analyse the legal framework and the requirements for the use of copyright-protected material in relation to a system for harvesting and monitoring social computing data.

One crucial result of the legal analysis is that social media content such as texts, images, videos, drawings, etc. are often deemed subject to protection. It depends on whether the material is the author's "own intellectual creation" and if a certain creative scope is present. In individual cases, it may be difficult to determine whether copyright protection exists. However, one must conclude that the use of social media content on a mass scale often comprises the use of protected works (cf. Section 4.3.1) and therefore requires a specific justification.

The ownership of copyright in social media content is of fundamental importance, in particular for the conclusion of a license agreement with the appropriate partner. First ownership rests with the author, which in the case of tweets and postings on social media is the public user of social media. On the basis of the general contractual terms and conditions, social media operators such as Facebook and Twitter can be granted rights of use. However, this is subject to the requirements of a simple and clear wording in the General Terms and the issue of reasonable remuneration of the author. Both questions have not yet been resolved, in particular due to a lack of court decisions on the issues. Hence, the question of ownership remains relevant.

Potentially relevant copyrights include the copyright-holder's exclusive right to reproduce, distribute and publicly communicate the content. The crucial question is whether the use of copyright material can be justified by law or by consent. Regarding specific limitations and exception on the basis of statutory copyright law, the basis for justification is relatively poor. Statutory copyright law does not address the specific issue of disaster management. Hence, the corresponding provisions are very narrow in scope and do not capture all conceivable scenarios. However, a justification of the use of copyright-protected material can be argued on the general justification of Section 904 of the GCC, according to which the owner of property is not entitled to prohibit the use by another person of the property if this use is necessary to ward off a present danger (e.g., for life and physical integrity). This statutory justification can be applied to copyright as well.

A further justification of the use of copyright-protected materials can be based on the fact that an implied consent by copyright holders can often be deemed to have been given (cf. Section 4.5.3). It can be presumed that anyone who posts disaster-related information in social networks must expect the acts of use which are usual under the specific circumstances and thus from an objective standpoint declares consent that this content will be shared with other users and in particular be used for managing the disaster.

On the other hand, the presumed intention of somebody who posts disaster-related content on social media is limited by the purpose of disaster management. Consequently, commercial use and preventive or precautionary monitoring of social networks cannot be justified by implied consent. Moreover, the consent is limited only to the time of the disaster management and thus requires that the copyright-protected materials are no longer used after the disaster has ended.

4.6.1 *Outlook: European Copyright Framework*

Our analysis suggests that copyright law, at least in certain fields, needs to be adjusted to the particularities of modern digital technology and communication methods. Our discussion in this chapter has shown that copyright law is highly relevant to the operation of a system for harvesting and monitoring social computing data. Copyright law as it stands now – as demonstrated by the example of German copyright law – can prove to be a significant hindrance to the use of social media content for the purpose of disaster management.

The extension of the scope of copyright protection driven by the rulings of the ECJ – we have seen that even a small number of words and plain portraits can be copyright protected (cf. Section 4.3.1) – is not reflected in an enlargement of limitations and exception, which remain still eclectic to a substantial degree, at least in the digital environment of creation and use. All uses of data and information within a system harvesting social media are by no means legitimised by limitations and implied consent.

To a certain degree, the European Commission has recognised the problem of copyright law in a digital context. In its communication "Towards a Modern, More European Copyright Framework", the Commission focuses on the issue of data mining in mass-scale digital content as follows:

The need to better reflect technological advances and avoid uneven situations in the single market is also clear with text-and-data mining (TDM), through which vast amounts of digital content are read and analysed by machines in the context of science and research. The lack of a clear EU provision on TDM for scientific research purposes creates uncertainties in the research community. This harms the EU's competitiveness and scientific leadership at a time when research and innovation (R&I) activities within the EU must increasingly take place through cross-border and cross-discipline collaboration and on a larger scale, in response to the major societal challenges that R&I addresses.[29]

The aforementioned lack of a clear statutory provision on text data mining which enhances scientific research is confirmed by the findings of this chapter. Furthermore, the regrettable deficiency of a copyright law adjusted to the needs of the digital context is not limited to *text* data mining and is not relevant in the field of *research* only.

The technical competence of generating information for the purpose of disaster management out of content on social media is not restricted to *text* analysis. A system for harvesting and monitoring social computing data can make use of the full range of social media content, which includes not only texts but photographs, videos and audio content as well. These types of "non-textual" content as well as texts are copyright protected. Consequently, this chapter suggests that the Commission's endeavour to initiate statutory provisions which enable data mining should be extended to these categories of copyright-protected material as well.

Furthermore, the scope of new provisions of use of social media should not remain restricted to research and innovation. It is not to be denied that research and innovation is the basis of new technology in the digital environment. However, with regard to a system that functions as an instrument for disaster management, the limitations and exceptions of copyright law should not only apply to the research phase of such a project, but to the deployment phase as well. In particular, the use of the system in a concrete disaster scenario should be enabled and facilitated by specific statutory legislation. Such a statutory provision could be developed in the framework of limitations and exception for copyright-protected works for the purpose of public security.

As of 2018, the newly adopted General Data Protection Regulation[30] provides an advanced framework for data protection which in particular addresses the needs of usage of personal data for the purpose of public security. In particular, the General Data Protection Regulation addresses data protection in the context of disaster response in Recital 73, according to which limitations of data protection responsibilities are possible in order to "safeguard public security, including the protection of human life especially in response to natural or manmade disasters". This can provide a legal basis for a system for harvesting and monitoring social computing data because it permits disaster management entities to access personal data in the case of disaster response.

Within the aforementioned initiative towards a modern, more European copyright framework, the Commission should consider a similar statutory exemption for the purpose of disaster management regarding copyright law. Such a provision would further enhance research and deployment of a system for harvesting and monitoring social computing data.

4.6.2 Outlook: Ethical Uses and Abuses

We have looked at the laws surrounding social computing systems as an artefact of the internet in general and at the interaction between laws designed to protect print material, items saved on magnetic material, audio formats and on paper, to the "copyright" of the data available on social computing systems. The key for us here is the notion of "right." There has been much discussion in terms of human rights, ranging from the right to hold beliefs, to own property, to access clear water and food and to enjoy privacy. The laws and protocols in the area of human rights – mostly internationally agreed – may be relevant to the protection of data on social computing streams and may help to protect citizens against the vagaries of national laws. This we discuss in the following chapter.

NOTES

1. In the UK, for example, the relevant legislation for emergency responders is the Civil Contingencies Act 2004, which outlines a legal obligation to prevent, reduce, mitigate and control the effects of an emergency (including "loss of human life, human illness and injury, homelessness, damage to property") (UK, 2004). In Italy, the law establishing the National Civil Protection Service in 1992 specifies the aim of "protecting the integrity of life, properties, settlements and the environment from damages or risk of damages arising from natural calamities, catastrophes and other calamitous events" (Italy, 1992).
2. The EU GDPR document referred to was published on 26 April 2016 and is available at http://data .consilium.europa.eu/doc/document/ST-5419-2016-INIT/en/pdf (last accessed 16 April 2018).
3. This definition of "personal data" is given in GDPR (2016) Article 4(1), p. 111.
4. Cited verbatim from GDPR (2016), Article 4(2), p. 111.
5. Paraphrased from GDPR (2016), Article 4(5), p. 112.
6. A consolidated version of TEFU is available on https://eur-lex.europa.eu/legal-content/EN/TXT/ PDF/?uri=CELEX:12012E/TXT&from=EN (last accessed 16 April 2018).
7. OJ L 167/10 as of 22.06.2001.
8. OJ L 199/40 as of 31.07.2007; van Engelen (2008), pp. 2 ff.
9. OJ L 177/6 as of 04.07.2008; Fiorini (2008), p. 94.
10. ECJ, 01.12.2011, C 145/10, ECLI:EU:C:2011:798.
11. ECJ, 16.07.2009, C-5/08, ECLI:EU:C:2009:465.
12. Sections 11(1) and 11(2) of the CDPA 1988 (as amended): Section 11(1): "The author of a work is the first owner of any copyright in it, subject to the following provisions". Section 11(2): "Where a literary, dramatic, musical or artistic work, or a film, is made by an employee in the course of his employment, his employer is the first owner of any copyright in the work subject to any agreement to the contrary."
13. Cited verbatim from Directive 2001/29/EC of the European Parliament and of the Council (22 May 2001), available at http://eur-lex.europa.eu/legal-content/EN/TXT/PDF/? uri=CELEX:32001L0029&from=EN (last accessed 16 April 2018).

14. Case 1:10-cv-02730 (AJN) (filed 13 August 2014).
15. OJ L111/16 as of 5 May 2009.
16. www.facebook.com/terms (Date of Last Revision: January 31, 2018; site visited 18 April 2018).
17. Kammergericht Berlin, Judgment of 24 January 2014 – File No 5 U 42/12.
18. Kammergericht Berlin, Judgment of 24 January 2014 – File No 5 U 42/12; for details of this concept cf. Berger and Wündisch (2015), chapter 2.
19. https://twitter.com/tos?lang=en#yourrights (last accessed 21 July 2016).
20. Kammergericht Berlin, Judgment of 24 January 2014 – File No 5 U 42/12; cf. footnote 19.
21. BGHZ 37, 1, 10 – *AKI*; BGH GRUR 1991, 449, 453 – *Betriebssystem*.
22. Joined Cases C-403/08 and C-429/08, court ruling as of 4 October 2011.
23. EJC, C-403/08 and C-429/03, margin note 159.
24. ECJ C-135/10, margin note 84 – *SCF*.
25. European Commission: Towards a modern, more European copyright framework, Communication from the Commission to the European Parliament, the Council, the European Economic and Social Committee and the Committee of the Regions, COM (2015), 626 final, pp. 6–7.
26. The Higher Regional Court Cologne, MMR 2007, 443, has answered this in the negative only for weather data which shall be communicated exclusively for aviation purposes; Raue (2013), p. 288.
27. ECJ C-5/08, margin note 62 et seq. – *Infopaq*.
28. BGH GRUR 2010, 628, margin note 36 – *Vorschaubilder*.
29. European Commission: Towards a modern, more European copyright framework, Communication from the Commission to the European Parliament, the Council, the European Economic and Social Committee and the Committee of the Regions, COM(2015), 626 final, page 5.
30. Regulation (EU) 2016/679 of the European Parliament and of the Council of 27 April 2016 on the protection of natural persons with regard to the processing of personal data and on the free movement of such data, and repealing Directive 95/46/EC (General Data Protection Regulation).

5

EU Human Rights Framework

Paolo de Stefani

University of Padova

5.1 INTRODUCTION

In this chapter we consider a human rights–based approach to personal data protection and privacy. Our analysis focuses on a legally less contentious scenario that relates to the state of exception during a natural disaster, in order to characterise the inherent limits and counter-limits of the rights claimed by different parties. In disaster situations, we can clearly see the tensions and necessary trade-offs between (a) privacy and dignity, and (b) other fundamental rights

Relief and rescue providers will invariably seek to remove any hindrance to their efforts and to avail themselves of any information, including personal and sensitive data, that is likely to facilitate access to people in need. As we discussed in Chapter 4 (Section 4.2), the primary objective and a mandatory requirement of emergency managers is to protect life and property. However, individuals in distress want to keep their dignified status of rights holders, and they wish to keep control over their personal data and avoid disclosing information that might expose them to any harm. In these circumstances privacy and personal data are to be protected as stand-alone fundamental rights, but they are also indispensable for the protection of other human rights, including perhaps the same rights to life and physical integrity that humanitarian operators seek to grant.

This tension can be seen in recent years as indicative of a global debate on dignity and privacy caused by technological advances in social computing systems. For example, one landmark US Appeals Court judgement (2nd Circuit, Case 14–42;05/2015) ruled that the seizure of bulk (meta) data by the US National Security Agency (NSA) from social media networks was illegal and affirmed that social media data belongs solely to the users and not to the social media companies or to communications firms (Barnett, 2015; Bekkers et al., 2013; Donohue, 2014;

Galicki, 2015). The reconciliation of the needs of public security agencies to tap into social media activity of citizens, and the privacy rights of citizens to their data, can be viewed as an attempt to resolve the conflict between any two parties whilst preserving the basic values held by both (Ramsbotham, Miall & Woodhouse, 2011).

The challenge, therefore, is one of negotiating the potential conflict between the right to privacy and control over one's personal data and the urgent need to process communications and information that may disclose personal and even sensitive data for the purpose of safeguarding the general interest during a natural disaster. Conflict resolution has been used in conflict prevention, in post-conflict rebuilding and in policing. It requires the use of an ethical framework based on value pluralism: here ethical theory and oral practice can help in resolving differences in value systems (de Graaf, 2015; Talisse, 2011) (however, for some, value pluralism cannot deal well with "incommensurable ideas" (Overeem & Verhoef, 2014)).

Whilst "public safety", "public order" and "public interest" clauses – not to mention derogation powers necessary to face major threats to the life of the nation – do allow for restrictions to the full implementation of most (though not all) individual rights, a blanket disregard for individual rights would be unacceptable in a democratic society. A proper human rights–based approach is therefore required to guarantee both effective humanitarian action and the dignity of affected people. In other words, the idea that an emergency caused by a natural disaster is a kind of zero-sum game between individual rights (privacy and data protection, individual freedoms, social rights, etc.) on the one hand and the public interest on the other should be rejected.

The following sections explore the legal scenario that may occur when a social media monitor[1] is deployed in support of emergency management, having as its terms of reference the overall spectrum of internationally recognised human rights, including EU human rights–related provisions. It is important for a system used to harvest and monitor social computing data to ensure that any foreseen activity fully complies with the human rights regime that underpins the EU.

The international legal landscape requiring consideration is composed of three components. The most directly relevant layer is human rights law, as articulated in the core UN-sponsored conventions and protocols and in some key regional instruments, including the EU Charter on Fundamental Rights. However the layer must also integrate norms and principles incorporated into international humanitarian law. In general, the humanitarian principles of humanity, neutrality, independence and non-discrimination apply also to emergency circumstances caused by a natural disaster. Finally, a further layer is represented by the international law on disasters, a set of norms, still lacking proper codification, that articulate the rights and duties of states, intergovernmental and non-governmental humanitarian actors, and affected populations in situations of natural (and man-made) disasters.

One of the most coherent ways of ethically and pragmatically handling this complex regulatory set is by adopting a human rights–based stance: the approach taken by, for example, the International Law Commission, which in 2014 adopted a consolidated version of the Draft Articles on the Protection of Persons in the Event of Disasters. The EU framework on human rights and, more specifically, on civil protection – a matter that is now within the remit of the EU law – partially confirms this trend towards an integrated concept of human rights, humanitarian and disaster law. The EU approach puts special emphasis on the dimension of solidarity, whilst the human rights dimension is relatively less developed.

A balanced and human-centric appraisal of the whole issue is also recommended in order to contrast a shared vision that disproportionately highlights the technological and "digital" dimensions of the humanitarian action, to the detriment of the societal impact of civil protection operations and the legal and institutional frameworks with which civil protection and humanitarian operators must interact.

Data harvesting and data processing – especially when "big data" are involved – raise ethical and legal challenges both to researchers and analysts and to the users (e.g., civil protection agencies). Social media may provide data that can and should be used, in accordance with applicable legal and ethical standards, to enhance emergency response. A system for harvesting and monitoring social computing data requires that users be endowed not only with proficiency in information and communications technology (ICT) and the skills needed to manage a complex information ecosystem, but also with an awareness of the broad societal implications of the technology they are using, including in the legal domain. Such awareness has to be instilled among researchers, stakeholders and users.

From a legal viewpoint, and having in mind the multilevel dimensions (global to local) of civil protection and risk-reduction policies (UNISDR, 2015; Decision No 1313/2013/EU of the European Parliament and of the Council of 17 December 2013 on a Union Civil Protection Mechanism, 2013), risks and areas of concern include copyright law, privacy and data protection law. Indirectly, however, many other fundamental rights are involved. Finally, legal matters relating to contract law are also relevant.

This chapter elaborates on the international and EU legal framework on human rights, developing the hypothesis that this is the normative and institutional environment that provides a system for monitoring and harvesting social computing data not only with a sound regulatory setting consistent with the domestic legislations of most states in Europe and outside Europe, but also with a reserve of legitimation and authoritativeness that may help support innovative undertakings and create consensus and trust within civil society around novel approaches.

Some fundamental rights are more likely to be affected by the functioning of a social media monitor. One of these is copyright because such a system collects and analyses data potentially covered by intellectual property laws; another is the right to privacy and personal data protection because the system analyses communications in the social media, where personal and even sensitive data may be exchanged. However, many other human rights are also involved in such a scenario. The right to life; the rights to food and water, housing, clothing, health and livelihood and the right not to be discriminated against are all of special relevance in the event of a humanitarian crisis. International human rights instruments, however, are generally reluctant to specify to what extent in humanitarian crises the individual interests of the affected persons are to be treated as rights, i.e., personal entitlements, rather than as expectations not creating state obligations vis-à-vis the individuals. If human rights (and not just "needs") are involved, then reparations and redress measures are also required; therefore, "secondary rules" of human rights protection are to be implemented.

The first part of this chapter illustrates the legal setting of international and EU law on human rights and disaster response. A short introduction to international human rights law (IHRL), international humanitarian law and disaster law is provided, with a special, although necessarily cursory, focus on the EU framework. The main goal is to delineate the boundaries and mutual interactions among the three main components of the relevant legal setting (Caron et al., 2014; De Guttry et al., 2012), the normative and institutional environment where disaster management activities are performed. Some further considerations are also provided in connection with the emerging phenomenon of "digital humanitarianism".

The second part entails a short discussion concerning the characteristics of the EU framework on civil protection in case of natural disaster, with the aim of assessing if and to what extent a human rights–based approach suits it. Finally, some human rights issues that are likely to emerge in relation to natural disaster response management are presented, along with their possible implications for the deployment of a social media monitor.

5.2 APPROACH

In this section we explore the legal territory of a human rights–based approach to civil protection in the context of the harvesting and monitoring of social computing data. This analysis seeks to characterise the inherent limits and counter-limits of the rights claimed by those on different sides of a natural disaster scenario. On the one hand, relief and rescue providers seek to remove any hindrance to their efforts – namely, to grasp and process any information, including personal and sensitive data, likely to facilitate access to people in need. On the other hand, individuals in distress keep their dignified status of rights holders and wish to keep control over their personal data and avoid disclosing information that might expose them to any harm.

Systematic and continuous monitoring of a public space through the surveillance of social computing transactions encroaches directly on the fundamental rights to privacy and dignity. For us, internet rights should not be viewed simply from a utilitarian standpoint. A proper human rights–based approach therefore is required to guarantee both effective humanitarian action and the dignity of affected people.

In this section a summary of international and EU sources relevant to the issue of disaster management and human rights is provided. The link between disaster management and human rights is rather obvious. However, a clear and articulated connection has not been fully explored until recently, as other paradigms, namely the "humanitarian" one, have monopolised the analysis and set the terms of the debate.

The main assumption is that a human rights–based approach allowing for a balance between the competing calls for public safety and individual rights usefully integrates and gives perspective to the humanitarian principles associated with emergency management. Human rights considerations are routinely embedded in sectorial legislation as well as in the practice of the relevant bodies, translating into operative provisions and principles derived from the various human rights instruments, including matters such as privacy and personal data protection.

5.2.1 *International Law of Human Rights*

The international law of human rights (Alston & Goodman, 2012; De Schutter, 2014; Shelton, 2014) is a set of public international law provisions, both customary (i.e., nonwritten principles and rules supported by consistent state practice and generalised conviction as to their binding nature) and conventional (i.e., written in treaties and other written binding instruments) law. State consent is therefore at the basis of such principles and norms, but what is peculiar to this branch of international law is that by entering a human rights regime, states consent to undergo obligations not only in respect of other states, but also ultimately vis-à-vis any individuals. As the Inter-American Court on human rights has stated with reference to conventional sources:

> Modern human rights treaties in general … are not multilateral treaties of the traditional type concluded to accomplish the reciprocal exchange of rights for the mutual benefit of the contracting states. Their object and purpose is the protection of the basic rights of individual human beings irrespective of their nationality, both against the state of their nationality and all other contracting states. In concluding these human rights treaties, the states can be deemed to submit themselves to a legal order within which they, for the common good, assume various obligations, not in relation to other states, but towards all individuals within their jurisdiction. (Inter-American Court of Human Rights, Advisory Opinion No. OC-2/82, 24 September 1982)[2]

Since the adoption of the Universal Declaration of Human Rights (1948), whose principles are now generally recognised as customary law, a web of multilateral conventions has gradually unfolded, with the support of the United Nations and other international organisations, involving virtually all states. As a matter of fact, each state is now a party to at least one of the nine core human rights conventions and protocols thereof, and bound to protect the rights of all human beings as a matter of international law. The core conventions and the respective protocols are the following (in parenthesis are the dates of adoption by the General Assembly of the UN and of entry into force):

- International Convention on the Elimination of All Forms of Racial Discrimination (7 March 1966–4 January 1969)
- International Covenant on Civil and Political Rights (16 December 1966–23 March 1976)
- International Covenant on Economic, Social and Cultural Rights (16 December 1966–3 January 1976)
- Convention on the Elimination of All Forms of Discrimination against Women (18 December 1979–3 September 1981)
- Convention against Torture and Other Cruel, Inhuman or Degrading Treatment or Punishment (10 December 1984–26 June 1987)
- Convention on the Rights of the Child (20 November 1989–2 September 1990)
- International Convention on the Protection of the Rights of All Migrant Workers and Members of Their Families (18 December 1990)
- International Convention for the Protection of All Persons from Enforced Disappearance (20 December 2006)
- Convention on the Rights of Persons with Disabilities (13 December 2006–3 May 2008)

Critical human rights provisions are also included in international law instruments dealing with asylum, repression of international crimes, labour rights, development cooperation and protection of the environment, including the global action on climate change. In addition to developments at the global level, regional organisations have adopted their own standards that are meant to integrate and enhance the protection afforded by the UN instruments just mentioned. The Council of Europe's Convention on human rights and fundamental freedoms (ECHR, 4 November 1950–3 November 1953) and its protocols constitute the most striking example of regional human rights instruments that have deeply influenced the law-making, jurisprudence and the policies of states parties.

Regional agreements have been adopted in the framework of the Organisation of American States, the African Union, the Arab League and the Association of South-East Asian Nations (in this last case, not as a binding legal instrument). The human rights standards appear, by and large, to have imposed international obligations on states and induced a harmonisation of their legal systems, but international bodies, including a few that are judicial in character, have also been established to apply those international norms. States and, most significantly, individuals may seize such international supervising bodies or courts, which have the authority to ascertain the violations of internationally recognised human rights and provide redress to the victims.

The EU, in particular, with the entry into force of the Lisbon Treaty, has incorporated as binding at the same level as the Treaties a Charter of Fundamental Rights, largely replicating the provisions of the European Convention on Human Rights (ECHR) and other instruments in the area of human rights to which the EU Member States are parties (De Schutter, 2013). In so doing it has explicitly expanded the repertoire of arguments at the disposal of the Court of Justice of the EU (CJEU) to include fundamental rights considerations, inasmuch as matters within the competence of the EU are at stake. The EU Charter of Fundamental Rights and the EU Treaties are explicit in maintaining that the new provisions do not imply any expansion of the EU competences (this is also reiterated in Protocol 30 to the Lisbon Treaty with reference to the position of United Kingdom, Poland and the Czech Republic). The CJEU, therefore, has become an important player in the domain of human rights judicial interpretation, adding its voice to that of the European Court of Human Rights (ECtHR).

The interests and values protected under international human rights regimes have gradually expanded over the years so as to embrace issues that some decades ago could hardly be associated with a state obligation to respect, protect and fulfil. This is to signal the evolutionary character of the human rights discourse. In addition to an ethically and politically strong kernel of human and peoples' rights whose denial would corrode the foundations of any modern society (a core set of norms sometimes referred to as part of *ius cogens*, or peremptory norms of international law), the recognition of other rights, as well as the interpretation and practical implementation of most of them, depends on historical, political and socio-economic factors and may vary *ratione temporis, loci and personae*.

That said, however, it must be pointed out that any limitation or restrictive interpretation of human rights standards motivated by economic, political or strategic interests of the states and other enterprises so mandated has to be carefully justified, as human rights are inherently associated with the basic interests, aspirations and needs of actual human beings. This human-centric stance explains why, although dispersed in a number of legal instruments, most of which focus on a specific subject (civil rights, torture, economic rights, etc.) or a particular target (children, women, persons with disabilities, etc.), all provisions do share a common pattern, and human rights have to be conceived of as "universal, indivisible and interdependent and interrelated".[3]

5.2.2 *International Humanitarian Law*

In the exceptional circumstances envisaged in the derogation clauses, namely in wartime, a more specific set of international rules apply: the international law of armed conflicts, also known as international humanitarian law (IHL). IHL originated in the nineteenth century with the fundamental aim of limiting and regulating the use of force in international armed conflict as *ius in bello*. Codification of IHL took place on the occasion of major international conferences (e.g., the Hague peace conferences of 1899 and 1907, the Geneva conferences of 1949 and 1977), often thanks to the input of the International Committee of the Red Cross (ICRC) and of the Red Cross and Red Crescent movement.

Many treaties and an expanding set of customary law constitute contemporary IHL, complemented by domestic laws and the jurisprudence of national and – especially after the 1990s – international criminal courts that have been applying humanitarian standards on war crimes. The most relevant instruments in the field of IHL are the four Geneva Conventions of 1949 – whose provisions have largely become general international law considering their virtually universal acceptance – and the Additional Protocols thereto, adopted in 1977 (on international and non-international armed conflicts) and in 2005 (on an additional distinctive emblem of the Geneva Conventions). While taking into account the "necessities of war", IHL provisions do include basic human rights and, generally speaking, the law or armed conflicts and human rights law are meant to be mutually supportive (Droege, 2007; Provost, 2002).

What is true in wartime also applies in other emergencies occurring in peacetime, including natural disasters. Humanitarian disaster response operations, therefore, are also aimed at human rights protection and promotion, in addition to re-establishing the conditions for the "life of a nation". Disaster response managers operating for the state may therefore trigger the state's international responsibility for human rights violations in cases where they do not meet the standards set forth in international law. Even in wartime, military personnel may commit war crimes (which involve the personal responsibility of the perpetrator but also may engage the international responsibility of the concerned state) as well as violations of human rights provisions from which the state has not derogated or that are non-derogable. Many judgements of the ECtHR, for example, have found Member States of the Council of Europe responsible for committing violations of the right to life or the right not be tortured while waging combat or other military operations, within or even outside the territory of the Council of Europe, in the context of an international or internal armed conflict (*Al-Skeini and Others v. the United Kingdom*, 2011; *Isayeva and Others v. Russia*, 2005). Connections between disaster situations and the international human rights framework will also be discussed in Section 5.2.3, after addressing the nature and content of the international law provisions dealing with disaster response.

In conclusion, it is safe to maintain that the web of human rights and humanitarian law provisions that have been quickly summarised in the preceding paragraphs confirms the assumption that any "exceptionalism" that would discard the relevance of law provisions and accountability thereof whenever patterns of emergency occur, including in natural disaster scenarios, is to be rejected. The *juridification* of facts such as armed conflicts and national emergencies is a consolidated reality in present day societies. A "law of disasters" is therefore not an oxymoron ("disasters know no law"), and managing a disaster situation in strict accordance with human rights is a real possibility.

5.2.3 *International Disaster Response Law*

In emergency situations (other than armed conflict), the applicable international legal framework is not fully articulated. Indeed, the area of "civil defence" has emerged as distinct from the domain of IHL during the first half of the twentieth century, but for many years it continued to be largely associated with the functions and methods of military or paramilitary forces. A clear separation from the military milieu was achieved in 2000 with the adoption of the Framework Convention on Civil Protection Assistance, which defines "civil defence service" as "a structure or any other state entity established with the aim of preventing disasters and mitigating the effects of such disasters on persons, on property and the environment" (Article 2).

A human rights approach to disaster management necessarily embraces the ethical and legal standpoint centred on basic needs and emergency and is epitomised in the triage process. Integrating human rights into civil protection activities does not change the priorities of relief officers. However, it makes them aware of the wider societal implications of their work, and it prevents the risk of giving full attention to fragmented, technical indicators of performance while neglecting human and social-centred indicators. In other words, "[i]ncorporating human rights, or adopting a human rights–based approach, does not necessarily mean that priority must shift away from the primary objective of saving lives: it simply requires that human rights be mainstreamed into each stage of the humanitarian relief effort" (Harper, 2009: 25). Looking at disaster management through the lens of human rights can help refocus some aspects of civil protection work, but it does not imply a dramatic shift of paradigm; indeed, the corresponding literature has argued for some caution in this regard. In particular, it is not obvious to conclude that a thing such as a human right to receive humanitarian assistance in case of a natural disaster is codified as such in international law.

Since the early decades of the twentieth century, a *corpus* of international disaster response law (IDRL) has been taking shape at a regional and global level, aiming at harmonising domestic legislations, facilitating international delivery of disaster response operations and coordinating activities performed by international actors operating both domestically and in transborder missions, in any phase of disaster management. The IDRL development, however, has been fragmented and inhomogeneous as well as negatively conditioned by political divides and lack of trust between states and groups of states. Evidence of this was, inter alia, the flop of the International Relief Union, an international organisation established in 1927 and eventually discontinued in 1982, which utterly failed to carry out its ambitious mandate of coordinating international assistance in disasters. Similarly, the Framework Convention on Civil Protection mentioned earlier, adopted in 2000 on the initiative of the Geneva-based International Civil Protection Organisation and entered into force in 2001 with the aim of reducing obstacles to offers and requests of assistance among states in case of natural or man-made disasters, has been ratified by only four states. The role of supplying soft-law instruments and political input, and of coordinating governmental and nongovernmental humanitarian actors in the field, when the affected state is overwhelmed by a crisis, has been taken up by the UN, especially after the enactment in 1992 of UNGA Resolution 46/182, which set up a comprehensive structure to address humanitarian crises and disasters. The UN currently ensures the coordination of humanitarian and disaster response activities through the Office of Coordination of Humanitarian Assistance (OCHA), established in 1998.

In contemporary state practice, IDRL is to be understood as encompassing not only the response phase of a disaster when strictly rescue or relief operations are performed, but also the phases of disaster prevention, mitigation and recovery (Farber, 2014). Relief interventions need be put into context; to this end, a thorough understanding of the disaster lifecycle is indispensable. The cycle includes pre-crisis risk mitigation efforts, as factors such as climate change and other large-scale environmental factors affect the unfolding of minor and major disasters. The 1992 UN Framework Convention on Climate Change and the subsequent agreements, including the 2015 Paris Agreement, have mandated states to undertake measures of adaptation to the adverse effects of climate change – namely, in the framework of the Cancún Agreements (UNFCCC, 2010) – by establishing, amongst other measures, early warning systems and enhancing emergency preparedness (Field, 2012).

I have suggested elsewhere (De Stefani 2017) that the EU and other international partners, in an effort to "achieve climate resilient sustainable development", have supported "the integration and building of climate resilience into relevant multilateral frameworks" for disaster risk reduction and sustainable development.[4] Furthermore, UN Sustainable Development Goals[5] link climate change adaptation, disaster risk reduction and development. The next layer in the crisis cycle is of course crisis response, the core of IDRL. A large number of treaties on diverse issues ranging from environment to aviation, from transboundary activities to trade include provisions of relevance for national civil protection services.

Even without a dedicated comprehensive framework, the IDRL has expanded and evolved in a wide web of bilateral and multilateral agreements, and a growing body of principles and soft law. The areas covered include states' international obligations in case of disasters affecting their territory, cooperation between states in delivering assistance and the rights of the populations and individual victims of the disaster (De Guttry, 2012). Examples of the renewed efforts towards a more consistent regulation of some key areas of the international disaster response frame are:

- Convention on Early Notification of a Nuclear Accident (1986)
- Convention on Assistance in the Case of Nuclear Accident or Radiological Emergency (1986)
- Convention on the Transboundary Effects of Industrial Incidents (1992)
- Tampere Convention on the Provision of Telecommunication Resources for Disaster Mitigation and Relief Operations (1998)
- Food Aid Convention (1999)
- Convention on the Safety of United Nations and Associated Personnel (9 December 1994) and the Optional Protocol thereto (2005)

The Optional Protocol specifically mandates for states parties to prevent crimes such as murder and hostage-taking committed against UN and UN-associated personnel (in addition to UN peacekeepers) who are "delivering emergency humanitarian assistance" and prosecute or extradite the authors of such crimes (the Convention does not cover the violations of humanitarian law). The International Law Commission of the UN has elaborated some draft articles on some aspects of IDRL, which will be presented in Section 5.2.4.

Not only states may be party to such agreements; in the European context in particular, a specific role is played by subnational authorities, who operate under the umbrella of the Council of Europe's Outline Convention on Transfrontier Co-operation between Territorial Communities or Authorities (adopted in 1980, entered into force in 1981, currently ratified by thirty-nine European states – the UK, Denmark and Greece being among the non-parties).

A powerful support to the development of IDRL, both world- and region-wise, has been provided by the UN – namely, the UN Office for Disaster Risk Reduction (UNISDR), a unit established in 1999 within the Secretariat-General to coordinate the International Strategy on Disaster Risk Reduction, and in particular to assist in implementing the Hyogo Framework for Action of 2005 and the Sendai Framework for Disaster Risk Reduction of 2015. An important contribution to IDRL has been provided by the Red Cross and Red Crescent Federation, under its Disaster Law Programme (formerly International Disaster Response Laws, Rules and Principles [IDRL] Programme),[6] which since 2001 has consistently fuelled research, publication and the sharing of good practice in this domain. The programme has prompted, among other things, the adoption in 2007 of the Guidelines for the Domestic Facilitation and Regulation of International Disaster Relief and Initial Recovery Assistance, a soft-law instrument that has inspired domestic legislation in many countries worldwide. Along with other humanitarian NGOs, the Red Cross and Red Crescent Federation has launched in 1997 and subsequently maintained and enhanced the Sphere Project, providing guidelines and evidence-based advice on how to bring humanitarian help in an ethically sound and victim-oriented fashion (Sphere Project, 2011).

Compensation, rebuilding and resettlement are aspects of the recovery phase of a disaster. They are clearly connected with the way relief is provided, as timeliness and effectiveness of previous measures necessarily condition the way disaster-affected individuals and communities receive redress. Rules and practices in this domain influence the whole cycle of the crisis, not only because the way in which reparations, rebuilding or resettlement matters are handled may condition the impact a subsequent emergency may have on the same community or territory, but also because the prospective post-event scenarios may retroactively influence the way civil protection actions are carried out during the relief delivery (response) phase.

5.2.4 *IDRL and Human Rights: The ILC Draft Articles on the Protection of Persons in the Event of Disasters*

Among the issues that international law instruments have addressed in connection with natural disasters, is the human rights dimension of disaster response operations.

As stated earlier, a disaster scenario necessarily involves human rights deprivations and creates material and socio-political conditions likely to trigger further human rights violations, including by exacerbating the weaknesses of the most vulnerable sections of a society. Human rights instruments have not articulated in detail their applicability in the context of emergencies, including natural and man-made disasters. Nevertheless, international practice and case law corroborate the idea that human rights are relevant entitlements in such circumstances.

Legal grounds for protection from natural disasters as a human right can be found in some conventions and declarations making reference to "the right to a standard of living adequate for the health and well-being of himself and of his family [...] and the right to security [...] *in circumstances beyond his control*" (Article 25 of the Universal Declaration of Human Rights, emphasis added). It may be assumed that such "circumstances beyond control" of the individual include natural disasters. A reference to the right to a special protection in case of emergency can be found in Article 22 of the Convention on the Rights of the Child, where refugee children are entitled to the right to receive humanitarian assistance and protection, especially if separated from the family. The Convention on the Rights of Persons with Disabilities has set forth a more focused language. Article 11 provides that:

> States Parties shall take, in accordance with their obligations under international law, including international humanitarian law and international human rights law, all necessary measures to ensure the protection and safety of persons with disabilities in situations of risk, including situations of armed conflict, humanitarian emergencies and the occurrence of natural disasters.

The treaty that perhaps most explicitly recognises the human right to receive assistance when in distress is the African Union Convention for the Protection and Assistance of Internally Displaced Persons in Africa (Kampala Convention), adopted in 2009 and entered into force in 2012. It states that "[a]ll persons have a right to be protected against arbitrary displacement, [including when forced evacuations are caused by] natural or human made disasters or other causes if the evacuations are not required by the safety and health of those affected" (Article 4.4 and (f)) and that internally displaced persons have the right "*to peacefully request or seek protection and assistance*, in accordance with relevant national and international laws, a right for which they shall not be persecuted, prosecuted or punished" (Article 5.9, emphasis added). The UN International Law Commission started a study project in 2007 aimed at better articulating the relationship between public safety and international standards on human rights and humanitarian action, including assistance for refugees and internally displaced persons. The study focused on the progressive codification of international law standards on the protection of persons in the event of natural or man-made disasters (Cubie & Hesselman, 2015; UNISDR, 2015).

The focus on human rights in the ILC Draft Articles on Protection of Persons in the Event of Disaster (DAPPED) is evident in the title. The word "protection", however, reveals the double-edged nature of the Draft Articles. On the one hand, the Draft Articles are intended to "facilitate an adequate and effective response to disasters that meets the *essential needs* of the persons concerned"; on the other, they aim at granting the "*full respect for [the] rights*" of the affected persons (Article 2 of the DAPPED, emphases added). "Rights" and "needs" are therefore equally relevant in the approach to disaster relief endorsed by the ILC. Similarly, the equal relevance of both a "technical" and "social" approach to catastrophes characterises the definition of "disaster": "'[d]isaster' means a calamitous event or series of events resulting in widespread loss of life, great human suffering and distress, or large-scale material or environmental damage, thereby seriously disrupting the functioning of society" (Article 3).

The principles of human dignity and human rights are the object of Articles 5 and 6 of the DAPPED: the "inherent dignity of the human person" is to be respected and protected by all relief actors, and "[p]ersons affected by disasters are entitled to respect for their human rights". "Dignity" is seen as the central principle not only in human rights, but also in humanitarian law. Human rights are referred to as encompassing all legal regimes applicable to any disaster situations. They also include the corresponding obligations on states and on any other entities that concur with the disaster response, according to the conventions that the concerned states have ratified, the legislation they have enacted, the restrictions or derogations that might apply and the responsibilities of international organisations or of non-governmental entities (such as the Red Cross and Red Crescent, which enjoy a specific international competence in this domain). As regards humanitarian principles, those are summarised in "humanity, neutrality and impartiality", to which are added the principle of non-discrimination and a mandate to take into account "the needs of the particularly vulnerable" (Article 7 of the DAPPED).

The fundamental provision of the DAPPED is the duty to cooperate in case of a disaster:

> States shall, as appropriate, cooperate among themselves, and with the United Nations and other competent intergovernmental organizations, the International Federation of the Red Cross and Red Crescent Societies and the International Committee of the Red Cross, and with relevant non-governmental organizations.

Other obligations codified in the Draft Articles are the duty to reduce the risk of disaster through measures aimed at preventing, mitigating and preparing for disasters (Article 11 of the DAPPED); the duty of the affected state to protect persons in its territory (Article 12 of the DAPPED) and to seek external assistance, in case the situation exceeds its response capacity (Article 13 of the DAPPED). A key principle then is Article 14, which establishes that "[t]he provision of external assistance requires the consent of the affected State"; the consent can be made conditional (Article 15). Reciprocally, "States, the United Nations, and other competent intergovernmental organisations have the right to offer assistance to the affected state. Relevant non-governmental organisations may also offer assistance to the affected state" (Article 16 of the DAPPED). Once the consent is granted, the affected state shall not withhold it arbitrarily and has the duty to facilitate the delivering of assistance and to protect the relief personnel provided by the assisting state (Articles 17–18).

The Draft Articles codify a number of norms scattered in treaties and soft-law instruments, seeking to draw a reasonable compromise between progressive development of international law and instances more inclined towards defending state sovereignty. Despite the emphasis placed on human dignity and human rights, however, the ILC has fallen short of affirming a right of affected persons to receive assistance in case of disaster. There is little consensus on the actual crystallisation of such a right in international law (Creta, 2012). In light of the trend illustrated earlier and leading to a human rights–based approach to humanitarian action, it might be maintained that humanitarian assistance from any competent actors, including foreign states, international organisations and non-governmental humanitarian organisations, is a crucial enabler for a range of human rights, from the right to life to the right to food, shelter, housing, etc. A right to seek and receive humanitarian assistance is therefore complementary to all these human rights.[7]

5.3 DISASTER MANAGEMENT AND HUMAN RIGHTS

Disaster management systems are grounded in humanitarian and human rights law. Under principles and norms of human rights and humanitarian law, states have a duty to protect the population from hazardous events, including natural disasters. Normative sources and case law provide examples of how disaster management systems address the issue. The very idea of establishing a law on disasters is premised on the hypothesis (though contentious) that disasters, including natural disasters, are social constructions: "disasters are social phenomena and should be understood through social systems' inability to encounter naturally occurring hazards or, more precisely, our social vulnerability" (Lauta, 2014: 36). In other words, despite the traditional notion that links any disaster to an unpredictable emergency situation where exceptional measures have to be "invented" and imposed, eventually displacing ordinary legal standards, the line of thought supported in this chapter is that disasters can be and are indeed managed under the rule of law and in accordance with human rights regimes. In this sense, it is argued that in disaster situations the humanitarian language, which implicitly incorporates emergency and extraordinary measures, is usefully complemented by a systematic reference to "ordinary" human rights standards and procedures.

5.3.1 *Disaster Management and Human Rights in European Case Law*

The jurisprudence of the ECtHR has tackled the balancing of civil protection emergency services against individual human rights. The most relevant case in this connection is *Budayeva and Others v. Russia* (Nos 15339/02, 21166/02, 20058/02, 11673/02 and 15343/02, ECHR 2008).

The events took place in the Russian city of Tyrnauz, situated in an area where mudslides were frequent since the 1930s. In 2000 a particularly destructive mudslide killed eight people, including the husband of Ms Budayeva, and injured the other applicants. A monetary compensation scheme and a relocation programme was set up for those families who had lost their homes and all their belongings, but the new houses were in extremely bad condition and caused a serious deterioration of the applicants' health, and the lump sum provided proved to be inadequate. The local prosecutor decided not to start any criminal investigation for either the disaster or the death of the husband of Ms Budayeva. Civil claims brought against the authorities were dismissed on the grounds that the risk of the mudslide in the area was well known and that all reasonable measures had been taken to mitigate it.

This position was also defended by the state before the ECtHR, maintaining that the mudslide of 2000 was unpredictable in its particularly devastating development and that the applicants on the occasion of the catastrophic event did not behave in accordance with the instructions given by civil protection. The applicants, for their part, accused the state authorities of ignoring specific warnings issued by a specialised agency since 1999, and of having failed for many years to make essential repairs and to implement a proper early-warning system. As a result, the court found Russia in breach of Article 2 of ECHR (right to life) and Article 1 of Protocol No 1 (right to the peaceful enjoyment of one's property).

The case is interesting as an example of how human rights obligations require states to implement positive measures of civil protection – risk prevention, mitigation, effective relief and reparation – as well as procedural measures aimed at ascertaining in an independent and effective way any criminal responsibility or civil liability for the death or injuries suffered by the claimants and their relatives. In particular, the responsibility of the state authorities for failing to take the legislative, administrative and technical measures that were reasonably likely to mitigate the risk and reduce the harm caused by the natural disaster had never been tackled. As a result, the right to life was seriously jeopardised. As for the right to property, the Strasbourg court found that the housing compensation offered by the state to those families that had their homes destroyed was not manifestly disproportionate and therefore concluded for a non-breach decision.

The adoption of a human rights approach to civil protection matters necessarily implies at any stage of the disaster response a requirement of awareness of the importance of the victims' right to an effective remedy – that is, to have their case heard before a court or an equally effective body – and to reparation – that is, to a redress in form of restitution, compensation, rehabilitation, satisfaction and/or guarantee of non-repetition. This right –arguably a non-derogable one, at least as far as it is necessary to guarantee substantial non-derogable rights (right to life, protection from torture, etc.) – is enshrined in all major human rights agreements (e.g., Article 13 of ECHR, Article 47 of the EU Charter of Fundamental Rights, Article 2.3 of the International Covenant on Civil and Political Rights). The importance of accompanying life-saving measures of a humanitarian nature with dignity-saving actions based on considerations of justice, equality and non-discrimination, can hardly be overestimated and is a cornerstone of a human rights approach to disaster management.

In some recent case law, the avenue of criminal prosecution has also been tested. Reference has been made to the judgement of an Italian court that in 2013 sentenced six scientists and a civil protection officer for manslaughter (Alemanno & Lauto, 2014; Lauta, 2014). The scientists and the officer, members of the National Commission for the Forecast and Prevention of Major Risks, a body of the Italian civil protection system, were allegedly responsible for downplaying in their public statements the likelihood that a strong earthquake would hit Central Italy within a short time, thus inducing the population of the city of L'Aquila to suspend some life-saving habits they had been observing, such as leaving home at any earth tremor above a given threshold. On 6 April 2009, a few days after the accused had released to the media some reassuring interviews (March 31), a devastating earthquake measuring 6.3 magnitude actually struck the city, killing 309 and almost completely destroying the old town. It was suspected that the death toll was so high because of the Committee members' gross negligence in evaluating the risk of a major earthquake and in conveying to the general public the message that the risk was diminishing. In 2011 the Prosecutor of L'Aquila issued an indictment against the seven members of the Committee who met and made public statements on 31 March, charging them with the death of a certain number of quake victims who, according to some evidentiary elements, failed to abandon their houses despite warnings about risks posed by unsafe buildings and who unfortunately died when their homes collapsed.

The judgement of first instance of the L'Aquila tribunal found that the incautious behaviour of the victims (especially considering that a swarm of low-intensity earthquakes had been shaking the area for months) was due to the reassurances provided by the media quoting the Committee members. The trial court eventually sentenced the seven defendants for manslaughter (*Barberi e a., Giud. Billi*, 2012). In the appeals, the six scientists were acquitted (Cartlidge, 2014). It was demonstrated that their statements had only concerned the scientific aspects of the issue and could not be interpreted as conveying any special message to the population concerning how to face the seismic risk. However, the civil protection officer – the highest representative of Protezione Civile, a Department of the Presidenza del Consiglio dei Ministri (Presidency of the Council of Ministers) in the area at that time – was found guilty. The Presidency was ordered to pay compensation to thirteen victims.

The Court found that in the statements the civil protection officer delivered to the media, the defendant contravened the professional standards that civil protection officers have to observe in their activities of risk prevention and protection. Communication to the public is indeed a risk prevention task. Finally, the Cassation Court endorsed the Appeals judgement,[8] arguing, among other things, that the ability of disaster response officers to condition the behaviour of citizens addressed through institutional communication, including press conferences, is confirmed by the language of the Italian law on civil protection, which lists "information to the population" among the "non-structural means" of disaster prevention. Negligence in performing communication tasks may therefore causally link (as a form of psychological causality) the officer's fault and the death of those individuals who omitted to take prudential measures on the eve of an earthquake because of the reassurances of an authoritative source.

The L'Aquila case illustrates not only the role that the judiciary – including criminal investigations – may play in connection with natural disasters in safeguarding the rights of individuals vis-à-vis the negligence of disaster response officers, but also the key relevance of communications to the public in disaster prevention and mitigation. It also evokes the issue of compensations that accompany findings of criminal liability.

An obvious problem arises when a state, ravaged by a disaster, cannot reasonably provide meaningful avenues of redress to its nationals who are victims of the event. As it has been pointed out,

[c]laiming a right to be guaranteed by the international community is nonsense according to present-day international law. Individuals may have a right vis-à-vis

their own State, but they are merely beneficiaries of external aid. At present, the international community does not guarantee any right which an individual may claim from a foreign State, unless a specific set of rules has been established. (Ronzitti, 2012)

European states are generally able to provide for the needs of most of their nationals who are victims of natural disaster, and have institutional and economic resources to provide them remedy and reparations, be it through tort litigation, government aid or private insurance schemes (Bruggeman, 2010).

For this reason provisions like those set forth in the EU Treaty, which connect disaster relief actions to solidarity, and potentially also extend solidarity to *third countries*,[9] (see Section 5.4), represent a valuable, principled and pragmatic response to the challenge posed by IDRL.

5.3.2 *Human Rights, Disaster Management and the Impact of ICT Digital Humanitarianism*

From the preceding analysis it can be inferred that disaster management is an activity infused with humanitarian and human rights values and that it should honour the dignity of human beings in all aspects of its deployment. As observed, however, a more "technocratic" approach to disaster response is also emerging (the same can be maintained for humanitarian aid and human rights activism, advocacy and litigation, of course). This trend has been induced in recent times by the massive incursion into disaster management of smart technologies, and specifically information and communication technologies.

Humanitarian work and disaster response is increasingly affected by information and communication technology (ICT) and "big data". ICT and big data are increasingly seen as crucial, not only in post-disaster scenarios as a tool to assess the effectiveness of emergency interventions and therefore improve preparedness and design risk-reduction and mitigation strategies, but also before a disaster as early-warning instruments and during a disaster to collect, process and dispatch real-time information and thereby influence how humanitarian operations are managed and affect the outcome of disaster management actions (Mans, Berens & Shimshon, 2015; OECD, 2015).

ICT, in particular, plays a key role in framing the overall discourse concerning natural disasters and emergencies and in creating the context in which disaster response activities, from early-warning to post-crisis measures, are carried out. The way a specific disaster situation is displayed on computer screens or on TV, captured in satellite images or reproduced through social media, is crucial for the unfolding of civil protection operations, for the social appraisal of the events, for shaping the post-disaster phases and for the overall aftermath and legacy of a crisis. As has been said,

ICT is often seen as a key element in improving sense-making before, during, and after crises. However, it is important to realise that although technology can greatly leverage capability, it can also be associated with various forms of vulnerability, the distraction of leaders away from their core role, and constitute a serious threat to privacy, civil liberties and trust. (OECD, 2015: 57)

The use of ever faster and interconnected computer systems, aided and perhaps abetted by artificial intelligence on the one hand and geographic information systems, to process the *big data* especially in a disaster emergency has led to many promises of immediate relief and rehabilitation of victims. For some, *digital humanitarianism* has substantial promise (PLoS Medicine Editors, 2012). This promise has to be viewed in the context of almost global levels of surveillance implicit in this connectivity between disaster victims and their helpers. Critics of digital humanitarianism present cogent arguments here: "While great developmental and humanitarian claims are made for connectivity, as a dual use technology, it is simultaneously a boon to global security governance. Unchecked by regulation or oversight, security concerns are encouraging the convergence of the localised humanitarian, development, government and security databases into a systems with a wide international reach" (Duffield, 2016: 161). In our view, the risk is that the "thick", context-based, socially embedded actuality of the "real" humanitarian work is overlooked and replaced by a narrative where the central role is played by smart "digital volunteers", with virtually infinite computing capacity at their disposal, potentially capable of solving any problem, as opposed to a wasted mass of *victims*, who can gain some relevance only by connecting to the web, turning into data producers or at least data-subjects that the digital hero can interrogate to predict how things will transform. This narrative stresses the lack of knowledge and intrinsic operational limits of disaster management agencies. It has been argued that "this configuration obscures the funding, resource, and skills constraints causing imperfect humanitarian response, instead positing volunteered labor as 'the solution'. This subjectivity formation carves a space in which digital humanitarians are necessary for effective humanitarian activities ... Within digital humanitarianism, the epistemologies privileged by Big Data are often data-centric and focused on correlations, rather than epistemologies highlighting qualitative understanding, communal and situated lay knowledges, and connections with social theory" (Burns, 2015: 486).

The technological revolution that is changing all sectors of economic and social life has reached also the domain of humanitarian action. Indeed, this domain was one of the first to be affected by the digital shift, although with huge diversities from one area to another, from one operative field to another. A giant digital divide exists between the technological capacities of the most modern structures of civil protection in some Western states – or more precisely in some developed areas of such states – and the ICT tools that disaster responders can access in remote areas of some of the least developed countries.

Despite the apparent disparity in resources, however, and narratives about the "new humanitarianism" (Terry, 2003) fostered in the last couple of decades, in which new technology, big data and the market have been portrayed as key elements for success in humanitarian action and disaster response, the gap between old and new forms of disaster response is not necessarily so stark. In particular, the emphasis put on the availability of ICT or other technological equipment and the scant consideration sometimes given to the institutional and legal landscape in which the disaster response activities take place, and to the human rights frame thereof, may turn out to be detrimental in the medium to long term to the effectiveness also of the most high-tech civil protection operations.

5.4 EU FUNDAMENTAL RIGHTS FRAMEWORK AND DISASTER MANAGEMENT

The EU has a relatively long history of engaging in disaster response activities. It has played a role both within the borders of its Member States – as an instance of coordination among the national civil protection systems – and in relationships with third countries in the context of humanitarian aid activities. The internal and external dimensions of the civil protection initiatives of the EU have been undergirded by the common ideal of solidarity. As we will see, however, in the EU system the solidarity claim is somehow detached from the dimension of human rights and therefore does not seem to fully express its own potential.

In addition to the many instruments that the EU has adopted in areas ranging from the protection of the natural environment to the handling of dangerous substances for industrial production, to anti-seismic standards in constructions, of special relevance for the aims of the present chapter are the provisions that first made possible, and then introduced and implemented, the EU Civil Protection Mechanism (UCPM).

5.4.1 *The Solidarity Clauses in the Treaty of Lisbon*

The steps that led to the UCPM began with a meeting at the ministerial level in 1985 and a Council Decision in 1997, establishing a ten-year Community action programme in the field of civil protection. In this framework, a Community Civil Protection Mechanism was set up by Council Decision 2001/792/EC, Euratom, 23 October 2001, replaced in 2007 by recast Council Decision 2007/779. Until the Treaty of Lisbon, however, the legal basis for the enactment of EU secondary legislation in this matter was uncertain. The new Treaty on the Functioning of the EU (TFEU), in its Articles 6 and 196, set forth solid legal bases for law making. Article 196 of the TFEU, in particular, stipulates that "[t]he Union shall encourage cooperation between Member States in order to improve the effectiveness of systems for preventing and protecting against natural or man-made disasters".

Before addressing the establishment of the UCPM, based on Article 196 of the TFEU, however, it is worth mentioning Article 222 of the TFEU, the Solidarity Clause. This provision mentions *disasters* (as well as *terrorist attacks*) as the events that may trigger the adoption of solidarity measures involving all Member States ("The Union and its Member States shall act jointly in a spirit of solidarity if a Member State is the object of a terrorist attack or the victim of a natural or man-made disaster"). It is also noteworthy that the solidarity clause can be triggered by both internal and external situations, to the effect that not only disasters occurring within the territory of the EU could be relevant, but also those taking place in third countries, provided that one or more Member States are "victims" of the events (Gestri, 2012). The intervention of the EU and of the Member States in any case is to be requested by the affected state, and states have a right to choose in which way their duty of solidarity can be discharged.[10] To implement Article 222 the Council will adopt decisions with a qualified majority or unanimity, if there is any implication for the common defence policy.

Besides Article 222, a "financial solidarity clause" is enshrined also in Article 122 of the TFEU. In particular, paragraph 2 of said Article provides that

> [w]here a Member State is in difficulties or is seriously threatened with severe difficulties caused by natural disasters or exceptional occurrences beyond its control, the Council, on a proposal from the Commission, may grant, under certain conditions, Union financial assistance to the Member State concerned.

Article 122 of the TFEU was the legal basis for the enactment of Council Regulation 2016/369 of 15 March 2016 on the provision of emergency support within the EU. This regulation is premised on the point that

> There is currently no appropriate instrument available at Union level to address on a sufficiently predictable and independent basis the humanitarian needs of disaster-stricken people within the Union, such as food assistance, emergency healthcare, shelter, water, sanitation and hygiene, protection and education. (Recital 5)

Actions financed by the general budget of the EU under this regulation include "assistance, relief and, where necessary, protection operations to save and preserve life in disasters or in their immediate aftermath" (Article 3). Since the envisaged operations to be carried out within the EU territory will be "need-based" and "humanitarian" in character, and comply with the "fundamental humanitarian principles of humanity, neutrality, impartiality and independence" (Article 3), for the implementation of such measures the EU will enter into framework partnership agreements with the same non-governmental organisations, specialised services of the Member States or international agencies and organisations that cooperate with the Commission in humanitarian projects in third countries, based on Council Regulation (EC) No 1257/96 of 20 June 1996 concerning humanitarian aid.

5.4.2 *The EU Civil Protection Mechanism*

Article 196 of the TFEU sets forth for the EU a complementary competence in the field of civil protection, especially aimed at supporting risk prevention and preparedness, also at subnational level. In this field the EU will adopt Decisions (the adoption of Directives or Regulations seems barred by Article 196.2, which excludes "any harmonisation of the laws and regulations of the Member States") according to the ordinary legislative procedure (unanimity not required).

The main outcome of EU actions under Article 196 of the TFEU is, as anticipated, the establishment of the Union Civil Protection Mechanism (UCPM), currently regulated by Decision 1313/2013 of the European Parliament and of the Council, of 17 December 2013. The UCPM is based on a structure articulated into "an Emergency Response Coordination Centre (ERCC), a European Emergency Response Capacity (EERC) in the form of a voluntary pool of pre-committed capacities from the Member States, trained experts, a Common Emergency Communication and Information System (CECIS) managed by the Commission and contact points in the Member States". The overall objective of the Union Mechanism is to "provide a framework for collecting validated information on the situation, for dissemination to the Member States and for sharing lessons learnt from interventions" (Decision 1313/2013, recital 12).

Decision 1313/2013 provides that the protection to be ensured by the UCPM primarily covers individuals, but will be extended also to properties and the environment, including cultural heritage. Natural and man-made disasters are in the remit of the Mechanism, whereas as far as the consequences of terrorism or radiological disasters are concerned, it may cover only preparedness and response actions (Article 2). The Decision indicates the types of activities that the Commission or the Member States can perform or finance in the areas of prevention and risk management [for example, the Commission shall "take action to improve the knowledge base on disaster risks and facilitate the sharing of knowledge, best practices and information, including among Member States that share common risks" (Article 5.1a); Member States shall "develop and refine their disaster risk management planning at national or appropriate sub-national level" (Article 6b)]; preparedness (Articles 7–12 emphasise the role of EERC, ERCC and CECIS) and response (especially Article 14).

In this last area, response, the Decision imposes on Member States the duty to notify all potentially affected Member States of the risk where a disaster occurs or is about to occur with transboundary effects. Moreover, any affected Member State may request the assistance of other Member States through the Commission, and the requested state "shall promptly determine whether it is in a position to render the assistance required" (Articles 14–15). Also, non-EU states may request assistance in cases where they are affected by a disaster, and the Commission will support the actions undertaken by the respondent states by granting coordination services

(Article 16). Finally, in the case of disasters in or outside the EU, the Commission may set up and dispatch teams composed of experts provided by Member States and support states in particular in obtaining access to equipment or transport resources (Articles 17–18). Substantial budgetary resources and lists of actions eligible for financing complete the text of the Decision.

There is no room in this chapter to enter into the details of the functioning of the UCPM and of the many policies and initiatives that the EU has been implementing in the area of humanitarian action. It should be noted, however, with reference to the overall approach adopted by the EU, that human rights do not feature prominently in the EU instruments on civil protection. Rather, a humanitarian paradigm is emphasised, whereby the safety/security dimensions (civil protection includes also response to acts of terrorism) almost dispel any human rights consideration. One of the few explicit – although very general – references to human rights in a document on civil protection can be found in a Resolution of the European Parliament on disaster prevention, where the text of a Commission Communication mentions the concept of "fundamental human rights".[11] The link established by the Parliament between risk prevention and human rights seems to have virtually disappeared in the EU documents. However, as earlier noticed, the solidarity principle, which potentially extends also to areas outside the EU territory, is a flagship of the EU approach to the issue.

5.4.3 *Human Dignity: Information and Access*

A system for monitoring and harvesting social computing data for emergency management is likely to enhance the capacity of civil protection officers to respond to natural disasters. It is also a technology that allows people who are victims or those potentially affected by disasters to share data and information and therefore contribute to the general humanitarian efforts. Inasmuch as the privacy and the personal data of individuals are not jeopardised, this form of agency that ICT-based systems assign to the individual, including people in distress, is likely to promote a sense of membership in a community, an ethic of solidarity, ownership and responsibility and ultimately human dignity. All of these elements are components of a human rights–based approach to disaster response operations and compatible with the principles of humanitarian action.

It is a specific responsibility of disaster management authorities, as part of risk prevention and mitigation action, to inform the public of the risks connected to old and new vulnerabilities of the territory and of the environment. Software for monitoring and harvesting social computing data, as a component of a broader system that integrates various sources of information and datasets, should increase the quantity and – more importantly – the quality of information at the disposal of the disaster managers as well as the general public. A wider and more reliable set of data has the potential to support finely tailored training activities, facilitate the sharing of good practices along the layers of the multilevel governance of civil protection policies in Europe, and eventually contribute to the implementation of the tasks set forth in the Decision on the UCPM. Interoperability between national systems could also be facilitated.

5.4.4 *Liability for Human Rights Infringements*

One of the most relevant findings in this chapter is the importance for users of a system for monitoring and harvesting data of having a clear idea of the nature of the web of legal obligations and opportunities in which they operate as disaster response officers. The stress here is put on "opportunities". The reference to the principles and norms of humanitarian law, human rights law and international disaster law is to be taken as a fresh opportunity to reassess the place of civil protection agencies in the current global debate on old and new risks connected to the natural environment, and to reframe the formerly narrowly construed approach to the legal dimension of humanitarian work.

Legal awareness also enables the realisation that individuals and organisations – including the state – can be held accountable for failing to appropriately respect and implement such legal standards. Although international case law concerning violations of European or global human rights standards in direct connection with civil protection actions or omissions is quite scant – as most litigations or prosecutions are understandably carried out at the state level – the principle of accountability is a natural counterpart to the right to an effective remedy and to reparation for breaches of human rights standards. Consistent with the legal background identified as most appropriate to the civil protection domain, the jurisprudence of the ECtHR has taken into account the right to life, violated under many aspects by state negligence in undertaking suitable risk mitigation or offering civil or penal procedures to provide remedy and reparation to the victims of such negligence.

Other cases, however, involving different human rights should be considered as plausible, namely those related to rights that have been dealt with in other chapters, such as the rights to personal data protection or to intellectual property. Violations of fundamental rights in natural disasters, however, are unlikely to be effectively handled by an international court. An international body such as the ECtHR can only ascertain the international liability of the State, with a very limited capacity to grant proper damages to the victims (eventually they are only entitled to a just satisfaction). Given the characteristics of the EU legal system, the CJEU is not the most plausible forum where civil protection cases will be heard, as the competence of the EU in this field is only complementary. National legal systems have the task of assessing the liability, under torts law or based on criminal charges, of the civil protection structure and its officers. In this connection, an important case that marked the recent Italian jurisprudence has been the one concerning the earthquake in L'Aquila, discussed in Section 5.3.1. Significantly, the criminal liability of the civil protection officer and the responsibility for damage of the national civil protection structure stemmed from negligence in delivering information to the public. The capacity to handle communication tools has proved to be critical in risk prevention and disaster response.

The preceding analysis has been undertaken with the aim of assessing whether a system for monitoring and harvesting social computing data has a positive role to play in an approach to disaster response that increasingly values the human rights dimension. It is therefore to be understood as an expansion of the analysis of the potentialities and associated risks of such a system from some more specific legal perspectives – namely, privacy and data protection rules, copyright and internet regulations. We explore the juridical implications (especially in light of EU law) of developing a web crawling software in support of civil protection functions, and test the "legal risks" of such an innovative technology. The reflection elaborated in this framework has transcended the limits of a strictly juridical discourse. The humanitarian and human rights dimensions tackled in the present chapter most conveniently capture the context that best suits the deployment of a social media monitor.

5.5 CONCLUSION

In this chapter the legal framework supporting a human rights–based approach to civil protection activities has been illustrated and analysed, with the aim of providing a sound normative and institutional context within which to locate the activity of a system for monitoring and harvesting social computing data.

The main findings that have been reached concern, first of all, the importance of fully integrating a system for monitoring and harvesting social computing data into the institutional and legal architecture of the civil protection structures at the local, national, European and international levels. Such a system seems equipped to make this multilevel and intersector integration a reality, as recommended by the most recent EU provisions. Secondly, we have observed that the dignity of the human person is a consensual principle underpinning the various legal regimes that are involved in framing civil protection functions. Thirdly, we found that transparency and the capacity to make a difference in quantity and quality of information processed is a key component of a civil protection system. Finally, legal awareness of civil protection officers is an added value that reflects the embodiment in the disaster response system of a genuine human rights–based approach to the delivery of humanitarian assistance.

In conclusion, it can be safely maintained that in the general framework of a human rights–sensitive understanding of civil protection and disaster response management, sound arguments can be found in support of testing and eventually implementing a software system for monitoring and harvesting social computing data.

NOTES

1. A social media monitor in this context is a monitoring system designed to analyse, aggregate, harvest and/or display information from social media.
2. The Opinion is available at www.corteidh.or.cr/docs/opiniones/seriea_02_ing.pdf (last accessed 25 April 2017).
3. Vienna Declaration and Plan of Action, adopted by the World Conference on Human Rights in Vienna on 25 June 1993, § I.5.
4. These frameworks include the Third World Conference on Disaster Risk Reduction that helped to formulate *Sendai Framework for Disaster Risk Reduction 2015–2030* and the post-2015 Development Agenda (UNFCCC & EU, 2015).
5. UNGA Resolution 70/1: Transforming Our World: The 2030 Agenda for Sustainable Development, 25 September 2015.
6. Information at www.ifrc.org/en/what-we-do/disaster-law (last accessed 25 April 2018).
7. IASC (2011). IASC Operational Guidelines on the Protection of Persons in Situation of Natural Disasters. Bern: The Brookings-Bern Project. Available at www.ohchr.org/Documents/Issues/IDPersons/OperationalGuidelines_IDP.pdf (last accessed 25 April 2017.
8. Cass., sez. IV, sent. 19 novembre 2015, n. 12478/16, Pres. Izzo, Rel. Dovere e Dell'Utri, P.G. in proc. *Barberi e a.*
9. A number of countries, such as Norway and other European countries in the European Free Trade Area, that are part of the enlargement of the EU, and others such as Russia that have or will soon have treaty arrangements with the EU.
10. See Declarations annexed to the Final Act of the Intergovernmental Conference which adopted the Treaty of Lisbon, signed on 13 December 2007, Declaration on Article 222 of the Treaty on the Functioning of the European Union (No 37).
11. "The main objective of disaster prevention is to safeguard human life, the safety and physical integrity of individuals, *fundamental human rights*, the environment, economic and social infrastructures, including basic utilities, housing, communications, transport and the cultural heritage" [European Parliament resolution of 21 September 2010 on the Commission communication: A Community Approach on the Prevention of Natural and Man-made Disasters (2009/2151(INI), emphasis added)].

6

Conclusion

Legally Using Social Computing Streams and Privacy Protection

Rob Corbet and Colm Maguire
Arthur Cox LLC, Dublin

6.1 INTRODUCTION

This chapter presents a synthesis of the three legal analyses presented thus far – internet law, copyright and data protection law, and human rights law – as applied to the use of social computing data, and is followed by a template legal agreement (Appendix A) that discourages improper use.

That there are benefits to monitoring and harvesting social computing data, particularly in circumstances in which this data may aid in the protection of life and property, is inconvertible. Social computing data should, however, be harvested in accordance with ethical principles; analysis systems should be required to keep track of the levels and details of data collection which has named entities and to produce an audit report. There are parallels in the use of lethal equipment by law enforcement and armed forces: bullets are counted when troops are sent out and recounted upon their return. This engenders a sense of accountability, and an awareness that one is being audited is amply demonstrated during the post-mortem of key events where lethal force has been used.

In the following sections, we briefly outline a social media monitor that can be used in a disaster scenario whilst complying with the three legal frameworks that have been the focus of this book. We show how the development of a model Licence Agreement was drafted from the synthesis of this legal research, referring to the EU General Data Protection Regulation (2016).

6.2 SOCIAL COMPUTING ANALYSIS IN EXCEPTIONAL CIRCUMSTANCES

Here, we analyse the legal scenario that a system harvesting social media data in exceptional circumstances will face, having as its terms of reference the overall spectrum of internationally recognised human rights and with a distinctive focus on privacy and data protection rights. As discussed earlier, disaster management presents an area in which a viable case for the use of data harvested from social computing systems can be made, and in which the need to protect the dignity and privacy of data subjects presents itself clearly.

The deluge of texts and – increasingly – images made voluntarily available by the public is perhaps at its most useful during a natural disaster. For example, an estimated 3.5 million tweets with the hashtag #sandy were generated in twenty-four hours during Hurricane Sandy (2012), and roughly ten pictures per second were uploaded using Instagram (Lindsay, 2016). In some significant cases, citizens on the ground were much better aware of the extent of the damage, whereas rescue authorities had incorrect estimates (Chatfield, Scholl & Brajawidagda, 2014).

Social computing systems carry an enormous volume of relevant and timely information, and they have proven to be a useful method for communicating when traditional lines of communication are unavailable or inoperable. There are strong indications that social media is playing an ever-increasing role in the management of emergencies, and it can play a key role in bridging the gap between traditional media reporting and adequate resource deployment (Young-McLear, Mazzuchi & Sarkani, 2015). By exploring the potential of modern computing systems to incorporate real-time feedback from the public, and by viewing the citizenry as a powerful, self-organizing and collectively intelligent force (as Palen et al., 2010 have influentially argued we should), we can add new tools to those currently available in disaster response.

When aggregated and integrated with geo-location systems already used by emergency managers, actionable information harvested from social media systems can be a vital resource for the coordination of emergency response (Chae et al., 2012; S. Kelly, Zhang & Ahmad, 2017; Stefanidis, Crooks & Radzikowski, 2013). During the Haitian crisis of 2010, for example, use was made of surviving mobile networks for exchanging information about the levels of disaster in remote areas between the English-speaking NGO volunteers and speakers of Haitian languages and dialects (Bengtsson, Lu, Thorson, Garfield & Von Schreeb, 2011). Locations of people, places and things were essential here, together with demographic data and details of medical needs established through access to medical and personal history. A combined geospatial information system and social computing system in emergency response will be the next step in the evolution of disaster management, allowing citizens to participate in the processes of gathering and sharing vital information (see, for instance, Maresh-Fuehrer & Smith, 2016).

During a disaster, the transparency, legality and morality of data harvesting and information dissemination of the biographical, biometric and geospatial data of an impacted population is secondary to the need for urgent protection of life and property. However, there is a need to ensure that the privacy and data of vulnerable individuals are respected to the highest degree possible. Information collected, processed, stored and eventually distributed for the purpose of protecting victims of natural disasters must be sourced and used in full compliance with privacy and personal data protection principles and rules.

This is particularly important for a system which harvests social media for the purposes of disaster management, since trust is a key resource for disaster response personnel (Busà, Musacchio, Finan & Fennell, 2015). People in positions of vulnerability have to trust those who are given the task of deploying rescue and relief activities and need to have confidence that their personal and sensitive data are handled according to the law and to the highest ethical standards. Trust implies transparency; lawfulness, fairness and transparency are the first fundamental principles that preside over data protection legislation in the EU (along with those of purpose limitation, data minimisation, accuracy, storage limitation, integrity and confidentiality, as stated in Article 5 of the EU General Data Protection Regulation).

6.2.1 *Slándáil: A System for Transparently and Ethically Sourcing Data from Social Computing Systems*

By way of example, we examine the case study of Slándáil, a research project funded by the EU's 7th Framework Programme in the areas of Trust and Security, aimed at maximising the use of social media in emergency management. The project explored the impact of social media in emergencies and built a social media monitor that would harness information generated during disaster events to enhance control room systems for emergency management. Project partners synthesised expertise in emergency management, text and image analytics, communication, ethics and law in order to not only present a system for leveraging social media data for the security of citizens in vulnerable areas, but also address the social and ethical implications of an integrated control room system for emergency management.

Slándáil produced a software system aimed at collecting and processing texts, images, video and other data circulating in formal and social media, including web-based social network services, in order to distil information that civil protection agencies in EU Member States may use in natural disaster scenarios. The software tools developed on the project work together to present fused data to create actionable location-specific information incorporating the EU geo-location framework, INSPIRE.[1] One of the project's key objectives was to "protect the rights of citizens and to manage the confidentiality of the collected data and processed information relating to individual citizens." This goal is premised on the assumption that social media may provide data that can and should be used, in accordance with applicable legal and ethical standards, to enhance emergency response. The project therefore incorporates the task of developing among researchers, stakeholders and users an awareness of the broad societal implications of the technological research being undertaken.

6.2.2 *Guidelines for Data Harvesting*

In the project's ethical analysis of the operation of a social media monitor, the following principles were identified as being essential.

First, data collected and harvested should maintain a high standard of security in order to prevent low-level security breaches. Access to this data should be restricted, particularly if it contains personally identifiable information. In situations where a natural disaster is occurring (and a State of Exception exists), personally identifiable information should only be stored if it may help to save life and property, after which it should be deleted or anonymised. Furthermore, proper procedures should be put in place to ensure that data cannot be easily retrieved by outside sources.

Second, data collected and harvested must be processed in a manner that ensures data confidentiality. Technical systems developed and manual procedures surrounding data obtained must comply with relevant law and institutional codes of ethics and data security practice.

Third, data collected should not be excessive. The derogations that exist during a State of Exception for police forces to save lives and property allow for the limitation of some civil rights. However, this suspension should be time-limited, and this data should *only* be used in relation to this derogation by official police forces. The data cannot be outsourced in a raw format to a third party without prior contractual agreement pertaining to the use of this data.

Past data protection breaches have shown that without proper logging and recording of who is using a system, major issues can occur. As such, it is suggested that systems for monitoring and harvesting social computing data include an in-depth logging system that will track and record all activities of the system. Thus any unauthorised use of the system outside of a natural disaster can be tracked, recorded and acted upon. Any log should be reported to an independent authority outside of government to ensure that the system is being properly regulated by a third-party source. Using login codes and saving a log of action to the system should ensure that no errors occur that would provide for a breach of data; should the system be inappropriately used, an individual could be held accountable for this.

6.2.3 *Operation of the Slándáil System*

End users of the Slándáil system are required to accept the terms of the Licence Agreement (presented in full in Appendix A) when logging on to the system (Figure 2). This mitigates the risk of infringement of the human rights of the data subject or owners, the copyright of the data owners and the relevant personal data protection and privacy provisions of the EU. The Licence highlights the fact that end user organisations have a responsibility to negotiate agreements to secure permission from the data owners (usually the social media providers) to collect and analyse the data, and a responsibility to provide training for users. It specifies when data should be archived from the live system and outlines the protocols that should be in place to provide for its appropriate handling by authorised persons prior to its timely destruction.

FIGURE 2 The login screen of the Slándáil system requires the user to agree to the Terms of Use, which highlight the legal obligations incorporated in the Licence Agreement that accompanies the system. (Image courtesy of Project Slándáil – EU-FP7 Project #607691)

The guidelines will work alongside the method of data harvesting, which incorporates a logging mechanism for tracking user activity. This includes the broad variety of data sources that will be used and couples them with information about the emergency management team. The user who operates the Slándáil system, and the start and end time of the session, will be recorded. Once filtered and stored, the information collected will include elements such as named entities and will account for the security of the data through encryption methods and a legally compliant standard of security. The stored data will be processed through a logging mechanism, and a log will be created that will have details on when, how and by whom the system was used. This log should not contain named entities, but it should contain encrypted data showing that a named entity appeared in the use of Slándáil. The log can then be passed to a third-party advisor, such as a data commissioner, should there be any breach of data security, to ensure the system was not misused.

Slándáil researchers also developed a privacy-preserving measure called the Intrusion Index to help identify when large bodies of automatically collected data contain sensitive personal information (see Appendix B). Personal information can identify and distinguish between individuals and even re-identify them in the case of anonymised data (Y. Liu, Gummadi, Krishnamurthy & Mislove, 2011), and those monitoring and harvesting social computing data need to be aware of the extent to which this activity intrudes upon the privacy of individuals. The Intrusion Index is a text analytical tool that detects and visualises the extent to which sensitive information (such as individual names, institutions and places) is being collected (Stephen Kelly & Ahmad, 2014, 2015) (Figure 3).

Using natural language processing techniques, the system can automatically track named entities such as those of people, places and organisations mentioned in social media conversations. A log of the frequency of these entities can be collected automatically by the system and the results can then be visualised. The Intrusion Index informs the end user when a large volume of personally identifying information is being collected. A geographical map illustrates how the Slándáil monitor uses the Intrusion Index to flag messages and their location on a map layer.

The index facilitates greater transparency in the type of analysis that is being performed and informs a decision maker of the potentially private information being aggregated so that he or she can act accordingly. This feature recognises the importance of building software tools with issues of trust and security in mind (Delgado, Torres, Llorente & Rodríguez, 2005). It functions as a moral mediator

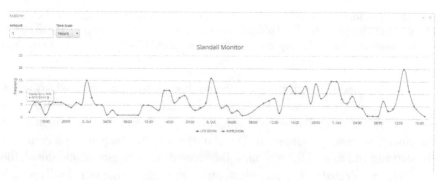

FIGURE 3 Intrusion Index showing frequency of sensitive entities detected by the Slándáil monitor. (Image courtesy of Project Slándáil – EU-FP7 Project #607691)

that preserves the discretion and decision-making abilities of end users while recognising the value of privacy and mitigating the risks of potential undesirable societal and ethical impacts of the system.

6.3 CHECKLIST OF LEGAL ISSUES

The project's ethical analysis and legal research culminated in a model Licence Agreement – the first of its kind – and an accompanying Legal Checklist incorporating all the legal requirements identified during the course of the project and representing the translation of this research into a practical and enforceable agreement. It was found that the system needed to deal with a complex but surmountable set of issues that could be dealt with using existing legal mechanisms. The Licence Agreement conforms to existing protocols in the field of data management and creates specific clauses for the field of disaster management. It specifies the scope of the system's use, limiting its deployment to humanitarian purposes and specific territories. It also points the end user towards the steps to be taken to access live social media data and comply with local statutes.

The accompanying checklist empowers users with information and awareness of the issues surrounding the use of social media data in an emergency management context. It functions to encourage diligence on the part of the licensee and to highlight areas – such as data security, privacy and copyright – in which particular safeguards are needed.

This licensing template incorporates the ethical demands and legal requirements identified during the course of the project, presenting a model for how social computing data can be monitored and harvested in an ethically robust and legally compliant manner.

The Checklist of Legal Issues is a guide for the licensee or end user on how to use the Slándáil software in a lawful manner without giving rise to potential legal issues relating to contract law, copyright infringement, data protection, privacy and human rights laws.

The checklist comprises invaluable pre-contract steps that the licensee should observe prior to committing to signing the Slándáil Software Licence Agreement. These include the following: that the licensee should ensure that they have secured the rights to use social media data and information; that the licensee have read, understood and signed the Slándáil Software end-user agreement; that the licensee should identify and comply with relevant privacy and national data protection laws; trans-border data transfer policies; secure personal data; and be apprised of data breach notification requirements.

Additionally, the licensee should be cognisant that Slándáil Software is protected by copyright; identify relevant national copyright laws and possible exceptions and lawful uses; and secure a Licence Agreement for the of copyright works. Furthermore, the licensee should be aware of the human rights implications of use of personal data for disaster management; conduct preliminary human rights assessments and comply with relevant human rights laws.

As noted earlier, the licence incorporates standard terms of a software licence that set out the contractual terms that establish and define the respective rights and obligations of the licensor and the licensee. In addition, there is a checklist of legal issues designed to help a licensee understand the legal landscape and legal implications of use of Slándáil Software. The primary aim is to ensure lawful use of Slándáil Software by the licensee and obviate possible infringements of copyright, human rights, and privacy and data protection laws.

6.4 RISK ANALYSIS

There are inherent legal risks and potential legal vulnerabilities that could potentially undermine some of the standard terms and clauses of the Template Licence Agreement, such as Clauses 4(a) and 4(b) on the restrictive uses of Slándáil Software by the licensee; and Clauses 10.1 and 10.2 on limitations of liability.

For example, Clause 4(a) of the agreement prohibits the licensee from modifying, adapting, disassembling, reverse engineering and discovering the source code "except as expressly allowed by applicable, mandatory law governing the rights of software licensees". Without a doubt, the clause is designed to ensure licensor's maximum control over Slándáil Software. However, this is impossible because there are indeed applicable and mandatory EU and national laws that give lawful users the right to make "error correction" in software or a computer program without prior authorisation of the licensor (Article 5(1) of Directive 2009/24/EC on the legal protection of computer program). Also, Article 5(2) of Directive 2009/24/EC permits the licensee to make "a back-up copy", whilst Article 6(1) permits the licensee to "decompile" a computer program or software without prior authorisation of the licensor, provided this was necessary to achieve interoperability (*SAS Institute, Inc. v. World Programming Limited*, 2016). Although these restrictions are anticipated by Clause 4(a) of the Template Licence Agreement, they clearly highlight its inherent limitations and the limits of the control exercisable by the licensor over their software.

There is another inherent limitation on the provisions of Clause 4(b) of the Template Licence Agreement, which provides that "the Licensor shall have no obligation to upgrade, bug-fix, provide support or maintenance services, or provide any information, assistance or consultancy in relation to the Software, unless agreed between the Parties". The legal challenge or risk here is that the software vendor or licensor does have an implied legal obligation in law to provide those services, irrespective of any express exclusionary clauses such as Clause 4(b) of the Template Licence Agreement. For example, Article 3(1) of Directive 93/13/EEC on unfair consumer contracts provides that "[a] contractual term which has not been individually negotiated shall be regarded as unfair if, contrary to the requirement of good faith, it causes a significant imbalance in the parties' rights and obligations arising under the contract, to the detriment of the consumer". However, in nearly all cases, it will not be "consumers" that will be using the Slándáil Software (a "consumer" is defined under the Directive as a person who is acting for purposes which are outside his trade, business or profession). Indeed, national laws require that goods or services must be of satisfactory quality and must be fit for purpose (UK Consumer Rights Act 2015). Thus, there is a risk that if challenged by the licensee, courts could strike down such clauses as an "unfair contract term", particularly if the licensee is a "consumer" (although this would be very unusual in practice) (Cusumano, 2004; Reed, 2012; *St Albans City and District Council v. International Computers Ltd*, 1996).

Similarly, although the provisions of Article 10.1 and Article 10.2 of the Template Licence Agreement, which respectively limit the liabilities of the licensor to a fixed sum, and exclude non-direct losses, are typical of standard terms of software licence agreements, they are equally vulnerable to implied terms of contract and the provisions of unfair contract terms in the laws of EU member states. For example, in *St Albans City and District Council v. International Computers Ltd* (1996), the UK Court of Appeal held that the liability limitation was unreasonable and in contravention of the provisions of the Unfair Contract Terms Act 1977; the court awarded £1,313,846 in damages, instead of the limited contractual liability of £100.000.

6.5 CONCLUSION

These inherent risks notwithstanding, the Slándáil Licence Agreement and accompanying checklist represent a model for the legal and ethical deployment of a social media monitor. The Licence Agreement incorporates a requirement for accountability and is based on key ethical principles identified in our research. It functions as a legal accompaniment to a software solution for accessing and processing social media information and data for disaster management by emergency responders. The Template Licence Agreement and Legal Checklist are indispensable to the operational deployment of a social media monitor. The results clearly define the legal obligations and rights of the licensor and licensee, and draw on extensive research to map an accurate legal landscape of privacy, data protection, copyright and human rights that the licensor and licensee must carefully navigate in order to obviate potential infringements and infractions.

The Licence Agreement comprises two distinct parts: (a) the Template Licence Agreement between the licensor and the licensee and (b) the Legal Checklist, which acts as a guide for the licensee or end user on how to use a software system for monitoring and harvesting social computing data in a lawful manner without giving rise to potential legal issues relating to contract law, copyright infringement, data protection, privacy and human rights laws. The work presented here shows a legal framework backed up by an ethical framework that can be practically applied to software systems that use social media in emergency management.

NOTES

1. INSPIRE, E. (2007). Directive 2007/2/EC of the European Parliament and of the Council of 14 March 2007 establishing an Infrastructure for Spatial Information in the European Community (INSPIRE). Official Journal of the European Union, L, 108(1), 50.

Licence Agreement for the Use of a Social Media Monitor in Disaster Management

This section comprises a Template Software Licence for the Slándáil System. The template licence presented here can be used as a model to license a social media monitor to end users. It is to be entered into by the relevant entity that has the necessary legal rights to license Slándáil (the "Licensor") and the relevant emergency services agency (the "Licensee"). Some of the provisions may be subject to negotiation and/or local law requirements.

At a high level, the Licensor grants to the Licensee the right to:

- use the "Software" (which is defined as the overall software solution known as Slándáil or any of its components that collects and processes Social Media Data for the Purpose);
- in the "Territory" (the relevant EU Member State(s) can be inserted here);
- for the "Purpose" (which is defined as receiving, processing and analysing the Social Media Data harvested by the Software for the purposes of preventing, managing and responding to natural disasters or for any other legal purpose).

Other key features of the licence include the following:

- Clause 3 (Conditions of Licence) makes it clear that the Licensee uses Slándáil entirely at their own risk and is responsible for ensuring that their use of the "Social Media Data" harvested through Slándáil complies with all applicable laws and other contractual restrictions or conditions imposed by social media companies.
- Clause 6 (Intellectual Property Rights) contains an express acknowledgement by the Licensee that the Licensor does not own any intellectual property rights in the Social Media Data.
- Clause 7 (Infringement of Intellectual Property Rights) provides that the Licensor shall have the exclusive right to determine whether or not any

litigation should be instituted or other action taken in connection with any infringement, or potential infringement, of the Software.

- Clause 8 (Indemnity) contains a wide-ranging indemnity in favour of the Licensor against third party claims brought against the Licensor arising from the Licensee's use of the Software.
- Clause 10 (Limitation of Liability) imposes a cap on the financial liability of both parties (which may be the subject of negotiation), but this cap does not apply to the indemnity in Clause 8.
- Clause 13.9 (Law and Jurisdiction) as requested and because Slándáil is an EU-funded project, the licence is governed by the laws of Belgium and each party agrees to submit to the exclusive jurisdiction of the courts of Brussels, Belgium.

The primary purpose or function of a software licence agreement, or an end user licence agreement (EULA), is to clearly set out the contractual terms and conditions that establish and define the respective rights and obligations of the licensor and the licensee. For in the absence of a written software agreement between the licensor and the licensee, the law could imply certain terms into the contract, which might run counter to the true intentions of the parties. A software licence agreement also pre-empts potential disputes between the parties by stipulating the terms and conditions attaching to the use of the software by the licensee and the modality for dispute resolution (Reed, 2012).

STANDARD TERMS OF CONTRACT FOR PROPRIETARY SOFTWARE

Clause 1 of the "template software licence" agreement for Slándáil incorporates standard terms of proprietary software licence by explaining the purpose of the licence and identifying and defining key concepts used in the licence such as "Claims"; "Effective Date"; "Intellectual Property Rights"; "Legal Checklist"; "Licence Fee"; "Purpose"; "Social Media Data"; "Software" and "Territory".

Clause 2 provides that the licence is "a non-exclusive, non-transferable, non-sub licensable, royalty-free licence". Clause 3 sets out the conditions for the grant of licence, which include standard disclaimers. Clause 4 provides restrictions on the scope of use of Slándáil Software by the licensee. Clause 5 deals with payment. Clause 6 makes it clear that the licensor owns the intellectual property rights in the Slándáil Software but does not own any rights in any "Social Media Data". Clause 7 deals with infringement of intellectual property rights and also third party rights. Clause 8 contains a broad indemnity in favour of the licensor. In Clause 9 both the licensor and licensee provide certain warranties. Clause 10 addresses limitation of liability issues. Duration and termination are dealt with in Clause 11. Data protection issues (if any) can be dealt with in Clause 12. Finally, Clause 13 contains some general terms, including jurisdiction and applicable law.

The aforementioned terms of the software licence agreement are typically generous to, and largely in favour of, the licensor. However, this is not uncommon for standard software licence terms drawn up solely by the lawyers for the licensor, because, invariably, software licence or end-user agreements are primarily designed for the licensor to gain control over their software (Reed, 2012: 60). Even so, Clause 13.2 of the Template Software Licence ostensibly seeks to balance the lopsided power and control dynamics by allowing for the possibility of an amendment or variation to the terms of the licence by authorised representatives of the licensor and the licensee.

DATED _____ 20_

[INSERT CONTRACTING ENTITY]

AND

[INSERT NAME OF RELEVANT EMERGENCY SERVICES AGENCY]

TEMPLATE SOFTWARE LICENCE

FOR SLÁNDÁIL

THIS AGREEMENT is made on the [•] day of [•] 20__ (the "**Agreement**")

BETWEEN

(1)   [Insert contracting entity] (the "**Licensor**"); and
(2)   [Insert emergency services agency] (the "**Licensee**" or "**you**")
      (each a "**Party**" and together the "**Parties**")

BACKGROUND

A.   The Licensor owns the Intellectual Property Rights in the Software and reserves the exclusive right to licence the Software.

B.   The Software can be lawfully and usefully deployed to assist civil protection and emergency response agencies in the EU to prevent, manage and respond to natural and man-made disasters.

C.   However, legal research has shown that improper use of the Software can give rise to legal issues, particularly with regard to the laws of copyright, data protection, human rights and privacy.

D.   The Licensee wishes to obtain the right to use the Software in the Territory for the Purpose.

E.   In order for the Licensee to use the Software in a lawful manner, the Licensor has provided the Licensee with the Legal Checklist.

F.   The Licensee is responsible for ensuring that the Software is used in a lawful manner and in accordance with all applicable laws, including all the laws referred to in the Legal Checklist.

NOW IT IS HEREBY AGREED as follows:

1. *Definitions*

In this Agreement, the following words shall have the following meanings:

"**Claims**" means all demands, claims and liabilities (whether criminal or civil, in contract, tort or otherwise, including negligence) for losses, costs, fees (including legal fees) and any other expenses relating to any actual or threatened claim or any actual or threatened proceedings;

"**Effective Date**" means the date on which this Agreement is signed by both Parties;

"Intellectual Property Rights" means all patents, patent applications, copyright works (including software), trade marks (whether registered or unregistered), trade secrets, database rights, know-how and any other intellectual property rights of a similar or corresponding nature;

"**Legal Checklist**" means the checklist of potential legal issues associated with using the Software, as provided by the Licensor to the Licensee, which is to be considered by the Licensee before using the Software;

"**Licence Fee**" means the fee of € [INSERT][1] paid by the Licensee to the Licensor for the use of the Software;

"**Purpose**" means receiving, processing and analysing the Social Media Data harvested by the Software for the purposes of preventing, managing and responding to natural disasters or for any other legal purpose;

"**Social Media Data**" means data made available by the public on formal and informal social media networks, including text, images, videos and sound recordings;

"**Software**" means the overall software solution known as Slándáil or its constitute components that collects and processes Social Media Data for the Purpose; and

"**Territory**" means [insert relevant EU Member State].

2. *Grant of Licence*

In consideration of the Licence Fee and subject to the conditions in Clause 3, the Licensor hereby grants to the Licensee a non-exclusive, non-transferable, non-sub-licensable, royalty-free licence to use the Software in the Territory for the Purpose.

3. *Conditions of Licence*

3.1   The Licensee is responsible for ensuring that their access to and use of the Social Media Data complies with all applicable laws, including, but not limited to, all laws that apply in emergency situations and the laws identified on the Legal Checklist, together with any other contractual restrictions or conditions on your use of the Social Media Data which may be imposed by the relevant owner, licensor or controller of the Social Media Data.

3.2   The Licensee acknowledges and accepts the following:
   a)   That the Licensee uses the Software entirely at their own risk;
   b)   That the Licensor does not create, edit, own, moderate or otherwise control the Social Media Data that is harvested via the Software;
   c)   That the Licensor does not guarantee or warrant that the Social Media Data is accurate or complete and expressly disclaims all liability for any loss or damage resulting from your reliance on the Software;
   d)   That the Licensee is entirely liable for any liabilities, damages, losses, costs, fees and any other expenses incurred as a result of using the Software and, in accordance with clause 4 shall indemnify the Licensor against any such losses incurred by it as a result of your use of the Software.

4. *Supply of Software*

a)   Except as expressly permitted by this Agreement, the Licensee shall not modify, adapt, disassemble, reverse engineer, decompile, translate or otherwise attempt to discover the source code of the Software or permit any of these things to happen, except as expressly authorised by applicable, mandatory law governing the rights of software licensees.

The Software is provided "as is" and the Licensor shall have no obligation to upgrade, bug-fix, provide support or maintenance services, or provide any information, assistance or consultancy in relation to the Software, unless agreed between the Parties.

5. *Payment*

Within thirty (30) days of the Effective Date, the Licensee shall pay the Licensor the agreed Licence Fee.

6. *Intellectual Property Rights*

6.1 **Intellectual Property Rights in the Software.** The Licensee acknowledges that the Licensor owns the Intellectual Property Rights in the Software and the Licensee has no rights in or to the Software other than the right to use it in the Territory for the Purpose in accordance with the terms of this Agreement.

6.2 **Intellectual Property Rights in the Social Media Data.** The Licensee acknowledges that the Licensor does not own any Intellectual Property Rights in the Social Media Data and that the Licensee is responsible for obtaining all necessary consents and permissions, including those identified on the Legal Checklist, that are required in order to lawfully use the Social Media Data in the Territory for the Purpose.

7. *Infringement of Intellectual Property Rights*

7.1 **Infringement of the Software**. The Licensee shall inform the Licensor promptly if it becomes aware of any third party infringement, or potential infringement, of the Software. The Licensor shall have the exclusive right to determine whether or not any litigation shall be instituted or other action taken in connection with any infringement, or potential infringement, of the Software.

7.2 **Infringement of Third Party Rights**. If any warning letter or other notice of infringement is received by a Party, or legal suit or other action is brought against a Party, alleging that the Software infringes the Intellectual Property Rights of any third Party, that Party shall promptly provide full details to the other Party and the Parties shall discuss the best way to respond. The Licensee shall not make any admissions in relation to such allegations, except with the prior written agreement of the Licensor. Unless otherwise agreed in writing by the Parties, the Licensor shall have the exclusive right to conduct any proceedings relating to the Software, including any proceedings relating to the alleged infringement of third party rights in the use of the Software.

8. *Indemnity*

8.1 The Licensee shall indemnify the Licensor against all Claims brought against the Licensor which relates to or is caused by:

    a) any decision or action taken by the Licensee (and any consequences that flow directly or indirectly from any such decision or action) based wholly or partly on the Software; or

b) any damage to, or loss of, life or property caused from the Licensee ordering an evacuation (or not ordering an evacuation) based wholly or partly on the Software; or

c) any breach by the Licensee of any laws or regulations applicable in the Territory, including, but not limited to, the laws of contract, data protection, privacy, copyright and human rights laws; or

d) the failure by the Licensee to secure all necessary consents and permissions required in order to lawfully use the Social Media Data in the Territory for the Purpose.

9. *Warranties*

9.1 The Licensor warrants and represents to the Licensee that:

a) it has the full power, capacity and authority to enter into this Agreement which has been signed by a duly authorised representative of the Licensor;

b) it has and will retain all necessary rights to grant the licence in Clause 2; and

c) it owns the Intellectual Property Rights in the Software, and is not aware of any claim that the Software infringes the Intellectual Property Rights of any third party.

9.2 The Licensee warrants and represents to the Licensor that:

a) it has read and understood the Legal Checklist;

b) it will take all measures necessary to ensure that its use of the Software accords with all applicable laws, regulations, authorisations and conditions; and

c) it has the full power, capacity and authority to enter into this Agreement which has been signed by a duly authorised representative of the Licensee.

d) Each of the Licensee and the Licensor acknowledges that, in entering into this Agreement, it does not do so in reliance on any representation, warranty or other provision except as expressly provided in this Agreement, and any conditions, warranties or other terms implied by statute or common law are excluded from this Agreement to the fullest extent permitted by law.

10. *Limitations of Liability*[2]

10.1 Except as provided for under Clause 3.2 Clause 8, neither Party shall be liable for any loss, damage, costs or expenses of any nature whatsoever incurred or suffered by the other Party that is (a) of an indirect, special or consequential nature or (b) any loss of profits, revenue, data, business opportunity or goodwill.

10.2   To the extent that either of the Parties has any liability in contract, tort (including negligence), or otherwise under or in connection with this Agreement, including any liability for breach of warranty, their liability shall be limited to [the Licence Fee].[3]

10.3   Nothing in this Agreement excludes or limits either Party's liability for:

    i.   death or personal injury resulting from its negligence or the negligence of its employees or agents; or

    ii.   fraud or fraudulent misrepresentation; or

    iii.   its obligations under Clause 8 (Indemnity); or

    iv.   matters for which liability cannot be excluded or limited under applicable law.[4]

11. *Duration and Termination*

11.1   This Agreement, and the licence granted in Clause 2, will commence on the Effective Date and, unless terminated earlier in accordance with this Clause 11, shall continue for a period of [1] year (the "**Initial Term**") and shall continue to renew for successive [1] year terms (the "**Renewal Period**") unless either Party terminates the Agreement in accordance with this Clause 11.

11.2   Either Party may terminate this Agreement at any time on thirty (30)[5] days' notice in writing to the other Party.

11.3   Either Party may terminate this Agreement at any time by notice in writing to the other Party (the "**Other Party**"), such termination to take effect as specified in the notice:

    i.   if the Other Party is in material breach of this Agreement and, in the case of a breach capable of remedy within ninety (90) days, the breach is not remedied within ninety (90) days of the Other Party receiving notice specifying the breach and requiring its remedy; or

    ii.   if the Other Party becomes insolvent or unable to pay its debts as and when they become due; an order is made or a resolution is passed for the winding up of the Other Party (other than voluntarily for the purpose of solvent amalgamation or reconstruction); a liquidator, examiner, receiver, receiver manager, or trustee is appointed in respect of the whole or any part of the Other Party's assets or business; the Other Party makes any composition with its creditors; the Other Party ceases to continue its business; or as a result of debt and/or maladministration the Other Party takes or suffers any similar or analogous action. A Party's right of termination under this Agreement, and the exercise of any such right, shall be without prejudice to any other right or remedy (including any right to claim damages) that such Party may have in the event of a breach of contract or other default by the other Party.

11.4 Consequences of Termination.

    a) Upon termination of this Agreement for any reason:

        i. the Licensee shall no longer be licensed to use or otherwise deal in any way, either directly or indirectly, with the Software; and

        ii. except in respect of any accrued rights, neither Party shall be under any further obligation to the other.

    b) Upon termination of this Agreement for any reason the provisions of Clauses 5, 6, 7, 8, 10 and 12 shall remain in force.

12. *Data Protection*

If the Licensor is processing personal data on behalf of the Licensee, then a data processing agreement should be put in place which includes the mandatory provisions of Article 28.3 of the EU GDPR (2016).

13. *General*

13.1 *Force Majeure*. Neither Party shall have any liability or be deemed to be in breach of this Agreement for any delays or failures in performance of this Agreement that result from circumstances beyond the reasonable control of that Party, including labour disputes involving that Party. The Party affected by such circumstances shall promptly notify the other Party in writing when such circumstances cause a delay or failure in performance and when they cease to do so.

13.2 **Amendment**. This Agreement may only be amended in writing signed by duly authorised representatives of the Licensor and the Licensee.

13.3 **Assignment**. The Licensee shall not assign, mortgage, charge or otherwise transfer any rights or obligations under this Agreement without the prior written consent of the Licensor. The Licensors may freely assign its rights or obligations under this Agreement.

13.4 **Waiver**. No failure or delay on the part of either Party to exercise any right or remedy under this Agreement shall be construed or operate as a waiver thereof, nor shall any single or partial exercise of any right or remedy preclude the further exercise of such right or remedy.

13.5 **Invalid Clauses**. If any provision or part of this Agreement is held to be invalid, amendments to this Agreement may be made by the addition or deletion of wording as appropriate to remove the invalid part or provision but otherwise retain the provision and the other provisions of this Agreement to the maximum extent permissible under applicable law.

13.6 **No Agency.** Neither Party shall act or describe itself as the agent of the other, nor shall it make or represent that it has authority to make any commitments on the other's behalf.

13.7 **Interpretation.** In this Agreement:

a) the headings are used for convenience only and shall not affect its interpretation;

b) references to persons shall include incorporated and unincorporated persons; references to the singular include the plural and vice versa; and references to the masculine include the feminine and vice versa;

c) references to Clauses and Schedules mean clauses of, and schedules to, this Agreement;

d) references in this Agreement to termination shall include termination by expiry; and

e) where the word "including" is used it shall be understood as meaning "including without limitation".

13.8 **Notices.**

a) Any notice or other communication given to a Party under or in connection with this Agreement shall be in writing in English (which shall include email).

b) Any notice or communication shall be deemed to have been received:

    i. if delivered by hand, on signature of a delivery receipt or at the time the notice is left at the proper address (being the address set out at 12.8(d) below);

    ii. if sent by pre-paid post or other next working day delivery service, to the proper address (being the address set out at 13.8(d) below) at 9:00 AM on the second business day after posting or at the time recorded by the delivery service;

    upon email delivery (to the email address set out at 12.8(d) below) and receipt of return receipt from the party to be notified if received by the recipient before 5:00 PM local time on a - business day, and if not, then the next business day.

c) This clause does not apply to the service of any proceedings or other documents in any legal action or, where applicable, any arbitration or other method of dispute resolution.

d) Contact details:[7]

    (i) Licensor:
       For the attention of:
       Email:

    (ii) Licensee:
       For the attention of:
       Email:

or to such other address(es) as may from time to time be notified by a party to the other Party.

13.9 **Law and Jurisdiction**.

   a) This Agreement shall be governed by and construed in accordance with the laws of [Belgium] and each Party agrees to submit to the exclusive jurisdiction of the courts of [Brussels, Belgium].[8]

   b) Notwithstanding 13.9(a), each Party shall consider in good faith whether it would be reasonable in the circumstances for the Parties to agree to pursue any alternative dispute resolution processes. Such alternative processes may include internal escalation procedures and/ or mediation in accordance with the WIPO mediation rules. For the avoidance of doubt, however, nothing in this Agreement shall prevent or delay a Party from seeking an interim injunction.

13.10 **Further Assurance**. Each Party agrees to execute, acknowledge and deliver such further instruments, and do all further similar acts, as may be necessary or appropriate to carry out the purposes and intent of this Agreement.

13.11 **Announcements**. Neither Party shall make any press or other public announcement concerning any aspect of this Agreement, or make any use of the name of the other Party in connection with or in consequence of this Agreement, without the prior written consent of the other Party.

13.12 **Entire Agreement**. This Agreement, including its Schedules, sets out the entire agreement between the Parties relating to its subject matter and supersedes all prior oral or written agreements, arrangements or under-standings between them relating to such subject matter.

13.13 **Export Control Regulations**.[9]

   a) "**Export Control Regulations**" mean any United Nations trade sanctions, Irish, or EU legislation or regulation, from time to time in force, which impose arms embargoes or control the export of goods, technology or software, including weapons of mass destruction and arms, military, paramilitary and security equipment and dual-use items (items designed for civil use but which can be used for military purposes) and certain drugs and chemicals.

   b) The Licensee shall ensure that, in exercising its rights pursuant to this Agreement including in using the Software, it shall not breach or compromise, directly or indirectly, compliance with any Export Control Regulations.

Agreed by the Parties through their authorised signatories:

For and on behalf of	For and on behalf of
[Full legal name of the Licensor]	*[Full legal name of the Licensee]*

Signed

Signed

Print name

Print name

Title

Title

Date

Date

NOTES

1. Fee to be inserted on final agreement following completion of the project.
2. Note: Clause 10 in its entirety will be the subject of negotiation between the parties and will be subject to local law requirements.
3. Note: Limitation of liability (if any) to be negotiated between the parties.
4. Note: To be amended/reviewed in accordance with applicable local law.
5. Note: To be agreed by the parties.
6. Note: Relevant details to be inserted.
7. Note: Belgian law and jurisdiction have been inserted on request as Slándáil is an EU-funded project.
8. Note: This may not be required but has been included for completeness sake.

Checklist of Legal Issues

The legal checklist presented here is a synthesis of the research undertaken by legal experts in the United Kingdom, Germany and Italy. The checklist has been designed to assist users in identifying and attending to key legal requirements prior to operational deployment of a social media monitor on the internet. The checklist covers five key legal areas as being particularly relevant: contract; data protection; privacy; copyright and human rights. These areas were identified by the Slándáil legal caucus as being most relevant to the use of Slándáil in emergency response situations.

1. Contract		
Please remember that the Software Licence Agreement between Slándáil and you grants you the right to use the Slándáil Software (see 1.4). However, it does not grant you any rights with respect to any content that comes from third parties, such as social media operators, even though this content may be capable of being processed on the Slándáil platform (see 1.1). This content is either owned or controlled by the third party operators (see 1.3) and accordingly you are responsible for engaging directly with them to negotiate the terms upon which you may use their content and for what purposes.		
No.	Action	Completed
1.1	Ensure that you have concluded an agreement with the relevant social media platforms from which content is harvested by Slándáil which grants you a licence to use this content for the purposes of preventing, managing and responding to natural and man-made disasters.	
1.2	Confirm whether or not the social media operators would be willing to offer "open source" type licences to you, considering you are committed to using Slándáil for humanitarian, non-commercial purposes. If so, this could enable you to streamline your deployments of Slándáil on standardised terms without incurring the cost and resources of negotiating bespoke Licence Agreements.	
		(Continued)

No.	Action	Completed
1.3	Consider the contractual relationship between the social media user and the social media company (and also any applicable third party rights) and, to the extent possible, confirm (or seek confirmation from the social media company) that the social media company has the right to grant the licence in 1.1 above.	
1.4	Confirm that you have read and signed an end-user licence agreement with Slándáil.	
1.5	Your software licence for Slándáil is limited to the purposes of enabling the prevention, management and response to natural and man-made disasters. Your agreements/licences above should limit the use of the social media content by you to these purposes and you should ensure that the data will not be used for commercial purposes.	
1.6	Check (or seek confirmation from the social media company) whether the terms of service of the relevant social media companies provide that content that is voluntarily uploaded and shared on their platforms can be used for civil protection / emergency purposes.	
1.7	Confirm that you shall only reverse engineer the Slándáil Software where such reverse engineering is necessary to achieve the interoperability (i.e., the ability to exchange information and mutually to use the information which has been exchanged) of the Slándáil Software with other computer programmes in accordance with Article 6 of the Software Directive 2009/24/EC.	
1.8	Confirm the law which governs your contractual obligations and use of the social media data. In relation to non-contractual obligations, consider the rules under Regulation No 864/2007 on the law applicable to non-contractual obligations (Rome II) and, in particular, Article 8 regarding infringement of intellectual property rights.	

2. Data Protection

Slándáil will enable you to collect, process, use and store a significant amount of information harvested from users of social media in areas affected by natural crises. The nature of this information will be varied; while some of it will be innocuous and anonymous, some will contain personal data. Personal data is information relating to an identified or identifiable natural person (i.e., someone who can be identified, directly or indirectly, by reference to an identifier such as a name, an identification number, location data or an online identifier). In the context of the data harvested by

(Continued)

2. Data Protection

Slándáil, an "online identifier" may include names, usernames, profile pictures, location data or such other data (or a combination of such data) which are capable of identifying a living person.

The protection of individuals in relation to the processing of personal data concerning him or her is a fundamental right, protected under Article 8(1) of the Charter of Fundamental Rights of the European Union and Article 16(1) of the Treaty on the Functioning of the European Union (see 3.1). With effect from 25 May 2018, the legal rules which serve to protect this fundamental right of citizens are set out in the General Data Protection Regulation (the "GDPR"); national laws should also be consulted (see 2.1) and appropriate legal advice be taken. You are responsible for ensuring that you collect, process, use and store personal data in accordance with the GDPR and applicable national laws.

No.	Action	Completed
	Identify Applicable Law	
2.1	Identify the national and EU data protection laws applicable to the processing of social media data harvested from Slándáil.	
2.2	Confirm that you are collecting, processing and storing data in accordance with the General Data Protection Regulation (the "**GDPR**").	
	Lawful Processing	
2.3	Confirm compliance with the principles for lawful processing of data outlined in Article 5 of the GDPR, which are as follows: (a) lawfulness, fairness and transparency; (b) purpose limitation; (c) data minimisation; (d) accuracy; (e) storage limitation; (f) integrity and (g) confidentiality.	
2.4	Confirm that data will only be collected and processed for the limited purpose as specified in the Software Licence for Slándáil and the licences with the social media companies and in accordance with relevant data protection laws.	
2.5	Confirm if there is a legal basis (e.g., consent, contractual necessity, legitimate interests, etc.) under the GDPR for the processing of personal data.	
2.6	If the answer to 2.5 above is no, confirm whether you intend to rely on either Article 6(d) of the GDPR – "*processing is necessary in order to protect the vital interests of the data subject or of another natural person*"; or Article 6(e) of the GDPR – "*processing is necessary for the performance of a task carried out in the public interest or in the exercise of official authority vested in the controller*" as a legal basis for the processing.	

(Continued)

No.	Action	Completed
2.7	Confirm that the following data subject rights will be respected: (a) the right to object to processing; (b) the right of access to data held by the controller; (c) the right of rectification of inaccurate data; (d) the right to erasure / right to be forgotten; (e) the right of restriction of processing; and (f) the right to data portability.	
2.8	To the extent that you process the data of minors, confirm what additional protective measures (if any) are required given the minor consent requirements of Article 8 of the GDPR.	
2.9	Profiling is defined under the GDPR as "any form of automated processing of personal data consisting of the use of personal data to evaluate certain personal aspects relating to a natural person, in particular to analyse or predict aspects concerning that natural person's performance at work, economic situation, health, personal preferences, interests, reliability, behaviour, location or movements". The Slándáil Software enables profiling for emergency response purposes. However, such profiling remains subject to data protection laws (e.g., privacy by design – see paragraph 15.15) and is required to be supported by national law which includes suitable measures to safeguard the data subject's rights. You should check what national law, if any, exists to support profiling for emergency response purposes in your jurisdiction and take independent legal advice.	
Data Security		
2.10	Confirm that you have adequate safeguards in place to protect data from access and use by unauthorised computer systems, public authorities, private bodies or individuals.	
2.11	Implement appropriate technical and organisational measures to ensure an adequate level of data security appropriate to the risk to the rights and freedoms of natural persons, taking into account the state of the art, the costs of implementation and the nature, scope, context and purposes of processing. Such data security measures may include pseudonymisation and encryption of data.	
2.12	If you are processing personal data in conjunction with other databases to which you have lawful access, ensure that you have appropriate technological safeguards in place to prevent access to the Slándáil data by unauthorised persons.	
2.13	Confirm that you are aware of data breach notification requirements under the GDPR and that you are in a position to comply with them.	
2.14	If you are using a third party processor, ensure that you have a binding agreement in place and that the processor provides sufficient guarantees to safeguard the data.	

(Continued)

No.	Action	Completed
2.15	Implement data protection by design and default as required under Article 25 of the GDPR.	
Procedural Requirements		
2.16	Confirm that you keep appropriate records of data processing activities for inspection by the relevant Supervisory Authority.	
2.17	Confirm that you aware of your obligations under the GDPR to cooperate with the relevant Supervisory Authority.	
2.18	Determine whether it is necessary to appoint a Data Protection Officer ("**DPO**"). The DPO should ensure compliance with national laws and the GDPR. The details of the DPO should be provided to the Supervisory Authority and made available to the public.	
2.19	Determine whether a data protection impact assessment is required and, assuming it is, prepare a DPIA in accordance with Article 35 of the GDPR.	
2.20	Ensure that you have a data retention policy in place which confirms how long the data will be stored. If you cannot provide the exact period, confirm the criteria that will be used to determine the period.	
2.21	Ensure that you have a data policy which provides all of the information specified under Article 13: *Information to be provided where personal data are collected from the data subject* and Article 14: *Information to be provided where personal data have not been obtained from the data subject* of the GDPR. This information should include, for example, the contact details of the controller, the purposes of the processing, the categories of the personal data and the recipients or categories of recipients of the personal data.	
Transfers of Data		
2.22	If you intend to transfer data to a third country (i.e., a country outside of the EU), ensure that adequate safeguards are in place. For example, consider if "Model Contractual Clauses", "Privacy Shield", "Binding Corporate Rules" or another mechanism is available to permit the transfer of data outside of the EU. Independent legal advice should be taken if you intend to transfer data to a third country.	
Fines		
2.23	Be aware that Member States may, under Article 83(7) of the GDPR, lay down rules on whether and to what extent administrative fines may be imposed on public authorities and bodies established in that Member State. You should familiarise yourself with the enforcement regime applicable to your jurisdiction.	

3. Privacy

The social media data harvested by Slándáil may contain private and personal information relating to individuals. All European citizens have a right to respect for their private and family lives under Article 8 of the European Convention on Human Rights. This right protects citizens from unnecessary interference in their private lives, including unnecessary surveillance. However, there is an exception under Article 8 for interference that is necessary for national security, public safety and the prevention of disorder or crime. If you wish to rely on this exception when using Slándáil, then you must take steps to ensure that you process and use social media data only for national security, public safety and the prevention of disorder or crime.

Further, the GDPR provides for security measures to protect the private data from unauthorised access. These security measures ensure that there is no unauthorised interference with the private and personal data beyond that which is permitted in the interests of national security, public safety and the prevention of disorder and crime.

No.	Action	Completed
3.1	Ensure that the social media data harvested from Slándáil will only be used by you in a way that respects a person's right to privacy under Article 8 of the European Convention on Human Rights which states that: 1. Everyone has the right to respect for his private and family life, his home and his correspondence. 2. There shall be no interference by a public authority with the exercise of this right except such as is in accordance with the law and is necessary in a democratic society in the interests of national security, public safety or the economic wellbeing of the country, for the prevention of disorder or crime, for the protection of health or morals, or for the protection of the rights and freedoms of others.	
3.2	Take measures to ensure against the accidental loss of data (e.g., from unsecured sources) and, in the event of a data breach, follow the data breach notification requirements under the GDPR (see above: Data Protection, 2.13).	
3.3	Take measures to ensure that the data is not used by you (or by any other entity or authority) for conducting illegal surveillance on citizens.	
3.4	Take measures to ensure that the data harvested from Slándáil is only used to prevent, manage and respond to natural and man-made disasters and for no other purposes.	

(Continued)

No.	Action	Completed
3.5	If you transfer the data to other computer systems, take measures to guard against accidental loss or cyber theft.	
3.6	Ensure that you have a privacy policy in place that the public can access.	
3.7	Use technical measures to adequately protect data and privacy without impinging on the ability of the Slándáil system to help save lives.	

4. Copyright

Copyright protects original literary and artistic works from unauthorised use by third parties. In the context of Slándáil, it should be assumed (unless the contrary can be proven) that copyright subsists in the wide range of content uploaded to social media platforms and harvested by Slándáil, which includes posts, tweets, photographs, videos and sound recordings. Accordingly, if you are to copy or communicate this content to the public, then you will require the permission of the copyright owner (see 4.3) or alternatively you must be able to rely on a limitation or exemption to the rights protected by copyright (see 4.4 and 4.5). If you use the copyright work without permission and no limitation or exemption applies, then you will be infringing the copyright, unless a defence is available (see 4.6).

The first owner of copyright is the author of the work, meaning that the person that uploads the content to the social media platform usually owns the copyright. However, under the terms of use for social media platforms, the user will almost always grant a licence to the social media company to reproduce, distribute and communicate the content to the public. Accordingly, it should be possible to obtain a sub-licence from the relevant social media companies to use the content uploaded to its platform instead of seeking permission from individual social media users (which is unworkable in practice) (see 4.3).

You are responsible for ensuring the lawful use of social media content protected by applicable copyright laws, and where you are in any doubt, appropriate independent legal advice should be taken.

No.	Action	Completed
4.1	Identify the national and EU copyright laws that are applicable to the reproduction and making available by you of the literary and artistic works harvested from Slándáil.	
4.2	Comply with the relevant copyright laws for the protection of those literary and artistic works (i.e., text, images, photos, videos and sound recordings) that are uploaded to social media platforms and harvested by Slándáil.	

(Continued)

No.	Action	Completed
4.3	Ensure that there is a contract / licensing arrangement in place between you and the owner / licensee of the copyright which authorises you to reproduce the copyright works and to make them available to the public.	
4.4	Check whether your use of the copyright works come within any national exemptions or limitations to copyright protection.	
4.5	Confirm whether any of the optional exemptions or limitations to copyright protection provided for under Article 5 of the Information Society Directive 2001/29/EC have been implemented under national law. In particular, confirm whether there is an exemption or limitation to copyright protection for the use of copyright works for the purposes of public security, and, if so, whether it applies in your case.	
4.6	Check whether there is a general right under national law to infringe copyright (and other rights) to safeguard life or to ward off a present danger.	
4.7	Check whether there is a "fair use" type exemption available in your jurisdiction.	
4.8	Check whether the right to freedom of panorama exists in your jurisdiction (to the extent that any pictures of videos of disaster-related events include copyright works).	
4.9	Confirm that legal entities can own copyright in your jurisdiction.	

5. Human Rights

Human rights are protected by a range of international, European and local laws, all of which must be considered by you when using Slándáil (see 5 generally). While the use of Slándáil may potentially threaten the right to privacy, dignity of the person and protection of personal data, as well as copyright of original literary and artistic works, this threat must be balanced against the social benefit that Slándáil offers in assisting civil protection and emergency response agencies in the EU to protect and uphold the other vitally important rights, such as the right to life and the right to humanitarian assistance in disaster situations. You are responsible for implementing a human rights–based approach which effectively balances these competing rights.

No.	Action	Completed
5.1	Where Slándáil is used by you to prevent, manage and respond to natural or man-made disasters, then you should ensure that your actions in responding to disasters respect human rights and, in particular, the dignity of the person.	

(Continued)

No.	Action	Completed
5.2	In particular, you should confirm that there is a sound ethical basis before you use Slándáil to respond to natural or man-made disasters.	
5.3	Concerns about data protection, copyright and privacy should be weighed against the rights of citizens (and the corresponding duty on emergency response agencies) to protection and relief from disasters.	
5.4	Consider whether the processing of social media data in emergency situations is necessary in order to protect the vital interests of the data subject or of another natural person [Article 6(d) of the GDPR].	
5.5	Comply with the European Union's human rights regime and, in particular, Article 1: *Human dignity*, Article 2: *Right to life*, Article 3: *Right to the integrity of the person*, Article 6: *Right to liberty and security*, Article 7: *Respect for family and private life* and Article 8: *Protection of personal data* of the EU Charter of Fundamental Rights of the European Union and Article 1: *Obligation to respect human rights*, Article 2: *Right to life*, Article 8: *Right to respect for private and family life*, Article 13: *Right to an effective remedy*, and Article 15: *Derogation in time of emergency* of the European Convention on Human Rights and that the relevant case law of the European Court of Human Rights is duly taken into account.	
5.6	Confirm that when responding to disasters you are acting in a way that respects international humanitarian law and the international law on disasters.	
5.7	Confirm that you are acting in accordance with the Universal Declaration of Human Rights.	
5.8	Confirm that you are clear on the types of emergency situations that lead to human rights' regimes being suspended.	
5.9	In the event of an armed conflict, ensure compliance with the four Geneva Conventions of 1949 on the law of armed conflicts, the other international Conventions and Protocols applicable in wartime, and with any relevant principles and rules of customary international humanitarian law.	
5.10	Confirm that you have considered and are acting in a manner that respects the following: the Convention on the Rights of the Child (in particular Article 22); the Convention on the Rights of Persons with Disabilities; the ILC Draft Articles on Protection of Persons in the Event of Disaster; and the International Covenant on Civil and Political Rights (in particular Article 2.3); and, as far as reproducing existing conventional and/or customary law provisions, the ILC Draft Articles on the Protection of Persons in the Event of Disaster.	

(Continued)

No.	Action	Completed
5.11	Conduct a preliminary human rights assessment of the legal and regulatory environment in which Slándáil will be used in accordance with the EU Civil Protection Mechanism. In 2001, the EU Civil Protection Mechanism was established, fostering cooperation among national civil protection authorities across Europe. The Mechanism currently includes all twenty-eight EU Member States in addition to Iceland, Montenegro, Norway, Serbia, the former Yugoslav Republic of Macedonia and Turkey. The Mechanism was set up to enable coordinated assistance from the participating states to victims of natural and man-made disasters in Europe and elsewhere.	

References

PRIMARY SOURCES

Ackerman, B. (2004). The Emergency Constitution. *Yale Law Journal*, 113(5), 1029–1091.

Agarwal, S., & Lau, C. T. (2010). Remote Health Monitoring Using Mobile Phones and Web Services. *Telemedicine and e-Health*, 16(5), 603–607.

Ahmad, K. (2017). Slándáil: A Security System for Language and Image Analysis-Final Report for EU FP7 Project no. 607691 (2014–2017). Available at https://papers.ssrn.com/sol3/papers.cfm?abstract_id=3060047 (last accessed 16 May 2018).

Alemanno, A., & Lauto, K. C. (2014). Opening Editorial. *European Journal of Risk Regulation*, 2, 129–132.

Alexander, D. E. (2014). Social Media in Disaster Risk Reduction and Crisis Management. *Science and Engineering Ethics*, 20(3), 717–733.

Alston, P., & Goodman, R. (2012). *International Human Rights*: Oxford University Press.

Andrejevic, M. (2011). Social Network Exploitation. In Z. Papacharissi (ed.), *A Networked Self: Identity, Community, and Culture on Social Network Sites* (pp. 82–101): Routledge.

Article 29 Data Protection Working Party. (2012). European Commission. Retrieved from http://ec.europa.eu/newsroom/document.cfm?doc_id=40100 (last accessed 16 May 2018).

Article 29 Data Protection Working Party: Preliminary EDPS Opinion on the Review of the ePrivacy Directive (2002). European Commission. Retrieved from https://edps.europa.eu/sites/edp/files/publication/16–07-22_opinion_eprivacy_en.pdf (last accessed 16 May 2018).

Austin, G. W. (2005). The Berne Convention as a Canon of Construction: Moral Rights after Dastar. *NYU Annual Survey of American Law*, 61(2),111–150.

Austin, L. M. (2014). Lawful Illegality: What Snowden Has Taught Us about the Legal Infrastructure of the Surveillance State. In M. Geist (ed.), *Law, Privacy and Surveillance in Canada in the Post-Snowden Era* (pp. 103–125): University of Ottawa Press.

Austin, L., Fisher Liu, B., & Jin, Y. (2012). How Audiences Seek Out Crisis Information: Exploring the Social-Mediated Crisis Communication Model. *Journal of Applied Communication Research*, 40(2), 188–207.

Bagh, M. T. (2007). *On-demand Anwendungen in Forschung und Lehre: die öffentliche Zugänglichmachung für Unterricht und Forschung im Rechtsvergleich zwischen Schweden und Deutschland* (vol. 6): Walter de Gruyter.

Barnett, R. (2015). Why the NSA Data Seizures Are Unconstitutional. *Harvard Journal of Law and Public Policy*, 38, 3–20.

Bartha, G., & Kocsis, S. (2011). Standardization of Geographic Data: The European Inspire Directive. *European Journal of Geography*, 2(2), 79–89.

Bekkers, V., Edwards, A., & de Kool, D. (2013). Social Media Monitoring: Responsive Governance in the Shadow of Surveillance? *Government Information Quarterly*, 30(4), 335–342.

Bengtsson, L., Lu, X., Thorson, A., Garfield, R., & Von Schreeb, J. (2011). Improved Response to Disasters and Outbreaks by Tracking Population Movements with Mobile Phone Network Data: A Post-Earthquake Geospatial Study in Haiti. *PLOS Medicine*, 8(8), e1001083.

Bently, L., & Sherman, B. (2014). *Intellectual Property Law*: Oxford University Press.

Berger, C. (2012). Aktuelle Entwicklungen im Urheberrecht – Der EuGH bestimmt die Richtung. *Zeitschrift für Urheber- und Medienrecht*, 56(5), 353–360.

(2014). European Copyright in Germany. In C. Enders, A. Kusumadara, & A. Mrozek (eds.), *United in Diversity: Freedom, Property and Human Rights* (pp. 89–108): Leipziger Universitätsverlag.

Berger, C. & Wündisch, S. (Des) (2015). *Handbuch des Urhebervertragsrechts*: Nomos Verlagsgesellschaft.

Berlin, I. (1958). *Two Concepts of Liberty*: Clarendon Press.

(2013). The Pursuit of the Ideal. In *The Crooked Timber of Humanity: Chapters in the History of Ideas*, 2nd edn., edited by H. Hardy (pp. 1–20): Princeton University Press.

Bernhöft, M. (2009). *Die urheberrechtliche Zulässigkeit der digitalen Aufzeichnung einer Sendung* (vol. 4942): Peter Lang.

Bigo, D., Carrera, S., Hernanz, N., Jeandesboz, J., Parkin, J., Ragazzi, F., & Scherrer, A. (2013). Mass Surveillance of Personal Data by EU Member States and Its Compatibility with EU Law. CEPS paper in Liberty and Security in Europe, no. 62, November 2013.

Bone, C., Ager, A., Bunzel, K., & Tierney, L. (2016). A Geospatial Search Engine for Discovering Multi-format Geospatial Data across the Web. *International Journal of Digital Earth*, 9(1), 47–62.

Boyd, D. & Ellison, N. B. (2007). Social Network Sites: Definition, History, and Scholarship. *Journal of Computer-Mediated Communication*, 13(1), 210–230.

Brayne, S. (2017). Big Data Surveillance: The Case of Policing. *American Sociological Review*, 82(5), 977–1008.

Brewer, I., & McNeese, M. (2003). Using Cognitive Systems Engineering to Develop Collaborative Geospatial Military Technologies. Paper presented at the Proceedings of the International Conference on Military Geology and Geography, United States Military Academy, West Point, NY.

Brownstein, J. S., Freifeld, C. C., & Madoff, L. C. (2009). Digital Disease Detection – Harnessing the Web for Public Health Surveillance. *New England Journal of Medicine*, 360(21), 2153–2157.

Bruggeman, V. (2010). *Compensating Catastrophe Victims: A Comparative Law and Economics Approach* (vol. 12): Kluwer Law International.

Burns, R. (2015). Rethinking Big Data in Digital Humanitarianism: Practices, Epistemologies, and Social Relations. *GeoJournal*, 80(4), 477–490.

Burton, E., Goldsmith, J., Koenig, S., Kuipers, B., Mattei, N., & Walsh, T. (2017). Ethical Considerations in Artificial Intelligence Courses. *AI Magazine*, 38(2), 22–34. Available at https://arxiv.org/pdf/1701.07769.pdf (last accessed 25 March 2018).

Busà, M. G., Musacchio, M. T., Finan, S., & Fennell, C. (2015). Trust-Building through Social Media Communications in Disaster Management. Paper presented at the 24th International Conference on World Wide Web, Florence, Italy.

Campbell, M. A. (2005). Cyber Bullying: An Old Problem in a New Guise? *Australian Journal of Guidance and Counselling*, 15(1), 68–76.

Caron, D. D., Kelly, M. J., & Telesetsky, A. (2014). *The International Law of Disaster Relief*: Cambridge University Press.

Cartlidge, E. (2014). Appeals Court Overturns Manslaughter Convictions of Six Earthquake Scientists. *Science*. Available at www.sciencemag.org/news/2014/11/updated-appeals-court -overturns-manslaughter-convictions-six-earthquake-scientists (last accessed 25 April 2018).

Cavoukian, A., & Castro, D. (2014). Big Data and Innovation, Setting the Record Straight: De-identification Does Work. White paper, 16 June 2014. Available at www2.itif.org/2014 -big-data-deidentification.pdf (last accessed 16 May 2018).

Chae, J., Thom, D., Bosch, H., Jang, Y., Maciejewski, R., Ebert, D. S., & Ertl, T. (2012). Spatiotemporal Social Media Analytics for Abnormal Event Detection and Examination Using Seasonal-Trend Decomposition. Paper presented at the 2012 IEEE Conference on Visual Analytics Science and Technology (VAST), 14–19 October 2012.

Chamlee-Wright, E., & Storr, V. H. (2009). "There's No Place Like New Orleans": Sense of Place and Community Recovery in the Ninth Ward after Hurricane Katrina. *Journal of Urban Affairs*, 31(5), 615–634.

Chatfield, A. T., Scholl, H. J., & Brajawidagda, U. (2014). #Sandy Tweets: Citizens' Co-Production of Time-Critical Information during an Unfolding Catastrophe. Paper presented at the System Sciences (HICSS), 2014 – 47th Hawaii International Conference.

Cherniss, J., & Hardy, H. (2004). *Isaiah Berlin*. Available at http://plato.stanford.edu/entries /berlin (last accessed 16 May 2018).

Citron, D. K. (2014). *Hate Crimes in Cyberspace*: Harvard University Press.

Cogburn, D. L., & Espinoza-Vasquez, F. K. (2011). From Networked Nominee to Networked Nation: Examining the Impact of Web 2.0 and Social Media on Political Participation and Civic Engagement in the 2008 Obama Campaign. *Journal of Political Marketing*, 10(1–2), 189–213.

Coile, R. C. (1997). The Role of Amateur Radio in Providing Emergency Electronic Communication for Disaster Management. *Disaster Prevention and Management: An International Journal*, 6(3), 176–185.

Coleman, D. J., & McLaughlin, J. (1998). Defining Global Geospatial Data Infrastructure (GGDI): Components, Stakeholders and Interfaces. *Geomatica*, 52(2), 129–143.

Cook, T. (2012). Exceptions and Limitations in European Union Copyright Law. *Journal of Intellectual Property Rights*, 17, 243–245.

Crackau, A. (2014). Zum europäischen Werkbegriff des Urheberrechts [On the European Definition of Works in Copyright Law]. *SSRN Electronic Journal*.

Creta, A. (2012). A (Human) Right to Humanitarian Assistance in Disaster Situations? Surveying Public International Law. In A. de Guttry, M. Gestri, & G. Venturini (eds.), *International Disaster Response Law* (pp. 353–379): Springer.

Criddle, E. J., & Fox-Decent, E. (2012). Human Rights, Emergencies, and the Rule of Law. *Human Rights Quarterly*, 34(1), 39–87.

Criddle, E. J., & Fox-Decent, E. (2016). *Fiduciaries of Humanity: How International Law Constitutes Authority*: Oxford University Press.

Cruz, A. M., & Krausmann, E. (2013). Vulnerability of the Oil and Gas Sector to Climate Change and Extreme Weather Events. *Climatic Change*, 121(1), 41–53.

Cubie, D., & Hesselman, M. (2015). Accountability for the Human Rights Implications of Natural Disasters: A Proposal for Systemic International Oversight. *Netherlands Quarterly of Human Rights*, 33(1), 9–41.

Cusumano, M. A. (2004). *The Business of Software*: Free Press.

De Franceschi, A., & Lehmann, M. (2015). Data as Tradeable Commodity and New Measures for Their Protection. *Italian Law Journal*, 1, 51.

de Graaf, G. (2015). The Bright Future of Value Pluralism in Public Administration. *Administration & Society*, 47(9), 1094–1102.

De Guttry, A., Gestri, M., & Venturini, G. (2012). *International Disaster Response Law*: Springer.

De Hert, P. (2015). The Right to Protection of Personal Data. Incapable of Autonomous Standing in the Basic EU Constituting Documents. HeinOnline.

De Schutter, O. (2013). *Fundamental Rights in the European Union*: Oxford University Press.
    (2014). *International Human Rights Law: Cases, Materials, Commentary*: Cambridge University Press.

De Stefani, P. (2017). Using Social Media in Natural Disaster Management: A Human-Rights Based Approach. *Peace Human Rights Governance*, 1(2), 195–221.

Delgado, J., Torres, V., Llorente, S., & Rodríguez, E. (2005). Rights and Trust in Multimedia Information Management. In J. Dittmann, S. Katzenbeisser, & A. Uhl (eds.), *Communications and Multimedia Security: 9th IFIP TC-6 TC-11International Conference, CMS 2005, Salzburg, Austria, September 19–21, 2005. Proceedings* (pp. 55–64): Springer.

Directive 2002/58/EC ePrivacy Directive. (2002).

Donohue, L. (2014). Bulk Metadata Collection: Statutory and Constitutional Considerations. *Harvard Journal of Law and Public Policy*, 37, 757–900.

Dreier, T., & Schulze, G. (2004). *Urheberrechtsgesetz. Urheberrechtswahrnehmungsgesetz, Kunsturhebergesetz. Kommentar*: Beck.
    (2015). *Urheberrechtsgesetz: UrhG*, 5th edn.: Beck.

Droege, C. (2007). The Interplay between International Humanitarian Law and International Human Rights Law in Situations of Armed Conflict. *Israel Law Review*, 40(2), 310–355.

Duffield, M. (2016). The Resilience of the Ruins: Towards a Critique of Digital Humanitarianism. *Resilience*, 4(3), 147–165.

Edwards, L. (2009). Coding Privacy. *Chicago-Kent Law Review*, 84(3), 861–873.

El Emam, K., & Álvarez, C. (2014). A Critical Appraisal of the Article 29 Working Party Opinion 05/2014 on Data Anonymization Techniques. *International Data Privacy Law*, ipu033.

Elliott, J. R. (2014). Natural Hazards and Residential Mobility: General Patterns and Racially Unequal Outcomes in the United States. *Social Forces*, sou120.

Elliott, J. R., & Pais, J. (2006). Race, Class, and Hurricane Katrina: Social Differences in Human Responses to Disaster. *Social Science Research*, 35(2), 295–321.

Ensthaler, J. (2009). Inhalte des Urheberrechts. In *Gewerblicher Rechtsschutz und Urheberrecht* (pp. 46–80): Springer.

Ess, C. (2013). *Digital Media Ethics*: Polity.

Farber, D. A. (2014). International Law and the Disaster Cycle. In K. Caron & A. Telesetksy (eds.), *The International Law of Disaster Relief* (pp. 7–20): Cambridge University Press.

Field, C. B. (2012). *Managing the Risks of Extreme Events and Disasters to Advance Climate Change Adaptation: Special Report of the Intergovernmental Panel on Climate Change*: Cambridge University Press.

Floridi, L. (2013). *The Ethics of Information*: Oxford University Press.

Förster, A. (2014). *Urheberrecht: eine Einführung in die rechtlichen Grundlagen kreativer Tätigkeit* (vol. 11): University of Bamberg Press.

Fraustino, J. D., & Ma, L. (2015). CDC's Use of Social Media and Humor in a Risk Campaign – "Preparedness 101: Zombie Apocalypse". *Journal of Applied Communication Research*, 43(2), 222–241.

Fuchs, T. (2006). Der Arbeitnehmerurheber im System des § 43 UrhG. *GRUR*, 561–565.

Galicki, A. (2015). The End of *Smith v. Maryland*: The NSA's Bulk Telephony Metadata Program and the Fourth Amendment in the Cyber Age. *American Criminal Law Review*, 52, 375–414.

Gestri, M. (2012). EU Disaster Response Law: Principles and Instruments. In A. De Guttry, M. Gestri, & G. Venturini (eds.), *International Disaster Response Law*: Springer.

Giegerich, T. (2012). Article 36 UN Charter. In A. Zimmermann (ed.), *The Statute of the International Court of Justice: A Commentary* (pp. 134–162): Oxford University Press.

Ginsburg, J. C. (1994). Global Use/Territorial Rights: Private International Law Questions of the Global Information Infrastructure. *Journal of the Copyright Society of the USA*, 42(4), 318–338.

(1999). The Cyberian Captivity of Copyright: Territoriality and Authors' Rights in a Networked World. *Santa Clara Computer & High Technology Law Journal*, 15(2), 347–362.

GNU. (1991). General public license.

Graham, C. (2016). Referendum Result Response [press release]. Retrieved from https://ico.org .uk/about-the-ico/news-and-events/news-and-blogs/2016/07/referendum-result-response (last accessed 16 May 2018).

Greaves, F., Ramirez-Cano, D., Millett, C., Darzi, A., & Donaldson, L. (2013). Harnessing the Cloud of Patient Experience: Using Social Media to Detect Poor Quality Healthcare. *BMJ Quality & Safety*, bmjqs–2012–001527.

Greenwald, G. (2013). NSA Collecting Phone Records of Millions of Verizon Customers Daily. *The Guardian*, 6(5), 13.

Griffiths, J. (2011). Infopaq, BSA and the "Europeanisation" of United Kingdom Copyright Law. *Media & Arts Law Review*, 16. Available at https://ssrn.com/abstract=1777027 (last accessed 16 May 2018).

Groot, R., & McLaughlin, J. D. (2000). *Geospatial Data Infrastructure: Concepts, Cases, and Good Practice*: Oxford University Press.

Gross, O., & Aolain, F. N. (2001). Emergency, War and International Law – Another Perspective. *Nordic Journal of International Law*, 70(1), 29–63.

Guadamuz, A. (2016). The Monkey Selfie: Copyright Lessons for Originality in Photographs and Internet Jurisdiction. *Internet Policy Review*, 5(1), DOI: 10.14763/2016.1.398.

Guibault, L. (2010). Why Cherry-Picking Never Leads to Harmonisation: The Case of the Limitations on Copyright under Directive 2001/29/EC. *Journal of Intellectual Property, Information Technology and Electronic Commerce Law*, 2, 55–66.

Gupta, R., & Brooks, H. (2013). *Using Social Media for Global Security*: John Wiley & Sons.

Handig, C. (2012). Erste Umrisse eines europäischen Werkbegriffs. *Wirtschaftsrechtliche Blätter*, 26(4), 191–197.

Hardin, R. (2002). *Trust and Trustworthiness*: Russell Sage Foundation.

Harper, E. (2009). *International Law and Standards Applicable in Natural Disaster Situations*: International Development Law Organization, Rome, Italy.

Hartig, O. (2009). Provenance Information in the Web of Data. *LDOW*, 538.

Hartzog, W. (2012). *Privacy and Terms of Use*. In D. Stewart (ed.), *Social Media and the Law: A Guidebook for Communication Students and Professionals*: Routledge.

Haupt, S., & Marschke, C. (2005). Urheberrecht für Autoren. Probleme des Urheberrechts bei wissenschaftlichen Publikationen. *Zeitschrift für Germanistik*, 15(2), 254–276.

Heipke, C. (2010). Crowdsourcing Geospatial Data. *ISPRS Journal of Photogrammetry and Remote Sensing*, 65(6), 550–557.

Henderson, J. J. (2013). The Boundaries of Free Speech in Social Media. In D. Stewart (ed.), *Social Media and the Law* (pp. 1–22): Routledge.

Herzberg, A. (2006). *Miturheberschaft, Bearbeiterurheberrecht, freie Benutzung und Plagiate*: GRIN.

Hetmank, S. (2016). Urheberrechtsverletzungen im Internet. In *Internetrecht* (pp. 117–145): Springer.

Hill, K. (2012). Max Schrems: The Austrian Thorn in Facebook's Side. *Forbes*, 7, 2012.

Hiller, J. S., & Russell, R. S. (2017). Privacy in Crises: The NIST Privacy Framework. *Journal of Contingencies and Crisis Management*, 25(1), 31–38.

Hoeren, T. (2013). Urheberrecht und Internetrecht. *Grundlagen der praktischen Information und Dokumentation. Handbuch zur Einführung in die Informationswissenschaft und-praxis*, 6, 39–55.

Holpuch, A. (2015, 19/02/2015). Native American Activist to Sue Facebook over Site's "Real Name" Policy. *The Guardian*. Available at www.theguardian.com/technology/2015/feb/19/native-american-activist-facebook-lawsuit-real-name (last accessed 16 May 2018).

Hu, M. (2015). *Small Data Surveillance v. Big Data Cybersurveillance. Big Data Cybersurveillance (28 November 2015). Washington & Lee Legal Studies Paper (2016–6)*.

Italy, Government of. (1992). *Law n. 225: Establishment of the National Civil Protection Service*. Available at www.protezionecivile.gov.it/jcms/it/view_prov.wp?contentId=LEG1602 (last accessed 16 May 2018).

Jackson, D., & Hayes, P. (2016). Ensuring Security of Data and Information Flow in Emergency Response Decision Support. Paper presented at the 11th International Conference on Availability, Reliability and Security (ARES) 2016, Salzburg, Austria.

Johnson, M., Ruess, P., & Coll, J. (2016). OPERA – Operational Platform for Emergency Response and Awareness: Reimagining Disaster Alerts. National Water Center Innovators Program Summer Institute Report 2016.

Kekes, J. (1996). *The Morality of Pluralism*: Princeton University Press.

Kelly, S., & Ahmad, K. (2014). Determining Levels of Urgency and Anxiety during a Natural Disaster: Noise, Affect, and News in Social Media. Paper presented at the DIMPLE: Disaster Management and Principled Large-scale information Extraction Workshop Programme, Reykjavik, Iceland.

(2015). Propagating Disaster Warnings on Social and Digital Media. *Intelligent Data Engineering and Automated Learning*, 9375, 475–484.

Kelly, S., Zhang, X., & Ahmad, K. (2017). Mining Multimodal Information on Social Media for Increased Situational Awareness. Paper presented at the 14th International Conference on Information Systems for Crisis Response and Management (ISCRAM), Albi, France.

Kerr, O. S. (2002). Internet Surveillance Law after the USA Patriot Act: The Big Brother that Isn't. *Northwestern University Law Review*, 97, 607–673.

King, I., Li, J., & Chan, K. T. (2009). *A Brief Survey of Computational Approaches in Social Computing*. Paper presented at the International Joint Conference on Neural Networks (IJCNN) 2009, Atlanta, Georgia.

Kinne, B. (1943). Voltaire Never Said It! *Modern Language Notes*, 58(7), 534–535.

Kramer, X. E. (2008). The Rome II Regulation on the Law Applicable to Non-Contractual Obligations: The European Private International Law Tradition Continued-Introductory Observations, Scope, System, and General Rules. *Nederlands Internationaal Privaatrecht*, 4, 414–424.

Kur, A., Planck, M., & Dreier, T. (2013). *European Intellectual Property Law: Text, Cases and Materials*: Edward Elgar Publishing.

Landau, S. (2014). Highlights from Making Sense of Snowden, Part II: What's Significant in the NSA Revelations. *IEEE Security & Privacy*, 12(1), 62–64.

Lauta, K. C. (2014). *Disaster Law*: Routledge.

Lee, D. (2014). Drag Queens in Facebook Name Row. *BBC News*, 12 September. Available at www.bbc.co.uk/news/technology-29175102 (last accessed 16 May 2018).

Leistner, M. (2014). Urheberrecht an der Schnittstelle zwischen Unionsrecht und nationalem Recht. *GRUR*, 1145–1155.

Lessig, L. (1999). *Code and Other Laws of Cyberspace*: Basic Books.

(2006). *Code and Other Laws of Cyberspace, Version 2.0*: Basic Books.

Lindsay, B. R. (2016). *Social Media for Emergencies and Disasters: Overview and Policy Considerations*: Congressional Research Service.

Lipton, J. (2001). Copyright in the Digital Age: A Comparative Survey. *Rutgers Computer & Technology Law Journal*, 27(2), 333.

Liu, S. B., Palen, L., Sutton, J., Hughes, A. L., & Vieweg, S. (2008). In Search of the Bigger Picture: The Emergent Role of On-line Photo Sharing in Times of Disaster. Paper presented at the Proceedings of the Information Systems for Crisis Response and Management conference (ISCRAM).

Liu, Y., Gummadi, K. P., Krishnamurthy, B., & Mislove, A. (2011). Analyzing Facebook Privacy Settings: User Expectations vs. Reality. Paper presented at the Proceedings of the 2011 ACM SIGCOMM conference on Internet Measurement Conference.

Lloyd, I. (2017). *Information Technology Law*: Oxford University Press.

Lo, C. P., & Yeung, A. K. (2007). *Concepts and Techniques of Geographic Information Systems*: Pearson Prentice Hall.

Loader, B. D., & Mercea, D. (2011). Networking Democracy? Social Media Innovations and Participatory Politics. *Information, Communication & Society*, 14(6), 757–769.

Longworth, E. (1999). *Possibilities of a Legal Framework for Cyberspace: Including a New Zealand Perspective: Prepared for the Unesco Experts Meetings on Cyberspace Law (in South Korea and the Republic of Monaco, September 1998)*: GP Publications.

Loos, M. (2016). European Harmonisation of Online and Distance Selling of Goods and the Supply of Digital Content. Amsterdam Law School Research Paper no. 2016-27; Centre for the Study of European Contract Law Working Paper Series no. 2016-08.

Luca, M. (2016). Reviews, Reputation, and Revenue: The Case of Yelp.com. Harvard Business School Working Paper no. 12-016.

Lutz, P. (2009). *Grundriss des Urheberrechts*: CF Müller GmbH.

Lyon, D. (2006). *Theorizing Surveillance*: Routledge.

(2014). Surveillance, Snowden, and Big Data: Capacities, Consequences, Critique. *Big Data & Society*, 1(2), DOI: 10.1177/2053951714541861.

Manning, C. (2016). Hyperlinks & Copyright Law. Available at https://ssrn.com /abstract=2781471 (last accessed 4 May 2018).

Mans, U., Berens, J., & Shimshon, G. (2015). *The New Humanitarian Data Ecosystem: Challenges and Opportunities to Increase Trust and Impact. World Humanitarian Summit White Paper*. Unpublished manuscript.

Maresh-Fuehrer, M., & Smith, R. (2016). Social Media Mapping Innovations for Crisis Prevention, Response, and Evaluation. *Computers in Human Behavior*, 54, 620–629.

Margoni, T. (2014). The Digitisation of Cultural Heritage: Originality, Derivative Works and (non-) Original Photographs. Available at https://ssrn.com/abstract=2573104 (last accessed 16 May 2018).

Mayer-Schönberger, V., & Cukier, K. (2013). *Big Data: A Revolution That Will Transform How We Live, Work, and Think*: Houghton Mifflin Harcourt.

McCaughey, M., & Ayers, M. D. (2013). *Cyberactivism: Online Activism in Theory and Practice*: Routledge.

McPherson, S. S. (2009). *Tim Berners-Lee: Inventor of the World Wide Web*: Twenty-First Century Books.

Menell, P. S. (2016). Economic Analysis of Copyright Notice: Tracing and Scope in the Digital Age. *Boston University Law Review*, 96(3), 967–1023.

Millman, R. (2016, 16/09/2016). Firefox and Chrome are Blocking Access to The Pirate Bay. *ITPRO*. Available at www.itpro.co.uk/security/27250/firefox-and-chrome-are-blocking-access-to-the-pirate-bay (last accessed 16 May 2018).

Mishna, F., Saini, M., & Solomon, S. (2009). Ongoing and Online: Children and Youth's Perceptions of Cyber Bullying. *Children and Youth Services Review*, 31(12), 1222–1228.

Mlot, S. (2016). Silence Instagram Trolls with Keyword Filters. *Entrepreneur.com*. Available at www.entrepreneur.com/article/282298 (last accessed 16 May 2018).

Moreau, L., Groth, P., Miles, S., Vazquez-Salceda, J., Ibbotson, J., Jiang, S., ... & Tan, V. (2008). The Provenance of Electronic Data. *Communications of the ACM*, 51(4), 52–58.

Morva, O. (2016). Are E-Petitions Operative for Change? On the Effectiveness and the Transformative Potential of E-Petitioning. Paper presented at the Proceedings of 22nd International Academic Conferences, Lisbon.

Netanel, N. W. (2000). Cyberspace Self-Governance: A Skeptical View from Liberal Democratic Theory. *California Law Review*, 88(2), 395–498.

Ni Loideain, N. (2016). The End of Safe Harbor: Implications for EU Digital Privacy and Data Protection Law. *Journal of Internet Law*, 19(8), 1, 8–14.

Nieuwenburg, P. (2004). The Agony of Choice: Isaiah Berlin and the Phenomenology of Conflict. *Administration & Society*, 35(6), 683–700.

Nissen, T. E. (2015). *#TheWeaponizationOfSocialMedia: @Characteristics_of_ Contemporary_ Conflicts*: Royal Danish Defence College.

OECD. (2015). *Changing Face of Strategic Crisis Management*: OECD Publishing.

Ohm, P. (2010). Broken Promises of Privacy: Responding to the Surprising Failure of Anonymization. *UCLA Law Review*, 57, 1701–1777.

(2012). The Fourth Amendment in a World without Privacy. *Mississippi Law Journal*, 81(5), 1309–1355.

Oriola, T. A. (2004). Electronic Database Protection and the Limits of Copyright. *Journal of World Intellectual Property*, 7(2), 201–228.

(2005). Regulating Unsolicited Commercial Electronic Mail in the United States and the European Union: Challenges and Prospects. *Tulane Journal of Technology & Intellectual Property*, 7, 113–166.

Overeem, P., & Verhoef, J. (2014). Moral Dilemmas, Theoretical Confusion: Value Pluralism and Its Supposed Implications for Public Administration. *Administration & Society*, 46(8), 986–1009.

Palen, L., Anderson, K. M., Mark, G., Martin, J., Sicker, D., Palmer, M., & Grunwald, D. (2010). A Vision for Technology-Mediated Support for Public Participation & Assistance in Mass Emergencies & Disasters. Paper presented at the Proceedings of the 2010 ACM-BCS Visions of Computer Science Conference, Edinburgh, United Kingdom.

Parameswaran, M., & Whinston, A. B. (2007). Social Computing: An Overview. *Communications of the Association for Information Systems*, 19, 762–780.

Pell, S. K., & Soghoian, C. (2014). A Lot More Than a Pen Register, and Less Than a Wiretap: What the Stingray Teaches Us about How Congress Should Approach the Reform of Law Enforcement Surveillance Authorities. *Yale Journal of Law and Technology*, 16(1), 134–171.

Peng, W., Li, F., Zou, X., & Wu, J. (2014). A Two-Stage Deanonymization Attack against Anonymized Social Networks. *IEEE Transactions on Computers*, 63(2), 290–303.

PLoS Medicine Editors. (2012). Digital Humanitarianism: Collective Intelligence Emerging. *PLoS Medicine*, 9(7), e1001278.

Poeppel, J. (2005). *Die Neuordnung der urheberrechtlichen Schranken im digitalen Umfeld* (vol. 11): V&R unipress GmbH.

Provost, R. (2002). *International Human Rights and Humanitarian Law* (vol. 22): Cambridge University Press.

Ramirez, E., Brill, J., Ohlhausen, M. K., Wright, J. D., & McSweeny, T. (2014). *Data Brokers: A Call for Transparency and Accountability*: Federal Trade Commission.

Ramsbotham, O., Miall, H., & Woodhouse, T. (2011). *Contemporary Conflict Resolution*: Polity.

Raue, B. (2013). Informationsfreiheit und Urheberrecht. *Juristenzeitung)*, 6, 280–288.

Reed, C. (2012). *Making Laws for Cyberspace*: Oxford University Press.

Reinemann, S., & Remmertz, F. (2012). Urheberrechte an User-generated Content. *Zeitschrift für Urheber-und Medien recht (ZUM)*, 55, 216–227.

Renda, A., Simonelli, F., Mazziotti, G., Bolognini, A., & Luchetta, G. (2015). The Implementation, Application and Effects of the EU Directive on Copyright in the Information Society. *CEPS Special Report No. 120*, 19 November 2015.

Rizza, C., Büscher, M., & Watson, H. (2017). Working with Data: Ethical Legal and Social Considerations Surrounding the Use of Crisis Data and Information Sharing during a Crisis. *Journal of Contingencies and Crisis Management*, 25(1), 2–6.

Ronzitti, N. (2012). Conclusion. In A. De Guttry, M. Gestri, & G. Venturini (eds.), *International Disaster Response Law*: Springer.

Rosati, E. (2013). *Originality in EU Copyright: Full Harmonization through Case Law*: Edward Elgar Publishing.

Rowland, D., Kohl, U., & Charlesworth, A. (2016). *Information Technology Law*, 5th edn.: Routledge.

Ryder, J., Longstaff, B., Reddy, S., & Estrin, D. (2009). Ambulation: A Tool for Monitoring Mobility Patterns over Time Using Mobile Phones. Paper presented at the 2009 International Conference on Computational Science and Engineering.

Schack, H. (2015). *Urheber-und Urhebervertragsrecht*, 7th edn.: Mohr Siebeck.

Sevignani, S. (2013). Facebook vs. Diaspora: A Critical Study. In G. Lovink, & M. Rasch (eds.), *Unlike Us Reader: Social Media Monopolies and Their Alternatives* (pp. 323–337): Institute of Network Cultures.

Shelton, D. L. (2014). *Advanced Introduction to International Human Rights Law*: Edward Elgar Publishing.

Shih, P. C., Han, K., & Carroll, J. M. (2014). Community Incident Chatter: Informing Local Incidents by Aggregating Local News and Social Media Content. Paper presented at the Proceedings of the International Conference on Information Systems for Crisis Response and Management.

Simon, H. A. (1982). *Models of Bounded Rationality: Empirically Grounded Economic Reason* (vol. 3): MIT Press.

Siracusa Principles. (1985). Symposium: Limitation and Derogation Provisions in the International Covenant on Civil and Political Rights: Principles. *Human Rights Quarterly*, 7(1), 3–14.

Solove, D. J. (2007). *The Future of Reputation: Gossip, Rumor, and Privacy on the Internet*: Yale University Press.

Sotto, L. J., & Simpson, A. P. (2015). United States. In R. P. Jay (ed.), *Data Protection and Privacy in 31 Jurisdictions Worldwide*: Law Business Research.

Sphere Project. (2011). *Humanitarian Charter and Minimum Standards in Humanitarian Response*: The Sphere Project.

Spicer, M. W. (2001). Value Pluralism and Its Implications for American Public Administration. *Administrative Theory & Praxis*, 23(4), 507–528.

Stallings, R. A., & Quarantelli, E. L. (1985). Emergent Citizen Groups and Emergency Management. *Public Administration Review*, 45, 93–100.

Stefanidis, A., Crooks, A., & Radzikowski, J. (2013). Harvesting Ambient Geospatial Information from Social Media Feeds. *GeoJournal*, 78(2), 319–338.

Stelter, B. (2009). Facebook's Users Ask Who Owns Information. *New York Times*, 16 February.

Stewart, D., ed. (2013). Preface. In *Social Media and The Law: A Guidebook for Communication Students and Professionals* (pp. vi–xxi): Routledge.

(2017). *Social Media and the Law: A Guidebook for Communication Students and Professionals*, 2nd edn.: Routledge.

Stieglitz, S., & Dang-Xuan, L. (2013). Emotions and Information Diffusion in Social Media – Sentiment of Microblogs and Sharing Behavior. *Journal of Management Information Systems*, 29(4), 217–248.

Sui, D. Z. (2008). *Geospatial Technologies and Homeland Security: Research Frontiers and Future Challenges* (vol. 94): Springer Science & Business Media.

Svensson-McCarthy, A.-L. (1998). *The International Law of Human Rights and States of Exception: With Special Reference to the Travaux Preparatoires and the Case-law of the International Monitoring Organs* (vol. 54): Martinus Nijhoff Publishers.

Sweeney, L. (2002). Achieving k-anonymity Privacy Protection Using Generalization and Suppression. *International Journal of Uncertainty, Fuzziness and Knowledge-Based Systems*, 10(5), 571–588.

Taddeo, M., & Floridi, L. (2017). The Moral Responsibilities of Online Service Providers. In M. Taddeo & L. Floridi (eds.), *The Responsibilities of Online Service Providers* (pp. 13–42): Springer.

Talisse, R. B. (2011). Value Pluralism and Liberal Politics. *Ethical Theory and Moral Practice*, 14(1), 87–100.

Tene, O., & Polonetsky, J. (2012). Big Data for All: Privacy and User Control in the Age of Analytics. *Northwestern Journal of Technology & Intellectual Property*, 11(5), 239–273.

Terry, F. (2003). Condemned to Repeat? The Paradox of Humanitarian Action. *Sydney Papers*, 15(2), 1–10.

Trudel, P. (2000). Liability in Cyberspace. In T. Fuentes-Camacho (ed.), *The International Dimension of Cyberspace Law* (pp. 189–211): Ashgate.

United Kingdom, Government of the. (2004). Civil Contingencies Act. Available at www.legislation.gov.uk/ukpga/2004/36/contents (last accessed 16 May 2018).

United Nations (UN). (1945). *Charter of the United Nations*.

(1976). *International Covenant on Civil and Political Rights*.

UN Commission on Human Rights. (1984). Siracusa Principles on the Limitation and Derogation of Provisions in the International Covenant on Civil and Political Rights. Geneva: United Nations Commission on Human Rights.

UN Framework Convention on Climate Change (UNFCCC). (2010). United Nations Climate Change Conference COP 16, 29 November–10 December 2010, Cancun, Mexico.

UNFCCC & EU. (2015). Submission-by-latvia-and-the-european-commission-on-behalf-of-the-european-union-and-its-member-states.html. Available at http://docplayer.net/amp/45102139 (last accessed 25 April 2017).

UN High Commissioner for Human Rights (OHCHR), Office of the. (2014). *The Right to Privacy in the Digital Age*. Available at www.ohchr.org/EN/Issues/Digital/Age/Pages/DigitalAgeIndex.aspx (last accessed 16 May 2018).

UN International Strategy for Disaster Recover (UNISDR). (2015). *Sendai Framework for Disaster Risk Reduction 2015–2030*: UNISDR.

US Department of Justice. (2006). Privacy Technology Focus Group: Final Report and Recommendations. Available at www.it.ojp.gov/documents/privacy_technology_focus_group_full_report.pdf (last accessed 16 May 2018).

Vallor, S. (2016). *Technology and the Virtues: A Philosophical Guide to a Future Worth Wanting*: Oxford University Press.

van Engelen, D. (2008). Rome II and Intellectual Property Rights: Choice of Law Brought to a Standstill. *Nederlands Internationaal Privaatrecht*, 4, 440–448.

Van Velze, S. C. (2015). *Communication to a New Public? A Critical Analysis of the CJEU's "New Public" Criterion in European Copyright Law*: Universiteit van Amsterdam.

Vandenbroucke, D., Zambon, M.-L., Crompvoets, J., & Dufourmont, H. (2008). INSPIRE Directive: Specific Requirements to Monitor Its Implementation. In J. Crompvoets, A. Rajabifard, B. van Loenen, & T. Delgado Fernández (eds.), *A Multi-View Framework to Assess Spatial Data Infrastructures* (pp. 327–355): Space for Geo-Information (RGI), Wageningen University and Centre for SDIs and Land Administration, Department of Geomatics, University of Melbourne.

Vitoria, M., Laddie, H. I. L., & Prescott, P. (2011). *Laddie, Prescott and Vitoria: The Modern Law of Copyright and Designs*, 4th edn.: LNUK.

von Lewinski, S., & Walter, M. (2010). Information Society Directive. In M. Walter & S. von Lewinski (eds.), *European Copyright Law: A Commentary* (pp. 921–1032): Oxford University Press.

Waelde, C., Laurie, G., Brown, A., Kheria, S., & Cornwell, J. (2013). *Contemporary Intellectual Property: Law and Policy*: Oxford University Press.

Wagenaar, H. (1999). Value Pluralism in Public Administration. *Administrative Theory & Praxis*, 21(4), 441–449.

Wagner, R. P. (2003). Information Wants to Be Free: Intellectual Property and the Mythologies of Control. *Columbia Law Review*, 103, 995–1034.

Wandtke, A.-A., Bullinger, W., Block, U., & Grunert, E. W. (2014). *Praxiskommentar zum Urheberrecht*, 4th edn.: Beck.

Wang, F.-Y., Carley, K. M., Zeng, D., & Mao, W. (2007). Social Computing: From Social Informatics to Social Intelligence. *IEEE Intelligent Systems*, 22(2). DOI: 10.1109/MIS.2007.41.

Warren, S. D., & Brandeis, L. D. (1890). The Right to Privacy. *Harvard Law Review*, 4(5), 193–220.

Weiss, M. A., & Archick, K. (2016). *US-EU Data Privacy: From Safe Harbor to Privacy Shield*: Congressional Research Service.

World Trade Organization (WTO). (1995). *Agreement on Trade-Related Aspects of Intellectual Property Rights*: WTO.

Xu, L., Jiang, C., Wang, J., Yuan, J., & Ren, Y. (2014). Information Security in Big Data: Privacy and Data Mining. *Access, IEEE*, 2, 1149–1176.

Yadron, D. (2016). Twitter Deletes 125,000 Isis Accounts and Expands Anti-Terror Teams. *The Guardian*. Available at www.theguardian.com/technology/2016/feb/05/twitter -deletes-isis-accounts-terrorism-online (last accessed 16 May 2018).

Young-McLear, K., Mazzuchi, T. A., & Sarkani, S. (2015). Large-Scale Disaster Response Management Social Media and Homeland Security. In *Social Media and the Transformation of Interaction in Society* (pp. 93–131): IGI Global.

Zeng, D., Wang, F.-Y., & Carley, K. M. (2007). Guest Editors' Introduction: Social Computing. *IEEE Intelligent Systems*, 22(5), 20–22.

Zhang, X., Kelly, S., & Ahmad, K. (2016). The Slandail Monitor: Real-Time Processing and Visualisation of Social Media Data for Emergency Management. Paper presented at the 11th International Conference on Availability, Reliability and Security (ARES) 2016, Salzburg, Austria.

Ziewitz, M., & Brown, I. (2011). A Prehistory of Internet Governance. In I. Brown (ed.), *Research Handbook on Governance of the Internet* (pp. 3–26): Edward Elgar.

Zimmer, M. (2010). "But the Data Is Already Public": On the Ethics of Research in Facebook. *Ethics and Information Technology*, 12(4), 313–325.

Zittrain, J. L. (2006). The Generative Internet. *Harvard Law Review*, 119, 1974–2040.

CASES

Agence France Presse v. Morel, No. 934 F.Supp.2d 547 (United States District Court 2013).

Al-Skeini and Others v. the United Kingdom, No. 55721/07 (European Court of Human Rights 2011).

The Amalgamated Transit Union, Local 113 v. Toronto Transit Commission (Use of Social Media Grievance), No. O.L.A.A No. 267 (Ontario Superior Court of Justice 2016).

Barberi e a., Giud. Billi (Trib. dell'Aquila 2012).

Beyond Systems, Inc. v. Realtime Gaming Holding Company, §878 A. 2d 567, at 579 (2005).

Campbell v. Mirror Group Newspapers Ltd, No. 2 AC 457 (UK House of Lords 2002).

Case C-335/12 Nintendo and Others v. PC Box Srl and Others (Court of Justice of the European Union 2014).

Cases C-293/12 and 594/12 Digital Rights Ireland and Seitlinger and Others (European Court of Justice 2014).

CBS Songs Ltd. v. Amstrad Consumer Electronics PLC, No. 1 AC 1013 (House of Lords 1988).

Craigslist Inc. v. 3Taps Inc., No. CV 12–03316 CRB (Northern District of California Court 2013).

Feist Publications, Inc., v. Rural Telephone Service Co, No. 499 U.S. 340 (Supreme Court of the United States 1991).

Government's Ex Parte Application for Order Compelling Apple Inc. to Assist Agents in Search (*Apple Inc. v. FBI*), No. ED No. 15-0451M (United States District Court 2016).

Independent Newspapers, Inc. v. Brodie, No. 966 A. 2d 432, 407 Md. 415 (Court of Appeals of Maryland 2009).

Isayeva and Others v. Russia, Nos. 57947/00, 57948/00 and 57949/00 (European Court of Human Rights 2005).

Largent v. Reed, No. 192009–1823 (Court of Common Pleas of the 29th Judicial District of Pennsylvania 2011).

Microsoft Corp. v. United States, No. 14-2985 (United States Court of Appeals for the Second Circuit 2016).

Nucci v. Target Corporation, No. 4D14-138, 162 So.3d 146 (District Court of Appeal of Florida, Fourth District 2015).

People of the State of New York v. Malcolm Harris, No. 192011NY080152 (Criminal Court of the City of New York 2012).

Pres. Francabandera, imp. Barberi e a, No. 3317 (Corte d'Appello dell'Aquila 2014).

Reno v. American Civil Liberties Union, 521 U.S. 844 (1997).

SAS Institute, Inc. v. World Programming Limited, No. 5: 10-CV-25-FL (Dist. Court, North Carolina 2016).

Sony Corp. of America v. Universal City Studios, Inc., No. 464 U.S. 417 (Supreme Court of the United States 1984).

St Albans City and District Council v. International Computers Ltd, No. EWCA Civ 1296 (UK Court of Appeal 1996).

Index